Jesus the Prophet

Jesus the Prophet

His Vision of the Kingdom on Earth

R. David Kaylor

Westminster/John Knox Press
Louisville, Kentucky

Scripture quotations from the New Revised Standard Version of the Bible are copyright © 1989 by the Division of Christian Education of the National Council of the Churches of Christ in the U.S.A., and are used by permission.

Quotations from Josephus' *Antiquities* reprinted with permission of Harvard University Press and the Loeb Classical Library from *Josephus,* vols. 2 and 5, translated by H. St. J. Thackeray. London: William Heinemann Ltd., 1930.

Book design by Laura Lee

Cover design by Susan E. Jackson

Cover illustration: Christ and the Tree of Life, woodcut, by R. F. McGovern, Narberth, Pennsylvania

First edition

Published by Westminster/John Knox Press
Louisville, Kentucky

This book is printed on acid-free paper that meets the American National Standards Institute Z39.48 standard. ∞

PRINTED IN THE UNITED STATES OF AMERICA

9   8   7   6   5   4   3   2   1

Library of Congress Cataloging-in-Publication Data

Kaylor, R. D.
   Jesus the prophet : His vision of the kingdom on earth / R. David Kaylor. — 1st ed.
     p.   cm.
   Includes bibliographical references and indexes.
   ISBN 0-664-25505-1 (alk. paper)

    1. Jesus Christ—Person and offices.   2. Jesus Christ—Political and social views.   3. Kingdom of God.   I. Title.
BT202.K34 1994
232'.8—dc20   93-31969

In loving memory of my father and mother
Lemuel Jefferson Kaylor
and Johnnie Hanson Kaylor
who taught me more about the Bible than they knew

Contents

Preface

The motivations for writing this book come primarily from the joys and frustrations of teaching an undergraduate course on Jesus for twenty-seven years: joy in seeing students discover that Jesus dealt as a human individual with a real world, inhabited by real people, torn by real problems; frustration in seeing how the joy some experience in that discovery is matched by the pain of others who feel that such a concrete image of Jesus may be inconsistent with their faith in a Christ who was God incarnate.

That feeling involves three questions about the relation between the Jesus of history and the Christ of faith. First, was Jesus really human, with endowments and limitations shared by other humans? To study Jesus concretely in his own environment assumes that he really was human, and that troubles the faith of some. Second, if one makes Jesus a *particular* human, is he less a universal figure either as a universal savior or a teacher of universal morality and value? Concern that the answer may be "no" creates both theological and ethical resistance to locating Jesus concretely in the conflicting world of first-century Roman Palestine. Third, if Jesus was really engaged with social and political conflicts in his society, does that make him less "spiritual"? This question implies a concern that spirituality, at least in its universal aspects, must be free from the particular conflicts that separate humans into differing camps.

Many of my students have at least a nominal connection with the kinds of churches in which I often teach or lecture. There too, not surprisingly, the universal Christ of faith is regarded as incompatible with a particular Jesus located in a particular history. What is not so evident to those who feel that way is the extent to which what they regard as a "universal" Christ actually mirrors the values they derive not from the New Testament but from their own culture. Thus, to challenge their universal Christ is not merely to challenge a theology thought to derive from the New Testament but also to call into question the concrete cultural values by which they live.

New Testament scholarship had its origins in the context of the church, and accordingly it has shared (and fostered) these same sorts of reservations. A great deal of New Testament study still is carried on by scholars with some sort of faith commitment, even if not "churchy," and though its theology may be much less confessional, it still often expresses a hidden theological agenda.[1] University-based New Testament study may provide more distance from confessional concerns, but it too may nonetheless carry agendas of universal applicability.

My intent in this book is to address a general audience of college and seminary students and other nonprofessionals. By presenting a historical understanding of Jesus, I wish to challenge those who have a commitment to Christian faith to take seriously a new look at the historical Jesus, to examine critically their modes of universalizing Jesus, and to reflect on the relationship of Jesus' vision of his world to the issues of their own time and place. I hope as well to provide an image of Jesus that will at least make convincing sense to those who do not share that faith commitment. Although I do not write for New Testament scholars, I hope my work will commend itself to them as a credible interpretation of the historical events and the documents that supply knowledge about those events.

A word of explanation is in order concerning the greater length of chapter 5, on parables. Since the parables offer, as most scholars think, the possibility of a closer approximation to Jesus' authentic words than any other form of the tradition, it seemed to me that close attention to them was required to sustain my thesis. For that reason, I have treated them in greater detail.

Many have contributed to this work: Davidson College granted a sabbatical leave. Students in my courses on Jesus and the Gospels have taught me

---
1. See David Stern's critique of Ricoeur's *logos* interpretation, which Stern thinks is an ideological interpretation based on Christian theology: "Jesus' Parables from the Perspective of Rabbinic Literature: The Example of the Wicked Husbandmen," in *Parable and Story in Judaism and Christianity,* ed. Clemens Thoma and Michael Wyschogrod (New York: Paulist Press, 1989), 56–58.

much. Bill Kaylor, Rebecca Gray, and Karl Plank read the manuscript; I thank them for their time and their many useful suggestions. Caroline Craig read drafts of each chapter as well as the whole manuscript, did the tedious work of checking all footnotes, and in many other ways gave encouragement and support; I am deeply grateful.

A Political Interpretation of Jesus

Scholarly interests and personal convictions converge in my desire to write this book. As one whose teaching concentrates on New Testament literature, I search for more adequate models for understanding the documents and persons who fascinate and elude. For many years my study and teaching of the Gospels reflected a strong influence by the New Testament scholar and theologian Rudolf Bultmann. I found—and still find—much to commend in Bultmann's persistent attempt to relate the tradition about Jesus to contemporary Western educated audiences. I learned from Bultmann that faith does not have to sacrifice intellectual integrity; that one can see profound meanings in narratives of "events" that did not literally happen; that the Gospels reflect the faith of the church and do not provide direct access to Jesus' words and deeds; that Jesus' proclamation of the kingdom of God comes to the hearer not as a concept but as a demand for decision about one's self.

In recent years, however, I have been troubled by Bultmann's overemphasis on the individual and the separation he made between Jesus and his social-political world. Renewed scholarly interest in the historical Jesus has come as a welcome change. Theology has rediscovered the importance of beginning with the historical Jesus as a basis for theological reflection.[1] Political theology and ethics, too, have found the need to locate contemporary models within Jesus' historical ministry more than in the incarnation.[2] Among New Testament scholars, a strong interest in the use of anthropological and sociological approaches has emerged as a means of clarifying historical movements, including the Jesus movement. The results include new questions and new ways of asking different questions of the texts concerning Jesus, with more promise of recovering valid knowledge of Jesus and his message.

Bultmann's radical historical skepticism still serves as a warning that our historical knowledge, even if improved, remains limited and that uncertainties are more numerous than certainties:

> I do indeed think that we can now know almost nothing concerning the life and personality of Jesus, since the early Christian sources show no interest in either, are moreover fragmentary and often legendary; and other sources about Jesus do not exist.[3]

Nonetheless, one may, with more confidence than Bultmann allowed, pursue a fuller understanding of Jesus in his social, political, and economic context.

In the following chapters I will attempt to delineate the political elements of Jesus' ministry and teaching. I intend to interpret the political dimensions of Jesus, not to reconstruct a political Jesus. Though closely related, the two

---

1. See, e.g., Jürgen Moltmann, *The Crucified God: The Cross of Christ as the Foundation and Criticism of Christian Theology,* tr. R. A. Wilson and John Bowden (New York: Harper & Row, 1974), 84: "The first task of christology is the critical verification of the Christian faith in its origin in Jesus and his history." As Moltmann proceeds, he seeks the historical reasons for Jesus' crucifixion; to some extent he violates his own insight when he says that the crucifixion must be understood both in light of Jesus' life *and his resurrection* (112). He more consistently follows that theme in his emphasis on "spirit Christology" rather than "cosmological Christology" in *The Way of Jesus Christ: Christology in Messianic Dimensions,* tr. Margaret Kohl (San Francisco: Harper, 1990).

2. See, e.g., Juan Segundo, *The Historical Jesus of the Synoptics,* tr. John Drury (Maryknoll, N.Y.: Orbis Books, 1985); Jon Sobrino, *Christology at the Crossroads: A Latin American Approach,* tr. John Drury (Maryknoll, N.Y.: Orbis Books, 1976); Leonardo Boff, *Jesus Christ, Liberator: A Critical Christology for Our Time* (Maryknoll, N.Y.: Orbis Books, 1978).

3. Rudolf Bultmann, *Jesus and the Word,* tr. Louise Pettibone Smith and Erminie Huntress Lantero (New York: Charles Scribner's Sons, 1958), 8.

are different. One can argue that Jesus' words and actions had political implications without arguing that Jesus was primarily a political actor. Few would totally deny the implications, though many would render it a relatively insignificant part of Jesus' intent. On the other hand, one could argue (like Reimarus and Brandon) that Jesus' political concerns provided the major motivation for his words and actions and that he deliberately intended his tactics to bring about political change—for example, by the expulsion of the Romans. I am not convinced that the available evidence supports the latter, but I do think that the repercussions of Jesus' political dimension are much more far-reaching than either popular understanding or past scholarly consensus would grant. I intend to show that that is the case.

The word "political" has so many connotations that its application to Jesus demands a definition. Dictionary definitions point to a theoretical meaning (relating to the science or theory of government) or to a practical meaning (being involved in political activities). I do not think Jesus was concerned with politics as a science. Was he "involved in politics"? If involvement means establishing a political party or seeking political office, my answer is "no." I doubt that Jesus put himself forward deliberately as Messiah or that he wished to establish an organization.

But I do believe that Jesus preached and taught a message that was thoroughly political, a message that demanded a social or political revolution. If Jesus had his way, the current ruling elites would no longer remain in their positions of power, or if they did, they would rule in a very different manner. In that sense he was political. Jesus operated out of a concern for justice and peace (*shalom*), not in a vague way, but on the basis of covenantal norms that had lapsed in the wake of the hellenization of Israel during and after the reign of Alexander the Great. Jesus was concerned for the healing of the body politic, the covenant community, and he had a clear vision of what that healing entailed in both the economic and the social sphere. On the basis of that vision, he addressed the social issues and tensions troubling the people.

Today when people hear that Jesus was political, many react immediately and say he was not political, he was spiritual. They have in mind what is meant by the often-repeated slogan, "The task of the church is spiritual; it is not to be involved in political matters." Such a dichotomy between social-political life and spiritual life contradicts the Israelite view that God gave the people their life together as a covenant people, and that their community life expressed or denied their covenant with God. I do not think that Jesus either invented that dichotomy or subscribed to it.[4]

To claim that Jesus was "political" is to say that Jesus promoted a restoration of the covenant community on the basis of the Torah and the prophets, both of which regarded the mundane aspects of life as "spiritual" issues. For him spiritual issues concern not merely the internal, private, and individual relationship between a person and God. The spiritual also governs interpersonal and community relations. This connection between political and spiritual was the standard understanding in the history of Israelite faith and life, as the voices of the prophets underscore again and again. Jesus was political in the same way the preexilic prophets in general were political: He believed that God's blessing of the people depended on their manifesting in the political sphere the justice God required of covenant people.

Although my interests in a political interpretation of Jesus are not merely academic, I do not intend to claim more than the available evidence justifies. I do not claim total "objectivity," nor do I think such a stance is possible. The lack of "objectivity" in our understanding of texts is more obvious in the work of others than in our own work. The self-delusion is clear when we notice how frequently the correct "historical understanding of Jesus" happens to coincide with the perspective of the interpreter; how often the "central meaning" of Jesus' teachings or Paul's letters coincides with the theological or faith convictions of the interpreter. How seldom do we find interpreters saying, "This is what Jesus or Paul really meant, and I disagree with him totally"? I hope that a recognition that personal convictions and perspectives shape our reading of history and texts will check me from simply writing my own viewpoints.

Another Book on Jesus?

Writing another book about Jesus indicates a belief that the definitive one has not yet been written. There are at least two reasons why no one will write the definitive one. First, historical subjects do not lend themselves to such certainty that further work becomes unnecessary. We may learn more and more facts about the past, but we never completely have the past open to us,

---

4. Martin Hengel does; see *Victory Over Violence: Jesus and the Revolutionaries,* tr. David Green (Philadelphia: Fortress Press, 1973), 1. Ellis Rivkin thinks the Pharisees already had; see *What Crucified Jesus? The Political Execution of a Charismatic* (Nashville: Abingdon Press, 1984), 47. I think both are wrong; see chapter 2 below.

with the actions, intentions, and motivations of the major actors laid bare for our critical or sympathetic gaze. Historians do not agree on the motivation of Julius Caesar, or what he would have done had he survived his attempt to control the Roman state. Similarly with Alexander the Great: Had he lived, what would he have done to consolidate the enormous territories he conquered? If agreement on such "academic" issues proves so difficult, it is even more true of those subjects that remain significant for our identity and our commitments in the present.

Abraham Lincoln and John Kennedy also remain subjects of discussion, difference of opinion, and disagreement. But for U.S. citizens, discussions about them are likely to be more heated because they are more immediately relevant to our understanding of ourselves and our nation than discussions of Julius Caesar or Alexander the Great.

This observation leads to a second reason we continue to write about historical subjects: We do so not merely to discover the past but also to discover ourselves. We investigate the past in part to see what it has to say. For millions in our culture, discussions about Jesus are even more important than discussions of Lincoln or Kennedy, and we are likely to carry them on with much more emotional fervor. When we say we cannot know all about him, his motives, his intentions, what he would have become had he not been executed, not only our minds but also our emotions and our convictions are engaged. But whether or not we are comfortable with the thought, we cannot know all about the human person Jesus. Scholars debate the degree of our knowledge or ignorance about Jesus, but no one would claim that we know Jesus completely, that we have his life laid bare for us to peruse and reflect upon. Thus, one reason for continuing to write about Jesus is that we are still trying to discover as much as we can about him as an important figure of our past and present.

The continuing discovery of Jesus takes place as a social process, not merely as an individual activity. I write as part of an intellectual and academic community that values truth that can stand in a public forum of competing claims above mere subjective opinion. Positions taken must be supported by evidence and rational argument. The desire to discover a Jesus concerned with political society is inadequate unless evidence and arguments support such a discovery. Neither can the wish to keep Jesus in a spiritual sphere divorced from the social tumult of his time provide a credible basis for valid interpretation of his life and work.

I write also as a member of a broad community that believes that Jesus and the religious movement that emerged from his historical ministry continue to have normative value. I write out of the conviction that the vision of the human individual and of social life that comes through the portraits of Jesus in the Gospels has the power to transform the world. But I write with the personal conviction that the very community that professes that vision often distorts it. As a defense against the moral decay in United States society and the meaninglessness that its materialism has spawned, many millions have turned to Christian faith seeking stability and goodness. While that turning has enabled meaningful lives for some, in other instances that faith appears to be a veneer over the dominant idols of American culture.

Uncritical acceptance in the name of Christian faith of a set of either "conservative" or "liberal" values, and the appeal to Jesus to justify those values, can only distort the historical Jesus and thwart genuine attempts to take seriously the vision of personal and social well-being that derives from the challenge he presented to his own time.

A historical study of Jesus will not bring to an end various misapplications of Christian faith, but such a concern nonetheless motivates this work. I do not think it would do justice to Jesus and his vision of the world to use him as an antidote to one misrepresentation by substituting another for it, and I have no desire to do that. I do wish, however, to assist a serious encounter with the Jesus who can be discovered through historical study as a reality test for the faith claims made on Jesus' behalf. Some visions of Jesus simply will not stand historical scrutiny, and they lead to theological and ethical distortions. Historical study provides a means to guard against such distortions by helping assure that the images today's followers have correspond to historical reality.

The personal subjectivity that each of us brings to the interpretive process often derives from the groups of which we are a part. Our religious tradition, our socioeconomic class, our race, and our political affiliation will significantly influence our reading of what any text says. Mainline Protestants in the United States, for example, are likely to think the biblical texts place supreme value on the individual. Personal sin and salvation and an ethic of individual responsibility are likely to be central to what such a Protestant hears the texts saying. A social construction that assumes the existence and primary importance of individual effort and initiative, and a corresponding affirmation of freedom of enterprise and freedom of choice, often forms a major part of that reading of the text.

Roman Catholics are more likely to emphasize concern for the church as the locus of God's action. Catholic interpretation more likely stresses the founding of the church and its endowment with power and authority for its eucharistic and priestly ministry. The apostles as a group with Peter at the head, rather than as individuals, are likely to be seen as the beginning of the church.

Radical Protestants such as Mennonites are likely to share the Catholic perception that the gospel concerns community and not merely individuals. They interpret that community differently, however, with less emphasis on the church as an institution in a world of institutions. For radical Protestants, the church forms an isolated and minority community that speaks to the world while deriving its values from its own internal life. As they read the Gospels, the institutional church, with its sacraments and priesthood, will seem less important to Jesus and his disciples than obedience to a radical ethic.

People who feel themselves victims of power structures are much more likely to see in the Gospels the theme of the liberation for the oppressed, to interpret Jesus as a deliverer who promises a new life of freedom and justice for those who have suffered injustice.[5] Central to their interpretation is likely to be Luke's account of Jesus' reading from the book of Isaiah in the synagogue as his first public act:

> The Spirit of the Lord is upon me,
>   because he has anointed me to bring good news to the poor.
> He has sent me to proclaim release to the captives
>   and recovery of sight to the blind,
>   to let the oppressed go free,
> to proclaim the year of the Lord's favor.
>   (Luke 4:18–19, alluding to Isa. 61:1–2; 58:6).

Such diversity in interpretation of the Gospels characterizes the modern Christian world; it is found also in the scholarly world. But it is nothing new. The Gospels themselves confirm the inevitability and the validity of differing interpretations. True, the Gospels attribute the "misunderstanding" to the hardness of heart of Jesus' hearers, to their refusal to hear the message with open minds, or to their inability during the course of events to know the full meaning of what they were seeing. But beyond the apologetic and theological explanations, we can detect individuals and groups reacting quite differently

---

5. See, for example, Ernesto Cardenal, *The Gospel in Solentiname* (Maryknoll, N.Y.: Orbis Books, 1976).

to the words and actions of Jesus, demonstrating that Jesus' intent and meanings were not unambiguously apparent to all.

The Gospels do more than show that individual hearers interpreted Jesus differently, for good or bad effect. The Gospels themselves do not view Jesus through a single lens. While the Gospels share much in common, each has a unique way of telling the same story of Jesus. In preserving these four portraits of Jesus and according them equal authority, the church accepted the reality and validity of differing interpretations and differing perspectives on the life and ministry of Jesus.

That fact alone should convince us the church did not regard precise historical accuracy as the most important element in the Gospels. The church regarded the Gospels as witnesses and understood them to contain both report and reflection. The Gospel writers certainly intended to present information about Jesus and his words, but they also intended to present testimony to their own experience and their own interpretation of the significance of those events and words. To excise from the Gospels the element of personal and communal witness and to make them into factual, objective accounts of Jesus is to turn them into something their authors did not intend them to be.

A Dialogical Approach

The recognition that the Gospels and their interpreters vary in their perspectives not only compounds our problem of knowing about Jesus; it also offers a useful insight in dealing with the problem. Like the Gospel writers, each reader of this book, as well as its author, has and will have a distinctive view of the matters it deals with. This fact suggests the need for a "dialogical interpretation." A dialogue is literally a talking through an issue. As seen in its classical form in Plato's dialogues, a dialogue involves conversation, a listening and a speaking in the presence of an other.[6]

Dialogue differs from monologue in that in the former one is open to another voice and in the latter one is isolated and can hear only one's own voice. A dialogical approach to biblical interpretation involves a genuine dialogue in which all are listeners and all are speakers assumed to have equal

---

6. The problem with the Platonic model is that usually one person does most of the speaking and the others the listening; one has all the major insights (even if he pretends they come from others) and the others are reluctantly or eagerly led along by him.

claim to be heard. The readers of this book are invited to a dialogical process of listening and speaking. Such a dialogue needs to be broadly based and to include elements that are historical, personal, communal, and ecumenical.

Historical dialogue involves an encounter with history, an interrogation *of* history and an interrogation *by* history. Even if the Gospel texts do not give us purely objective history, they do contain history. There is record of event and word, mediated through the words of those who saw, heard, and interpreted what was going on. If the Gospels simply gave us the words of Jesus, the task of historical dialogue would be much simpler: We could encounter Jesus' words directly and seek their meaning, which even then might not be transparent. The Gospels, however, provide a written culmination of a process of remembering and interpreting Jesus. The texts thus bring the reader into the world of Jesus but also into the worlds of the communities whose experiences lie behind the written texts. The interpreter's own world provides another major ingredient in the historical dialogue between reader and text. As the interpreter moves within these various horizons, both a distancing and an approaching are necessary.

Even though we cannot ferret out with certainty "what it meant"[7] or give an account of "what really happened" or "what was actually said," it is both instructive and legitimate to distance ourselves momentarily and ask questions. In what context might Jesus have said or done this? Presumably Jesus intended to impart some teaching or to affect his hearers in some fashion. What might he have intended by "Love your enemies" in the context of the Roman occupation of an internally conflictive Palestine? Were his words and actions intended to influence individual and community life within a concretely real world of political, economic, social, and religious strife and confusion? Or was Jesus disengaged from that history, offering a spiritual haven for those who looked for escape from it?

Even though we can never know the precise occasion for a specific word, the more we can know the general historical context, the more nearly we can approach a historical understanding of Jesus' meaning. The nuances of his words will be quite different depending on how we question the history within whose context they were given or recorded. Different interpretations of "what it meant" by authors using similar methods of inquiry demonstrate

---

7. Krister Stendahl made a useful distinction between "what it meant" and "what it means" in "Biblical Theology, Contemporary," *The Interpreter's Dictionary of the Bible,* ed. George Buttrick et al. (Nashville: Abingdon Press, 1962), 1:418–32. These two are not merely chronologically successive stages but interactive.

that laying out the original meaning of the text is finally impossible. That can mean texts have plural rather than single meanings, or that the interpreters' own perceptions and convictions color their readings of the texts, or both. In either event precisely "what it meant" always eludes. But that does not mean we should give up the question, for the question itself reminds us that the text has its own horizons and its own integrity apart from our encounter with it. The act of historical distancing helps check our tendency to bring the text so completely into our horizon that the text has little chance of providing the possibility of new insight, growth, and change.[8]

If distancing were the final act of interpretation, texts would remain as dry bones. A second stage in historical dialogue with a text is drawing near, asking "what it means." As interpreters interrogate the texts concerning history, texts are also interrogating the interpreters concerning their history. The process of drawing near moves the interpreter from historical to *personal dialogue*. The texts do not finally say anything significant to the readers unless they speak to present existence in the world. The reader inevitably brings his or her own presuppositions, questions, anxieties, hopes, and fears to the reading of the text. The text does not merely provide information about the world outside or about past or future events. It gives insight into present existence, challenges our perceptions and convictions, and opens up new possibilities for shaping our future.

The danger of subjectivity here is obvious: The text can be reduced to speaking only of those matters that the reader brings to it. The word the text gives may be predetermined by the way the reader has phrased the questions. Nevertheless, the way out of the subjectivity trap is not the way of objective interpretation. The way forward involves recognizing the danger posed and recognizing the other dimensions of dialogical interpretation that lead the reader to further reflection.

Historical and personal dialogue can be individual exercises in interpretation; that is both their strength and their weakness. Engagement with the texts must be individual, but it must be not only individual. The texts derive from social and political contexts and cannot finally be limited to individual interpretation. Further, personal existence and personal faith happen in a communal context of some kind. Thus personal dialogue with texts needs also to be *communal dialogue*. Most people have heard the texts first in a

---

8. Patrick Henry, *New Directions in New Testament Study* (Philadelphia: Westminster Press, 1979), 64.

communal setting, and along with the texts they have learned a communal interpretation prior to developing a personal interpretation. We live in communities that can enhance our perception of texts and challenge our personal interpretations. Our reading of texts needs to be subjected to conversation with our communities, whether the communities are ecclesiastical, social, political, or academic. At the same time, the dialogical process demands that communal understandings be tested by personal and historical dialogue.

The communal reading has wider components than merely the denomination or the social or family group to which one belongs. In interpreting the texts, personal views shaped in small communities need correction by those larger communities. Personal struggles to understand the texts also need to keep those larger communities in mind. That means that social as well as personal concerns and questions are appropriate to the interpreter's search for the meaning of texts. What do the texts have to say regarding the issues facing those national and political structures to which we belong?

Communal experience can be liberating or stultifying. Communities can bind their members within their own dogmas, or they can allow persons the freedom to express themselves. They can lead their members to accept or reject new ideas and strange people; read texts with eagerness for insight or with fear of change; view texts with a politics of challenge or a politics of conformity. Whether religious, political, or academic, communities can be hospitable places of renewal or bastions of the status quo. Communal interpretation is therefore necessary and promising, providing it embodies the requisite openness to the challenge of the texts it preserves and seeks to hear. To guard against its abuses and to secure its promise, communal dialogue needs always to take place along with other dialogical dimensions.

Dialogical interpretation is therefore appropriately *ecumenical*. As interpreters we are easily entrapped in our own communities; as we read the texts we are likely to hear mostly the echoes of the traditions that have been accepted within those communities. Ecumenical dialogue offers a challenge and a promise to the biblical interpreter. It challenges by providing new angles of vision. It has been too easy for Protestant, Catholic, and Jew to dismiss the interpretations of the others as representing biases of their traditions; it is more difficult to allow others' visions to challenge one's own. A recognition that the meaning and interpretation of a text does not lie on the surface, and a recognition of the importance and relativity of various perspectives, allows even remote or strange interpretations to challenge one's views. That challenge contains within it the assurance that the reading will be both more reliable and more relevant to the world inhabited by other communities together with one's own.

In principle that dialogue ought to include communities outside the Jewish and Christian traditions. Listening to Muslim, Hindu, or Buddhist responses to the traditions about Jesus can sharpen the questions and suggest different perspectives. Reading S. Radhakrishnan's interpretation of Jesus as a mystic provides insight into the issues facing the interpreter of John's Gospel. Mohandas Gandhi's radical understanding of Jesus as a source of courage for political change challenges more timid Christian responses.

This interpretation of Jesus intends to be a part of such a broadly dialogical approach and to invite the reader to participate in it as fully as possible. I will not be satisfied to dialogue only within the context of a religious community or only within a community of New Testament scholars. I hope to have connection to both. Too often wide gulfs separate what we do in the classroom and library from what happens in the ongoing communities who claim allegiance to Jesus in one form or another. A genuinely political interpretation of Jesus must take place within and for the various communities in which we live.

The Necessary Peril of Modernizing Jesus

Dialogical interpretation can benefit from the warning Henry Cadbury gave a previous generation about the "peril of modernizing Jesus." Cadbury recognized that the tendency to modernize arose almost immediately. There is no Gospel account of Jesus that does not contain the efforts of Jesus' followers to keep him current, to keep him in the context of their own changing lives.

Modernizing in that sense means maintaining a dialogical relationship with a past event or person. If persons bring Jesus into their sphere and engage him in serious dialogue about issues of importance, that very process has at least some aspects of modernizing. In that sense modernizing is nothing other than seeking relevance. The problem is how to keep Jesus relevant without distorting him and his message.

The peril of modernizing is also the necessity of modernizing: If one cannot bring the past into the present through dialogue with it, the past has lost its significance. For that reason biblical interpretation is never finished. Texts are open-ended because life continues. We keep writing books and articles on the biblical material although much of what we write has been said many times over. We can, of course, argue that past interpreters have missed the point at many places, that we have new and better information or improved methods of getting at the meaning of texts. While all of that is true, the real reason we keep up the task of interpretation is that we ourselves want to continue the dialogue. Even individually, as our experience continues, as our perspectives broaden or change, we see new meanings in texts. We could say that those new meanings were there all the time and we simply did not recognize them, and that may be partially true. But it is even more true that those meanings have emerged in the dialogical process of interpreting the texts and ourselves.

Jesus and the Gospels

The Gospels of the New Testament are the major source of our knowledge of Jesus. Other New Testament writings, such as Paul's letters, reflect on the meaning of Jesus but rarely present stories or sayings purporting to come from his earthly ministry. From them we learn about the movement initiated by his followers after Jesus' death. These writings, in other words, present the emerging Christian communities, their establishment, struggles, attempts to define themselves in relation to their culture, theological and ethical disputes, and testimony to their faith.

Sources outside the New Testament present very meager direct historical information about Jesus and his teachings. Among noncanonical Christian writings, the *Gospel of Thomas* has gained increasing recognition as a valuable source for Jesus' sayings. This early Christian writing, discovered in Egypt in 1945, contains 114 sayings attributed to Jesus. It includes no narratives about Jesus, not even of his miracles or his death. In that regard it is very much like the hypothetical Q, but with its own distinctive flavor that separates it from the Synoptic Gospels and from Q. Some have thought that the sayings in *Thomas* derive from the Synoptics, but now some scholars regard it as an independent and equally valuable source for Jesus' words.[9]

Roman and Jewish historians provide confirmation of Jesus' historical existence and location but provide little specific information that would

---

9. This is the judgment of the "Jesus Seminar" as reflected in Robert W. Funk and Mahlon H. Smith, *The Gospel of Mark: Red Letter Edition* (Sonoma, Calif.: Polebridge Press, 1991), 10–11. See also H. W. Attridge, "Gospel of Thomas," *Harper's Bible Dictionary,* ed. Paul J. Achtemeier et al. (San Francisco: Harper & Row, 1985), 355–56; John Dominic Crossan, *The Historical Jesus* (San Francisco: Harper, 1991), 427–28.

confirm or contradict the Gospels. The Jewish historian Josephus tells of the stoning of James "the brother of Jesus, who was called Christ."[10] Josephus's writings contain a second reference to Jesus that is of questionable value:

> About this time there lived Jesus, a wise man, if indeed one ought to call him a man. For he was one who wrought surprising feats and was a teacher of such people as accept the truth gladly. He won over many Jews and many of the Greeks. He was the Messiah. When Pilate, upon hearing him accused by men of the highest standing amongst us, had condemned him to be crucified, those who had in the first place come to love him did not give up their affection for him. On the third day he appeared to them restored to life, for the prophets of God had prophesied these and countless other marvellous things about him. And the tribe of Christians, so called after him, has still to this day not disappeared.[11]

Because of the strong Christian flavor of this passage, scholars believe it is a Christian insertion. The Roman historian Tacitus reports that "Christus . . . was executed at the hands of the procurator Pontius Pilate in the reign of Tiberius."[12]

More valuable than this direct evidence are the rich sources of information about the Jewish world of Jesus' time provided by Josephus's extensive writings and by the ancient documents from Qumran known as the Dead Sea Scrolls. While Josephus is by no means an objective reporter, he provides invaluable information about historical events as well as the social, political, economic, and religious context within which Jesus' active ministry took place. The Dead Sea Scrolls provide insight into the thought and practice of a disaffected Jewish sect whose concerns and ideals have an affinity with the movements associated with John the Baptist and Jesus. Not merely the religious thought and practice but also the social ferment expressed through religious faith during the time of Jesus has become much more available.

The following interpretation of Jesus presupposes certain understandings of the Gospels and their relation to Jesus' own history. I share much of the broad consensus of New Testament scholarship. Robert W. Funk and Mahlon H. Smith provide a valuable presentation of that consensus in a work

---

10. *Jewish Antiquities* XX.200.
11. *Jewish Antiquities* XVIII.63–64.
12. Tacitus, *Annals* XV.44, quoted in C. K. Barrett, *New Testament Background: Selected Documents* (New York: Harper & Brothers, 1961), 15.

deriving from the "Jesus Seminar."[13] The following summary is based on or is consistent with the "premises" from that account.

1. "The historical Jesus is to be distinguished from the Gospel portraits of him."[14]
2. The tradition about Jesus circulated orally before it was written down.
3. The traditions about Jesus were preserved in the context of the church's life and work; thus they reflect not only the historical situation of Jesus but also the changing situation, beliefs, and problems of the church.
4. The *Gospel of Thomas* and the Q document were among the earliest written accounts of Jesus' teaching; both were composed during the period 50–60 C.E.
5. Mark, the earliest of the canonical Gospels, was composed around 70 C.E.
6. Matthew and Luke, using Mark and Q as primary sources, were composed around 85–90 C.E.
7. The Gospel of John, composed around 80–100 C.E., used an earlier "book of signs" and differs substantially in the mode and content of Jesus' words.
8. Only a part of the sayings and parables attributed to Jesus were actually spoken by him.[15]
9. The Gospels and Jesus should be studied by the same methods by which other ancient texts and persons are studied.
10. Like other persons, Jesus is best understood within the context of the Jewish social and religious milieu of which he was a part.
11. Historical research results in probabilities rather than in certainties.

Criteria of Authenticity

Critical scholars differ in regard to the degree of their skepticism regarding the reliability of the tradition. Various attempts have been made to establish criteria by which to distinguish between authentic and inauthentic material. Though by no means universally accepted, the following criteria have been widely used. With modifications and reservations stated, they will provide guidelines for my interpretation of the Gospels.

1. Criterion of multiple attestation. Attitudes, teachings, and actions found

---

13. Funk and Smith, *The Gospel of Mark*, 1–26.
14. Funk and Smith, *Gospel of Mark*, 2.
15. The Jesus Seminar states it more skeptically: "Only a small portion of the sayings attributed to Jesus in the gospels was actually spoken by him. . . . A larger portion of the parables goes back to Jesus." See Funk and Smith, *Gospel of Mark*, 17.

in multiple, independent layers of tradition (for example, Mark, Q, *Thomas*) and/or in different types of traditions (for example, in parables, aphorisms, apocalyptic pronouncements) have stronger claim to be authentic than a point made, for example, in a single miracle story in Mark, even if Luke and Matthew follow Mark in using it.

2. Criterion of dissimilarity. According to this test, if possible derivation from Judaism or the early church cannot account for any saying attributed to Jesus, it has a good claim to authenticity.

Although it is useful, problems attend this criterion. First, our records of Judaism and the early church are too incomplete to rely fully on this test. Second, it posits too radical a difference between Jesus and his contemporaries in Judaism and too radical a difference between him and his successors in the church. Third, this criterion assumes that what is most central to Jesus is what most distinguishes him from Judaism.[16] That posits a break between Jesus and Judaism such as we find in the Gospel of John but which is unlikely to be historically warranted. Thus, this criterion must be applied critically. It does provide one particular measure that can prove useful for purposes of exploring my thesis: Since the church as it moved outside the Palestinian context did not continue to be concerned about the social and political issues of Palestine, any materials manifesting such an interest have a strong claim to be authentic. The church tended to eschew political involvements and thus to remove rather than to introduce such concerns.

3. Criterion of coherence. As usually stated, this criterion logically follows the criterion of dissimilarity. The latter helps to establish a "critically assured minimum" of authentic materials. This third criterion can add to that minimum additional materials that may not on their own account have sufficient claim to authenticity but that cohere with the minimum, are consistent with it, and thus help to enlarge the picture provided.

While such a criterion is difficult to use, it does have a specific application to our question. A well-substantiated fact is that Jesus was crucified by the Romans as a politically dangerous person. A credible interpretation of his words and actions must "cohere" with that fact in an intelligible fashion. Then, too, the overall presentation of Jesus must have coherence and consistency enough to commend itself to rational inquirers.

---

16. Marcus J. Borg, *Conflict, Holiness and Politics in the Teachings of Jesus* (Lewiston, N.Y.: Edwin Mellen Press, 1984), 21.

What Lies Ahead

Chapter 1 presents the historical context in which Jesus' ministry took place, not merely so the reader will have a backdrop against which to view Jesus, but so that the social issues and tensions that Jesus himself addressed are clear.

Chapter 2 investigates the critical issue of Jesus' execution by the Romans, which is the most critically assured fact we can know about Jesus. That execution provides the most assured historical fact we have in the Gospels. It must be fully accounted for in any credible interpretations of Jesus. Both historical and theological interpretations of Jesus have a large stake in his death.

Chapter 3 concentrates on the central symbol in Jesus' message, the kingdom of God. Jesus proclaims the kingdom as promise, implying that the present conditions did not conform to the kingdom. Jesus' execution expressed the response of political powers to Jesus' preaching of the kingdom. I will ask how Jesus' critique of social, political, economic, and religious conditions and his announcement of a coming kingdom generated fear and opposition. Interpretations of Jesus divide primarily in their understanding of what Jesus meant by the kingdom. A historical understanding must trace the connection between Jesus' understanding of the kingdom and his execution.

Chapter 4 will present an exposition of Jesus' nonparabolic teachings. I will attempt to show how his teachings confirm that Jesus used the kingdom of God as a political metaphor to convey a social-political message and thus how his teachings were a significant factor in leading to his execution as an agitator of the people. Only if that is the case can one understand why the Romans would have crucified him.

Chapter 5 will present an interpretation of some of Jesus' parables that I believe inform us both of the circumstances in which Jesus worked and of the politically oriented message that he delivered. I will offer an interpretation of selected parables to show how Jesus understood the social and economic issues that the parables point to.

Chapter 6 will interpret the meaning of discipleship reflected in Jesus' call, teaching, and commissioning disciples as he did. The Twelve symbolize the renewal of all Israel. The radical demands made of disciples, the tasks they were assigned, and their extension of Jesus' work reveal further the nature of Jesus' message and the reasons for his execution.

Chapter 7 will interpret the spirituality that integrates and motivates Jesus' political teaching. Focusing on the "Lord's Prayer," I will show how Jesus' piety engaged the social and political issues, holding together God's kingdom and God's will for the covenant people.

Chapter 8 will address the question of Jesus' identity. It will argue that Jesus' identity is attached less to titles than to his actions, and that his actions show that social revolution, and not simply personal renewal, was his intent.

CHAPTER ONE

"We Have No King but Caesar"

The Gospel of John portrays a scene during the proceedings against Jesus in which Pilate asks in response to the crowd's demand that he crucify Jesus, "Shall I crucify your King?" The people reply, "We have no king but Caesar" (John 19:13–16, RSV). The scene provides an outstanding example of John's use of irony in which the speaker stands self-condemned. The Johannine irony raises historical and theological questions: Would it be possible to have any other king as long as Caesar was king? Could a messiah of any sort coexist with Caesar's rule? Could God's kingdom, with or without a messiah, coexist with Caesar's rule? If Jesus were identified as Messiah, or if Jesus preached the kingdom of God, was execution the inevitable result, or was Jesus executed because the Romans misunderstood him and his message?

The Romans did crucify Jesus. Any credible interpretation of Jesus must account for that indisputable fact. Crucifixion was political execution, a death penalty meted out by the Romans to those whose activities showed them to be dangerous to civil order. Did the Roman governor have any sufficient reason for this political execution?

Most traditional and most scholarly interpretations of Jesus say no: Jesus' execution took place either because his intentions were misunderstood or because the religious leaders were jealous or afraid of his influence with the people. The thesis of this book is that as a matter of historical truth, the Romans, in conjunction with Jewish political leaders, had good reason to execute Jesus. Jesus' words and actions called for radical social and political change. In addressing concrete social and political issues of his day, Jesus posed a sufficient threat to the authorities that they feared his influence.

Any attempt to answer questions about Jesus' execution demands knowledge of the circumstances of his life and ministry. Though the Gospels do not intentionally portray the historical background of Jesus or the historical events leading to his death, they provide information necessary for investigating those events.

The Jewish historian Josephus provides much fuller information in his two long works, *Jewish Antiquities* and *The Jewish War.* Josephus belonged to the elite groups in Roman Palestine, having family connections with priestly and royal (Hasmonaean) families. Born in 37–38 C.E., he participated as a young commander of Jewish troops during the war with Rome in 66–67. After the Romans captured him, he ingratiated himself with them, and following the war he went to live in Rome. He enjoyed the patronage of the imperial court, which enabled him to write extensive histories of the Jewish people. He held strong opinions about the causes of the unrest that led to the war against Rome. He wanted to show Jews in a favorable light, and thus he interpreted the conflict as the result of a small group of fanatics.[1] Although Josephus's views need to be judged critically, he provides a wealth of historical information.

David Rhoads,[2] Richard Horsley,[3] and John Dominic Crossan[4] employ Josephus's writings extensively to describe the social and political environment of Jesus. An invaluable two-volume work by an international and ecumenical team of scholars, edited by S. Safrai and M. Stern,[5] also uses Josephus extensively. The latter enlarges the base to include a wealth of Jewish, Christian, and Roman sources to describe Jewish life in Jesus' time. In what follows, I draw extensively on these works not merely to paint the background against which Jesus worked but to show the social and political tensions that engaged his attention. Jesus' world was in the midst of social revolution, and Jesus was executed because of his participation in it.

---

1. H. W. Attridge, "Josephus," *Harper's Bible Dictionary,* 508.
2. David M. Rhoads, *Israel in Revolution: 6–74 C.E.: A Political History Based on the Writings of Josephus* (Philadelphia: Fortress Press, 1976).
3. Richard Horsley, *Jesus and the Spiral of Violence* (San Francisco: Harper & Row, 1987); see also Richard A. Horsley and John S. Hanson, *Bandits, Prophets, and Messiahs: Popular Movements in the Time of Jesus* (Minneapolis: Winston Press, 1985), 31.
4. Crossan, *Historical Jesus.*
5. *The Jewish People in the First Century: Historical Geography, Political History, Social, Cultural, and Religious Life and Institutions* (Philadelphia: Fortress Press, 1974).

Rome as the Superpower

In Jesus' day Rome was the master of the world, and Rome intended to maintain that position. All who dared to challenge Rome were dealt with severely. Rome's rule was not all bad: Peace was maintained, travel was safe, taxes were not more excessive than under other world rulers, order and new opportunity were there for many. There were, however, negative consequences of Rome's rule of Palestine. Social, political, and economic circumstances within Israel worsened under Roman rule. Those circumstances led to a Jewish revolt some thirty-five years after Jesus' death, with disastrous consequences for the Jews. The revolt was already brewing in Jesus' day. The conditions that led to it claimed Jesus' prophetic attention and thus were among the causes of his death.

Rome had taken control of Palestine in 63 B.C.E. The takeover resulted from factors both external and internal to Palestine. Rome's growing power in the eastern Mediterranean world made it almost inevitable that Rome would rule Palestine. Internal circumstances within Palestine provided the occasion for it to happen. Contending factions of the ruling Jewish family, the Hasmonaeans, had in fact invited the Romans to intervene and to settle their internal dispute.

The Roman general Pompey, stationed in Syria, acceded to their request. Pompey wanted to reduce the size and influence of the Hasmonaean kingdom. He invaded, besieged, then took Jerusalem, and, according to Josephus, promptly violated the Holy of Holies.[6] He freed those Greek cities in the Decapolis and on the coast that the Hasmonaeans had brought under Jewish control; Jews from those cities crowded into Judea.[7]

The presence of Rome did not end the struggle for political control of Palestine. Rival factions among both the Hasmonaeans and the Romans vied for control for nearly a generation, repeatedly devastated the land, imposed heavy taxes, and generated more social unrest.[8] The Romans brutally subjugated the people, crucifying or enslaving large numbers.[9] By 55 B.C.E. Rome had gained sufficient control to appoint as procurator an Idumean with connections to the Hasmonaean family, named Antipater. At Antipater's

---

6. *Jewish Antiquities* XIV.105.

7. John E. Stambaugh and David L. Balch, *The New Testament in Its Social Environment* (Philadelphia: Westminster Press, 1986), 23.

8. Horsley and Hanson, *Bandits, Prophets, and Messiahs,* 31.

9. Horsley and Hanson, *Bandits, Prophets, and Messiahs,* 31, citing Josephus, *Jewish Antiquities* XIV.120, 272–75; XVII.288–89, 295; and *Jewish War* I.180, 219–20.

death in 43, Rome appointed his son Herod as king, though it took several years and Roman assistance for Herod to subdue all opponents and establish his control over Palestine. His marriage in 37 to a princess of the Jewish royal family gave some semblance of legitimacy to his title as king of the Jews.

Herod proved to be a reliable ally of the Roman Empire, endeavoring through his policies and his ambitious building program to make Palestine a reflection of Roman greatness. Both inside and outside Palestine, Herod undertook major building projects.[10] His Temple in Jerusalem set a world record for overall size, even though the sanctuary was similar in size to Solomon's Temple.[11]

Herod's palace had the reputation of being the largest in the world until Nero built a larger one in Rome. Josephus describes it as "baffling all description," as more extravagant than any other, with immense banquet halls, splendid decorations, and rare stones. Josephus laments that it was destroyed, not by the Romans, but by the rebels when the revolt against Rome broke out.[12] Herod also constructed a remarkable harbor of Caesarea, which Broshi describes as "the most technologically advanced . . . in antiquity."[13]

Herod sought to maintain good relations with Jewish leadership, as his professed belief in the Torah indicates. Neither that profession nor the rebuilding the Temple on such a grand scale necessarily shows a genuine interest in Jewish faith. The Temple certainly provided an opportunity to court Jewish favor, and not incidentally its lavish style and size brought increased prestige to Herod.

Herod died in 4 B.C.E. Rome rewarded his faithfulness and expressed its preferred policy of governing through local client kings by appointing Herod's sons to succeed him. However, Rome did not fully honor Herod's request regarding titles his sons should have. Three sons ruled his divided kingdom: Herod Antipas ruled Galilee and Perea; Philip ruled northeast of Galilee, in an area without many Jews; and Archaelaus ruled Samaria, Judea, Idumaea.

Herod Antipas and Philip succeeded in holding on to their kingdoms, Herod Antipas ruling in Galilee during Jesus' ministry in the late twenties.

---

10. Magen Broshi, "The Role of the Temple in the Herodian Economy," *Journal of Jewish Studies* 38 (1987): 31, describes Herod's projects as "showy." For a fuller description of Herod's building projects, see G. Foerster, "Art and Architecture in Palestine," in Safrai and Stern, *Jewish People in the First Century*.

11. For the details, see Carol L. Myers, "The Temple," *Harper's Bible Dictionary*, 1028.

12. Josephus, *Jewish War* V.176–83.

13. Broshi, "The Role of the Temple," 31.

Archelaus was less fortunate: Scandal and internal tension worsened to the point that the Romans removed him in 6 C.E. They established direct Roman rule in Judea with procurators from Rome. The Apostles' Creed enshrines the fifth and most famous of the Roman governors in describing Jesus as "crucified under Pontius Pilate."

Any Roman governor of Judea was bound to have a difficult time because of the social conditions there and because of the desire for independence. But Pilate made his task more difficult than necessary by ignoring Jewish sensibilities concerning their religion. On one occasion he brought Roman troops with military insignia bearing the image of the emperor into Jerusalem against the sage advice of Jewish and Roman advisers. When the Jews protested this "idolatry," Pilate surrounded them with troops and threatened to slaughter them. He relented only when the demonstrators extended their necks and offered to die rather than have the Torah transgressed.[14] On another occasion Pilate expropriated funds from the Temple treasury to build an aqueduct to bring water into Jerusalem. Since these funds were designated to support Temple sacrifices, it is no wonder the Jews protested vehemently. Pilate put down the protest with force.[15]

The Romans removed Pilate from office in 36 after he sent cavalry and heavy infantry against a large crowd at Mount Gerizim. The crowd had gathered in response to a Samaritan prophet who promised to show them holy vessels he claimed Moses had hidden there.[16]

The Challenge of Hellenism

Roman rule, whether direct or indirect, posed a threat to traditional Jewish values. That threat was not new, since Israel had never been isolated from the influence of its neighbors. Many traditionalists in Israel believed its future as God's people depended on shielding the people from the idolatries of the Gentiles. Prophets and priests said the destruction of the nation by the Babylonians (586 B.C.E.) was due to the corrupting influence of foreign neighbors. After the Babylonian exile, the Torah provided a shield, as the small Jewish community sought to maintain its identity and integrity regardless of the foreign rulers who held political power over it. The Jews became more and more a community of the Torah.

---

14. Josephus, *Jewish War* II.169–74; *Jewish Antiquities* XVIII.55–59.
15. Josephus, *Jewish War* II.175–77; *Jewish Antiquities* XVIII.60–62.
16. Josephus, *Jewish Antiquities* XVIII.85–89.

During their rule over the Jews, the Persians (538–332 B.C.E.) left them free to pursue their religious traditions without major interference. New threats came with the conquests of Alexander the Great, who set in motion political and cultural forces that had severe impact on Jewish society. Following Alexander's death in 323, political control of Palestine passed to the dynasties his generals set up: The Seleucids in Syria and the Ptolemies in Egypt vied for control of the politically and commercially strategic land. Like Alexander, they promoted Greek language, Greek culture, and Greek ways.

Whether under Syrian or Egyptian domination, many among Palestine's leading classes were attracted to the modernity that Hellenistic civilization represented. Then, too, not all the people of Palestine were Jews. Jewish settlements throughout Palestine were surrounded by a diverse Gentile population whose upper classes were thoroughly hellenized. The Jews could easily have lost their distinct identity and become amalgamated into the Hellenistic culture of the Near East.[17]

Hellenism was especially attractive to the Jewish upper classes, among whom were the main priestly families. Influential Jewish families such as the wealthy Tobiads and some of the high priestly Oniads were inclined to transform Jewish society so that its distinctiveness was replaced by Hellenistic institutions and values. As part of a ruling class, the high priest no longer spoke to the secular ruler on behalf of the people but spoke to the people on behalf of the ruler.[18]

The Maccabean revolt in 167 B.C.E. expressed strong opposition to hellenization. Led by country priests affirming traditional ways, the revolt represented an attempt to maintain a Jewish nation committed to the distinctive faith of a covenant people. As a significant part of this attempt, the revolutionaries changed the high priestly families who controlled the Temple.[19] Stern believes that the Hasmonaean revolt enabled Judaism as a national and religious entity to survive.[20]

The revolt intended to establish the kingdom of God. As the book of Daniel expressed the convictions of those who precipitated it, the kingdom was to be in the hands of a "son of man" in contrast to the animals who

17. M. Stern, "Aspects of Jewish Society: The Priesthood and Other Classes," in *The Jewish People in the First Century,* ed. S. Safrai and M. Stern (Assen and Amsterdam: Van Gorcum, 1976), 2:564.

18. Stern, "Aspects of Jewish Society," 2:565–67. Onias III "was loyal to Judaism," but others of his house were not, according to Stern.

19. Stern, "Aspects of Jewish Society," 2:566.

20. Stern, "Aspects of Jewish Society," 2:566.

symbolized foreign rule (Dan. 7:13, RSV). That human figure represented "people of the holy ones of the Most High," whose dominion God will establish forever (Dan. 7:27).

Regardless of its intent, that revolt did not establish God's kingdom, nor did it end the tendency toward hellenization, nor does it seem to have brought about a genuine social revolution. Even if pressure from the peasant population spurred it on, the change that occurred was more political than social: One ruling group supplanted another, but rule remained in the hands of the same social class.

The truth of this statement is seen in the fact that later Hasmonaeans brought into alliance with Jewish elites other important families on the borders of Palestine, such as the family of Antipas, father of Antipater, and thus the ancestor of Herod.[21] Herod continued the policy of realigning the ruling elites. As part of his struggle against the Hasmonaeans, he brought Diaspora Jews from Egypt and Babylon to be high priests, leading to the establishment of the high priestly oligarchies that remained until the revolt against Rome in 66.[22]

The drive toward hellenization of Palestine continued under Herod. He promoted Hellenistic ideas and practices, established gymnasia, stadia, and theaters to encourage cosmopolitan ways. In Gentile areas of Palestine he built Roman temples and promoted the imperial cult, though he avoided doing so in Jewish areas. Just as he built Roman temples in his new cities, Herod rebuilt the Jerusalem Temple (23 B.C.E.). The style of that Temple conformed to the plans of Roman temples. The Temple itself thus provides "additional evidence of [Herod's] utter subjection to Augustus and of the impact of Hellenistic Roman styles on the character of his buildings even in his people's most sacred places."[23]

Residences in the Herodian quarter of Jerusalem show the influence of Hellenistic architecture and luxury on Herod.[24] The subjection is evidenced also by his building temples to Augustus at Caesarea and Sebaste (Samaria), towns that Herod named in honor of Augustus.

Herod strengthened the Hellenistic development of Palestine by the cultivation of good relations with elite families from among Diaspora Jews

21. Josephus, *Jewish Antiquities* XIV.10, cited by Stern, "Aspects of Jewish Society," 2:569.
22. Stern, "Aspects of Jewish Society," 2:570. Stern notes that the famous House of Hillel also came from Babylonia.
23. Foerster, "Art and Architecture in Palestine," 980.
24. For an indication of the Hellenistic influence in architecture, see N. Avigad, *The Herodian Quarter in Jerusalem* (Jerusalem: Keter Publishing House, 1989).

and from non-Jewish parts of Palestine.[25] Whether Herod tried to fuse
Hellenism and Judaism, or how successful he might have been in doing so, or
to what extent his activities profoundly affected Jewish society are subject to
debate.[26] However, it is difficult to see how the placing of hellenized Jews in
the high priesthood and promoting an elite society with a Hellenistic spirit
could avoid having significant impact on Jewish society. Perhaps Herod's
actions in promoting Hellenism among the upper classes so outraged those
who were not already thoroughly hellenized that his efforts had little
influence among ordinary people. Near the end of his reign his conflict with
the Pharisees and with the whole nation was such that revolts broke out
against the Herodian dynasty. Though a large part of the motivation for revolt
was due to economic and political tensions, Herod's promotion of alien
values and attitudes increased the tensions.

At Herod's death, the people were not only thoroughly alienated from his
regime due to his excesses, intrigues, and remoteness from Judaic values
(even though he affirmed his allegiance to Torah), they were also exhausted
economically. Economic factors were not the least of the reasons for the
revolt that broke out at his death. For his massive building projects, inside
and outside Palestine, he relied on lands he had acquired in gaining his
kingdom and on heavy taxation.

Herod's building in Hellenistic style continued during the reign of his son
Antipas in Galilee. The Hasmonaeans had expanded Jewish control into
Galilee, forcing Judaism on the inhabitants, and encouraging Judean Jews to
settle there. Thus Galilee had become largely Jewish in its religious orientation, even though the population was mixed. Antipas promoted Hellenistic
cities in Galilee, including Tiberias on Lake Galilee (renamed Lake Tiberias).
He rebuilt Sepphoris, which the Romans had destroyed in 4 B.C.E. during the
uprising that occurred after Herod's death. He made Sepphoris into the
showcase of Galilee.[27]

These two cities became centers of Hellenistic culture.[28] This area of
Galilee was heavily populated, urbanized, and urbane.[29] Sepphoris is only
two miles from Nazareth, and even if they avoided such Gentile centers, Jesus

25. M. Stern, "The Reign of Herod and the Herodian Dynasty," in *The Jewish People in the First Century*, ed. S. Safrai and M. Stern (Assen and Amsterdam: Van Gorcum, 1976), 1:273.
26. Stern, "Reign of Herod," 1:273, says that in spite of the rise of Hellenes in Herod's kingdom, there is no evidence that he attempted a fusion.
27. Crossan, *Historical Jesus*, 18.
28. Horsley and Hanson, *Bandits, Prophets, and Messiahs*, 34.
29. Crossan, *Historical Jesus*, 19, citing a study by J. A. Overman.

and his disciples would have inevitably been in contact with the Hellenistic civilization they represent. The way of life in such cities stood in conflict with the traditional rural values of the Galilean peasants.

The negative economic forces in place at Herod's death continued to cause social unrest during and after the period of his sons' reigns. Finally (in 66) conditions had reached such a point that direct rebellion broke out against Rome and Rome's allies among the Jewish leadership. Those economic forces helped shape the world Jesus inhabited and were at the base of much of the social tension that strained the fabric of Jewish society. Jesus' teachings and actions are so directly related to those economic stresses that a further exploration of economic conditions is necessary to understanding Jesus.

Economic Conditions in Jesus' Time

Roman rule brought prosperity to Palestine. Even before the coming of Roman rule, Israel had become, as Applebaum puts it, "an integral part of the Hellenistic economy of the Eastern Mediterranean, and of the Roman Empire that succeeded it."[30] Participation in Palestinian prosperity was unequal, with the coastal cities and some towns of the Transjordan area receiving the major benefits of increased trade, leaving other towns behind.[31] The countryside did not share equally with towns and cities, and except for Jerusalem, Judea did not fare well. Increasing trade and commerce led to an increasingly cosmopolitan society that more and more adopted Hellenistic ways.

The Temple itself played an important role in urban prosperity in Jerusalem, both by attracting numerous pilgrims to the city[32] and by receiving payments of the Temple tax. Both Julius and Augustus Caesar allowed the half-shekel Temple tax; Broshi estimates that it could have amounted to as much as a million drachmas (denarii) annually.[33] The funds were to maintain the Temple, the aqueduct, the city wall, and to provide for "all the needs of the city."[34]

Priests and Levites received other income, some discretionary and some

---

30. S. Applebaum, "Economic Life in Palestine," in *The Jewish People in the First Century*, ed. S. Safrai and M. Stern (Assen and Amsterdam: Van Gorcum, 1976), 2:631.

31. Stern, "Aspects of Jewish Society," 2:574.

32. Although there are no data on the number of pilgrims to Jerusalem, Broshi says they "must have made Jerusalem an important commercial centre" (Broshi, "The Role of the Temple," 34).

33. Broshi, "The Role of the Temple," 34.

34. Broshi, "The Role of the Temple," quoting from the Mishna.

obligatory. Altogether, the Temple income amounted to a high sum. While the priests benefited most from this income, it would have also had a considerable impact on the economy of the whole city, enhancing trade, commerce, and employment. Rural priests did not share equally in the income to the Temple. Although the Temple tithes were intended to support rural priests (like John the Baptist's father, Zechariah, in Luke 1) as well as the city priests, it is likely that the urban priestly group controlled most of it.

Israel remained primarily agricultural, not manufacturing or commercial, and thus the rural areas did not realize direct benefits from increased economic activity. Instead, the influx of wealth enabled the well-to-do to buy up large estates, replacing landholding peasants. Agriculture flourished during Hellenistic and Roman times. New crops were introduced, new land was brought under cultivation, mountainous regions were terraced, and irrigation was expanded to the maximum.[35]

These developments changed the nature of Palestinian agriculture and fostered the conditions leading to the revolt of 66.[36] According to Stern, the process of hellenization as early as the Hasmonaean rulers disrupted traditional patterns of agriculture, with small farmers working their own lands with their families. Large landowners became more common:

> Beth Shearim was the centre of a private estate that had been inherited by Berenice from her forebears, the Hasmonaean kings and the kings of the Herodian house. Some agricultural lands, such as the famous balsam groves [which provided one of the few exports], passed directly into the hands of the Roman authorities.[37]

Herod's ambitious building projects provided employment for many laborers and those skilled in various crafts, bringing many people into the cities where the projects were taking place. When direct Roman rule ended the Herodian projects in Judea, the unemployed work force, with no other jobs and no land to turn to, formed a discontented urban population.[38]

Economic development and the process of Hellenistic influence did not

---

35. Broshi, "The Role of the Temple," 32. Broshi says that "almost all the arable land was cultivated, and almost all available water was used for irrigation." Mountainous areas were terraced in the early Iron Age. He cites Josephus's account in *Jewish Antiquities* XVI.145, which tells of an irrigation project near Jericho. See also Applebaum, "Economic Life in Palestine," 2:641, who attributes the extensive irrigation in Transjordan to the Roman period.
36. Stern, "Aspects of Jewish Society," 2:574.
37. Stern, "Aspects of Jewish Society," 2:575.
38. Stern, "Aspects of Jewish Society," 2:577.

mesh easily with much of Israelite social and religious tradition. Thus there developed a dichotomy in Israelite society between many who resisted Hellenistic influence in social and religious life and those who supported the modernizing process. In some ways this dichotomy was also one between the poor and the rich, in part because adaptation to new modes of life was required to participate in the new developments, and in part because to those who have more will be given.

Who Owns the Land?

Even with the increase of trade and enterprise Roman occupation encouraged, agriculture remained the base of the economy. It provided the source of income for most of the people. Land remained in short supply even after more arable land was brought under cultivation. Many were left landless. Changing patterns of agriculture and land tenure drove others off the land. Growth in indebtedness, resulting in the loss of land, added to the problem.

The land was increasingly in the hands of wealthy landowners and decreasingly tilled by small farmers working their own family plots.[39] That change did not begin in the Roman period. The Hasmonaeans had gained control of large tracts of land, including an area extending over the foothills of Judea and Samaria and to Caesarea on the coast.[40] Thus, while it is likely that the Hasmonaeans had the initial support of rural people in their revolt against the Hellenistic monarch Antiochus IV, they too moved more toward a Hellenistic pattern of land tenure. That change could explain why the Hasmonaean dynasty lost support among the people.

Herod took over lands occupied by the Hasmonaeans and undoubtedly increased his holdings through confiscating the lands of his political opponents. Herod and his sons regarded the whole countryside as at their own disposal and removed peasants at will.[41] Oakman estimates that Herod's territory covered about 2.6 million acres, of which he himself owned enough

---

39. See the studies of this issue in Douglas E. Oakman, *Jesus and the Economic Questions of His Day*, Studies in the Bible and Early Christianity, 8 (Lewiston, N.Y.: Edwin Mellen Press, 1986); Applebaum, "Economic Life in Palestine," 2:631–700; Horsley, *Jesus and the Spiral of Violence;* Richard A. Horsley, *Sociology and the Jesus Movement* (New York: Crossroad, 1989); Crossan, *Historical Jesus.*
40. Applebaum, "Economic Life in Palestine," 2:634–36.
41. Applebaum, "Economic Life in Palestine," 2:657–58.

to receive about 20 percent of the annual agricultural production in Palestine.[42]

When Rome took direct control, they leased out Herodian lands to those best able to pay for them, that is, to the elites of the towns and cities. The general prosperity of the Roman period provided them with the resources to purchase and exploit the land. The landless peasantry did not benefit from the redistribution of royal lands. Several factors increased the peasants' loss of land. High taxes under the Romans were one factor. According to one estimate, direct income tax ranged as high as one-fourth to one-third on cereals and one-half on fruit. In addition, indirect taxes, and temporary taxes ("gifts") increased the pressure on farmers.[43] Even so, taxation probably was no higher under the Romans than in earlier times, and thus taxes may not have been the primary cause of debt. Population pressure led to a reduction in the size of small farms, placing farmers on the margin of economic collapse. Bad harvests may also have contributed, but the persistence of the problem among urban and rural poor suggests the need for a further explanation.

Goodman argues that the crucial element in the growing problem of landlessness was increased wealth and its uneven distribution. He reasons that the debt of farmers increased not only because the poor needed loans but also because the wealthy needed places to invest surplus income profitably. Judea offered too few opportunities to invest in enterprises; lending provided the best available option.[44] Thus it was to the advantage of those with surplus funds to keep indebtedness high. The wealthy in towns and cities had the power to maintain the poor in a state of indebtedness, for it was they who controlled prices of agricultural products.[45] It is no wonder that peasants identified the ruling group in the towns and cities as the main oppressors, and that the "powerful revolutionary movement in 66 . . . was very largely the reaction of rural Judaism to social injustice."[46] The ruling groups were allied with the Romans, but it was the Jewish elites more than the Romans with whom the peasants had their dealings.

---

42. Oakman, *Jesus and the Economic Questions of His Day*, 70–71.
43. Broshi, "The Role of the Temple," 31.
44. Martin Goodman, "The First Jewish Revolt: Social Conflict and the Problem of Debt," *Journal of Jewish Studies* 33 (1982): 418–19.
45. Applebaum, "Economic Life in Palestine," 2:663.
46. Applebaum, "Economic Life in Palestine," 2:664.

Economic Conditions and Social Justice

The complex of factors leading to the revolt of 66–70 were ingredients in the daily life of people in Jesus' time. Poverty, indebtedness, and their consequences for rural people were nothing new. Why in this case did the conditions finally lead to attempts at political and social revolution? As the revolts at the death of Herod show, there were underlying problems that came to the fore in different ways in different times. Analyses of these factors by authors cited above enables us to see better what concerned Jesus and what led him to actions and words that brought about his death.

This attention to the economic conditions shows that it is not enough to fall back on simple religious explanations for the revolt against Rome in 66, as if the only real issue were religious freedom. But it would be equally inadequate to neglect the part covenant norms derived from scripture and tradition played in that revolt. Religious issues concerned not only modes of worship, aspects of personal piety, and study of scripture. Modes of organizing the political life of the people of God were also religious matters. Traditions rooted in the distant past formed the attitudes of common people and provided standards for social justice and economic equity.

Those traditions shaped the way people regarded the crucial issue of land: Whose is it, how is it to be used, and for whose benefit? Fundamental to Israel's notion of covenant community is the idea that the land is a gift from God for the well-being of the community as a whole. Possession of a part of the land is not an absolute right but a trust and a responsibility.

The patriarchal period portrayed in Genesis suggests a nomadic life in which tribal groups held land in common (see the stories of Abraham and Lot in Genesis 12–19). The book of Joshua shows how in more settled times one gained possession of communal land by casting lots (Joshua 18). That method does not intend to make the process merely random; God manipulates the casting of lots and thus determines land allocation.

Families were to guard property and keep it within the family as inheritance. "The peasant was deeply attached to the piece of ground he had inherited from his fathers: Naboth refused to surrender his vineyard at Yizreel to Achab, and the king could not legally force him to do so (1 Kings 21). The social ideal was that every man should live 'under his vine and under his fig-tree' " (1 Kings 5:5; Micah 4:4; Zech. 3:10).[47] Marriage laws were set up to

---

47. Roland de Vaux, *Ancient Israel, Its Life and Institutions,* tr. John McHugh (New York: McGraw-Hill, 1961), 166.

ensure keeping the land within the family. Thus sons normally inherited from fathers, though a daughter could inherit if there were no sons and if she married within the tribe. The custom that a brother marry his deceased brother's widow in order to raise posterity for the brother also has the purpose of preventing loss of tribal or family property. One who became so poor and in debt that holding on to family property became impossible looked for a "redeemer" (go'el) within the family. This person would buy the property until the owner could afford to regain possession.

The egalitarianism of this early system began to break down under the hereditary monarchy founded by David. Only military necessity caused a reluctant Israel to adopt that system of government. A new wealthy class associated with royalty began to develop large land holdings in spite of prophetic denunciations (see Isa. 5:8; Micah 2:2; and Amos 5:11). Israelite kings themselves came to own large estates, worked by slaves or levies of (temporary) forced labor. Such labor practices helped account for the breakup of the Davidic monarchy after the death of only its second king, Solomon. "Alienation of family property and the development of lending at interest led to the growth of pauperism and the enslavement of defaulting debtors or their dependants. This destroyed that social equality which had existed at the time of the tribal federation."[48]

The ideal of social equality remained, especially in the northern kingdom of Israel, even after the development of monarchy. The accounts of such early prophets as Elijah and Elisha show strong challenges to monarchy from the point of view of the older, more egalitarian ways. They assert the power and authority of God over the land, its fertility, and its just use (see especially 1 Kings 17:1–19:21; 21:1–29).

Social legislation at least as early as the late fifth century B.C.E. protected those egalitarian ideals and limited the impact of poverty and indebtedness. (1) Fields were left fallow in the sabbatical year, and the poor could harvest them for their own use (Ex. 23:10–11). (2) Those who had sold themselves into slavery were to gain release after seven years (Ex. 21:2–6). The effect was that one could buy the labor of an Israelite for seven years but never own the person or have a right to the person's labor indefinitely. (3) After forty-nine years, the Jubilee year required that all land be returned to its ancestral owners, all Israelite slaves be freed, and all debts canceled (Lev. 25:8–17,

---

48. Vaux, *Ancient Israel*, 173.

23–55; 27:16–25; Num. 36:4). Such laws provided opportunity for those who fell into poverty to regain their economic position.

Whether the sabbatical and Jubilee laws were ever fully functional in fact, or whether they merely stated ideals in the form of legislation, is a topic of debate. Written laws governing these practices date after the Babylonian exile and thus may not have been in operation when Israel was self-governing. However, Jeremiah 34 suggests that they were partially recognized earlier. He reports that faced with the threat of a Babylonian attack on Jerusalem, King Zedekiah "made a covenant with all the people in Jerusalem to make a proclamation of liberty to them, that all should set free their Hebrew slaves" (34:8–9). Jeremiah then complains that the people rescinded their actions after the threat passed. He reminded the people of the law (34:12–14) and condemned them for having violated the covenant. Nehemiah 10:31 suggests that Nehemiah enforced the Sabbath year. 1 Maccabees 6:49 provides evidence for the sabbatical fallow year, for it states that the town of Beth-zur had no food to withstand a siege "since it was a sabbatical year for the land." Josephus confirms the practice by noting that Julius Caesar did not collect a particular tax in the sabbatical year, "for in this time they neither take fruit from the trees nor do they sow."[49] Whether the remission of sabbatical-year taxes continued under Herod and the procurators is not known. Failure to excuse the tax might have sparked Judah the Galilean to revolt when Judea became a province.[50] Further evidence that sabbatical years were observed comes from the reign of Herod, when Rabbi Hillel invented *prosbol*[51] as a way of avoiding the difficulty of making and receiving loans in times near a Sabbath year. This evidence shows that the Jews took the sabbatical year seriously, though it is impossible to say how widely they observed it in Jesus' day. Some of the evidence comes from "periods of national and religious fervor."[52] In times of national crisis and renewal, a reformer like Jesus might well have called for its observance.[53]

The Jubilee year as a "Sabbath of Sabbaths" might have begun after the

---

49. *Jewish Antiquities* XIV.202.

50. Applebaum, "Economic Life in Palestine," 2:652.

51. The *prosbol* was a piece of legislation that allowed loans to avoid cancellation in a sabbatical year.

52. Vaux, *Ancient Israel*, 175.

53. See the study by Sharon Ringe, *Jesus, Liberation, and the Biblical Jubilee* (Philadelphia: Fortress Press, 1985). She thinks examples belong to royal proclamations of release and not to legislation being enforced.

Babylonian exile. According to Jubilee traditions, the fiftieth[54] year was a time to "proclaim liberty throughout the land to all its inhabitants" (Lev. 25:10). All Israelites must return all land to its ancestral owners, cancel all debts, and free all Israelite slaves. Jubilee legislation assumes that "the land shall not be sold in perpetuity, for the land is mine; . . . you are but aliens and tenants" (Lev. 25:23). Even houses in towns that have no walls were to be returned in the Jubilee year along with all houses belonging to Levites (Lev. 25:29, 33). Israelite slaves were to be freed to "return to their ancestral property" (Lev. 25:41). Thus, every fifty years society begins again on a more even playing field for everyone. Theoretically in Israel one did not buy the land but a certain number of harvests until Jubilee. As in the case of the Sabbath year, it is difficult to know whether Jubilee was put into practice or whether it expresses an ideal of social justice never fully carried out.[55]

The importance of these traditions for the present purpose does not depend on whether Sabbath year and Jubilee were observed regularly or at all. The point is that they provided a basis for prophetic appeals for covenant justice in a time of crisis, when injustice and inequity were rampant and on the rise. The economic conditions existing during Jesus' ministry fell far short of the standards of justice these traditions sought to establish in Israel. The failure to maintain them falls upon the elite Jewish class in Roman Palestine.

The Priestly Establishment

The priestly establishment in Jerusalem provided an important, even indispensable, part of Roman control. The Romans were building on a practice that goes back at least to the Hasmonaeans who combined political and religious authority in one person: The kings were also high priests. Even though the Hasmonaeans had replaced earlier powerful priestly families (including the house of Zadok, whose lineage went back to David), and even though Herod had done a similar thing, the same priestly *class* exercised political power during all this period. Changes in priestly authority were merely changes within that class. As Stern says, "The priesthood constituted

---

54. Whether it was reckoned as 49 or 50 years is discussed (J. Morgenstern, "Jubilee," *Interpreter's Dictionary of the Bible*, 2:1001–2).
55. Vaux, *Ancient Israel*, 176–77.

the upper stratum of Jewish society in the Second Temple period. It was a kind of Jewish nobility," with large landholdings.[56]

N. Avigad's description of the Herodian Quarter shows that the opulence of Herod's temple extended to the residences of the priestly class as well. Archaeological excavations have uncovered evidence in Jerusalem of large villas in Roman style with mosaic floors and frescoed walls, along with amphorae of fine blown glass. Avigad describes these residences as so spacious that they had

> the character of luxurious villas. The houses were decorated with wall frescoes, and with stucco modeled in relief, and were paved with colorful mosaics; they were equipped with ritual baths and elaborate bathing installations; they contained stone furniture, luxury goods, ornaments, and the like, indicating a high standard of living. Thus it can be assumed that this was an upper-class quarter inhabited by wealthy families of the Jerusalem aristocracy. Here they built their houses and decorated their homes according to the fashion of that time and in the style of the Hellenistic-Roman period.[57]

The presence of vessels for ritual ablutions shows that the houses were for priests. They enjoyed luxurious living equivalent to the wealthy elsewhere in Roman society.[58] Priests with Hellenistic tastes thus had a monopoly on forgiveness of sins and controlled a large proportion of the wealth.[59]

The priestly aristocracy received their support from rural areas, primarily through the tax on agricultural products intended to support the Temple. The Romans backed the arrangement by decreeing that the people should bring their tithes to the Temple.[60] Roman backing was necessary because, since Hasmonaean days, the sympathy of the people for supporting the

---

56. Stern, "Aspects of Jewish Society," 2:580. In regard to landowning, Stern cites Hacataeus, in Diodorus Siculus XL, 3,7, and concludes, "In light of the preponderant position of priests in Jewish society at the time, it may be assumed that not a few of them attained to the status of wealthy landowners" (Stern, 2:587). Josephus, who was of priestly aristocracy, received compensation from the Romans for the loss of an estate he owned near Jerusalem (Josephus, *Life*, 422).

57. Avigad, *The Herodian Quarter in Jerusalem*, 10.

58. Ian Wilson, *Jesus: The Evidence* (San Francisco: Harper & Row, 1984), 80.

59. Stern, "Aspects of Jewish Society," 2:587, cites particular examples of notable wealth, one example being the high priest Ananias, whose generosity during the Roman attack on Jerusalem is mentioned in Josephus, *Jewish Antiquities*, XX.205.

60. Josephus, *Jewish Antiquities* XIV.203, cited by Horsley, *Jesus and the Spiral of Violence*, 286.

Temple establishment had diminished.[61] The residents of Qumran completely withdrew their support from the Jerusalem priests as illegitimate. The Temple undoubtedly maintained its symbolic value (as Jesus' visit and the Qumran desire to return to a purified Temple show), but that value was not identified with the incumbent priestly groups that controlled it. In such circumstances the peasant population would have made little distinction between the Roman rulers and the high priestly rulers.

The priestly establishment cannot be identified with the Sadducees, but the two are closely connected. According to Josephus, the Sadducees had close relations with the wealthy families and vied for political and social power. The Gospels associate the Sadducees with the Temple, the priesthood, and the Sanhedrin.[62]

Reactions to the Situation

The priestly aristocracy, along with the Sadducees, accommodated themselves to Roman rule and the hellenization it promoted. As members of the elite and prosperous, they had no interest in ridding the nation of the political and social situation that guaranteed their own position.

The Pharisees as a group accommodated Roman rule by concentrating on personal piety, purity, tithing, and Sabbath observance. Neither pro-Roman nor anti-Roman as such, they tended to "live and let live" as long as they were free to live faithfully to the Torah as they interpreted it. As Rivkin expresses it, "they urged their followers to render unto Caesar what was Caesar's, so that they would be able to render unto God what was God's."[63]

At the other extreme from the priestly aristocracy stood various resistance and renewal movements. John the Baptist and Jesus of Nazareth provide the best-known examples of those whose proclamations and actions so ran afoul of Roman authorities or Rome's surrogates that they were killed as politically dangerous.

The movements of John and Jesus were not isolated ones. They rather represent particular expressions of a larger movement or set of movements that took place over several decades and eventually led to the revolt of 66.

---

61. Sean Freyne, *Galilee, Jesus, and the Gospels: Literary Approaches and Historical Investigations* (Philadelphia: Fortress Press, 1988), 188.

62. Anthony J. Saldarini, "Sadducees," *Harper's Bible Dictionary*, 891–92.

63. Rivkin, *What Crucified Jesus?*, 39.

The historian Josephus provides the main information for reconstructing the history of those movements. He regarded most of the resistance to Roman rule as expressions of bad motivation and bad character, a view not necessarily shared by ordinary people of the time or by scholars today.

Essene Withdrawal

Some Essenes answered the need for renewal by withdrawing from society into a close-knit and tightly controlled community.[64] Their action was a short-term tactic more than a long-term commitment to a monastic life. Their writings show that they wished to return to society, but only when they could control it according to their own ideals. Whether they would have carried their ideal of common ownership of community property over into the larger society cannot be determined, but the nature of the community indicates that had they gained control, society would have changed radically.

As a renewal movement, the Essene community offered its own definition of Israel as the people of God. Whether they were an "evasive group," as Theissen thinks, or whether they were an "aggressive group"[65] (as the battle plans in their War Scroll and their destruction during the revolt of 66–70 suggest), they had their own program to offer. That program included strictly following the Torah as the leaders of the community interpreted it. It rejected the hellenization of Israel represented in the Jerusalem priestly aristocracy. It sought to draw the covenant community together as a solid front against the inroads of Gentile ways. They believed God ruled within their community, while Satan ruled the world outside.[66]

They applied strict discipline to keep the community pure. Unlike Pharisees, who thought purity was possible within life in the world, the Essenes withdrew. In effect, the Essenes thought of purity in communal terms, while the Pharisees thought in more individual terms.

The Essene practice of common ownership of all property was not a rejection of material wealth but of the current means the ruling elites used to control and distribute that wealth. They harked back to the more egalitarian

---

64. Other Essenes or their sympathizers lived in more ordinary circumstances.

65. Gerd Theissen, *Sociology of Early Palestinian Christianity*, tr. John Bowden (Philadelphia: Fortress Press, 1978), 34. Hengel, *Victory Over Violence*, 15, points out that the pacifism attributed to Essenes by Josephus and Philo contrasts with the War Scroll. Also the Manual of Discipline ix.21ff. advocates eternal hatred of all those of perdition.

66. John Riches, *Jesus and the Transformation of Judaism* (New York: Seabury Press, 1982), 95.

strains in Israel's economic thinking, even though their government was very
hierarchical. New members of the community had to pass through a period of
training as novitiates to learn the community's understanding of covenant
standards. Only then could they participate in the community.

Peasant Unrest in Roman Palestine

Not all responses to the social crisis facing Roman Palestine were as
carefully organized as the Essene movement. Some were sporadic and
short-lived reactions to particular incidents, and some continued over a
longer period. On the surface these movements reveal little commonality
among them; they are alike in that they arise in response to a common core of
social and religious problems. Crossan discusses at some length the various
protest and resistance activities and movements in early Roman Palestine and
provides in an appendix[67] a catalog that includes

> protesters, of which there were seven cases between 4 B.C.E. and 65 C.E.;
> prophets, of which there were ten cases between c. 30 C.E. and 73 C.E.,
>   excluding Jesus;
> [social] bandits, of which there were eleven cases between 47 B.C.E. and 68–69
>   C.E.; and
> messiahs, of which there were five cases between 4 B.C.E. and 68–70 C.E.

Josephus describes these in his accounts of the events leading up to the
Jewish revolt against Rome. They represent not merely isolated miscreants (as
Josephus suggests). Rather, they were varied reactions to continuing tensions
within Roman Palestine, particularly the tensions between the peasant
population and the urban elites, including the Jerusalem priestly aristocracy.
I will give only some pertinent examples here that provide partial parallels to
Jesus' activity or to the way it was perceived.

Prophetic Protests

1. Theudas. According to Josephus, when Fadus was procurator of all
Palestine (44–46 C.E.),

---

67. Crossan, *Historical Jesus*, 451–52. The following description depends heavily on
Crossan.

A certain impostor named Theudas persuaded the majority of the masses to take up their possessions and to follow him to the Jordan River. He stated that he was a prophet and that at his command the river would be parted and would provide them an easy passage. With this talk he deceived many. Fadus, however, did not permit them to reap the fruit of their folly, but sent against them a squadron of cavalry. These fell upon them unexpectedly, slew many of them and took many prisoners. Theudas himself was captured, whereupon they cut off his head and brought it to Jerusalem.[68]

This demonstration carries clear overtones of the exodus under Moses and the crossing of the Jordan under Joshua. It echoes with themes of liberation from oppression and renewal of the covenant community. Josephus does not indicate that the followers of Theudas were armed or that they intended to carry out any military action. Probably Theudas expected God to provide miraculously as in the past. They would enter again the land of promise, free to be God's people. Even if this was a completely peaceful demonstration, Rome would not perceive it as purely religious, since it has far-reaching political implications. Death to the leader and repression of the followers was Rome's natural and understandable reaction.[69]

2. The Egyptian. Josephus reports that "impostors and deceivers called upon the mob to follow them into the desert," promising signs and wonders. According to Josephus, they were promoting revolution under a claim to divine inspiration. Felix, the procurator from 52 to 60, punished them, and put a number to death by the sword.[70]

The unrest continued under new leadership:

At this time there came to Jerusalem from Egypt a man who declared that he was a prophet and advised the masses of the common people to go out with him to the mountain called the Mount of Olives, which lies opposite the city at a distance of five furlongs. For he asserted that he wished to demonstrate from there that at his command Jerusalem's walls would fall down, through which he promised to provide them an entrance into the city. When Felix heard of this he ordered his soldiers to take up their arms. Setting out from Jerusalem with a large force of cavalry and infantry, he fell upon the Egyptian and his followers, slaying four hundred of them and taking two hundred prisoners. The Egyptian himself escaped from the battle and disappeared. And now the

---

68. Josephus, *Jewish Antiquities* XX.97–99.
69. See further, Crossan, *Historical Jesus,* 162.
70. Josephus, *Jewish Antiquities* XX.167; *Jewish War* II.167–72.

brigands once more incited the populace to war with Rome, telling them not
to obey them. They also fired and pillaged the villages of those who refused to
comply.[71]

Threatening Jerusalem's walls, as Joshua threatened Jericho's, suggests that
God's deliverance of the people requires overcoming the city's leadership.
The event posed a threat not merely against the Romans but also against those
who assisted Rome's control. Josephus regards the protesters, not the Romans
or the Jewish aristocracy, as in the wrong. Less privileged people would not
likely have shared Josephus's view. Many must have regarded them as
spirit-filled prophets sent by God to deliver the people as God had delivered
them in the past.[72] To follow such a person as the Egyptian risked danger.
Only a conviction that God was about to act through such a person, just as
God had acted through Joshua, could prompt one to join these protesters.

3. John the Baptist. Josephus also tells about an earlier prophet whom the
political authorities executed. In this case, Josephus says some Jews regarded
the destruction of Herod Antipas's army by King Aretas as "divine [and] . . .
just vengeance" because of Herod's treatment of John the Baptist:

> For Herod had put him to death, though he was a good man and had exhorted
> the Jews to lead righteous lives, to practise justice towards their fellows and
> piety towards God. . . . When others too joined the crowds about him, because
> they were aroused to the highest degree by his sermons, Herod became
> alarmed. Eloquence that had so great an effect on mankind might lead to some
> form of sedition, for it looked as if they would be guided by John in everything
> that they did. Herod decided therefore that it would be much better to strike
> first and be rid of him before his work led to an uprising, than to wait for an
> upheaval, get involved in a difficult situation and see his mistake. . . . John . . .
> was brought in chains to Machaerus . . . and there put to death.[73]

Josephus shows the close connection between popular prophecy and
seditious activity, and the fear that ruling powers had of such movements,

---

71. Josephus, *Jewish Antiquities* XX.169–72. Cf. *Jewish War* II.261–63. Horsley, *Sociology and the Jesus Movement*, 55, speaks of "prophetic" movements that were drawn mostly from rural people who abandoned their roots and went into the wilderness. "The one prophetic movement (led by the 'Egyptian' Jew) that did not go out into the wilderness marched about Jerusalem" perhaps to see it liberated by God rather than to see it destroyed because they were opposed to city life as such.

72. Horsley and Hanson, *Bandits, Prophets, and Messiahs*, 161.

73. Josephus, *Jewish Antiquities* XVIII.116–19.

whether they were armed or not. He does not directly describe John's activity as political, but the description clearly shows that he had a political effect. John aroused his hearers and created in Herod a fear of sedition. Neither the followers of such prophets nor the authorities they made nervous would have separated calls to repentance and renewal from political activity.

Social Banditry

Josephus reports many instances of what he calls bandits and brigands from the time of Herod the Great down through the revolt of 66–70. They lived in caves or received protection from the citizens and "eminent men" in villages and towns. In several instances the Romans took direct action against the bandits and in some cases against those who had protected them. Both *Jewish Antiquities* and *Jewish War* report that "brigands" or "seditious revolutionaries" attacked and robbed "a slave of Caesar, named Stephen."[74]

The procurator Cumanus "sent troops round the neighboring villages, with orders to bring up the inhabitants to him in chains, reprimanding them for not having pursued and arrested the robbers."[75] In *Jewish Antiquities* Josephus says the Romans also brought "eminent men" in chains. Such outlaw activities were forms of social protest, according to Horsley[76] and Crossan.[77] Josephus's reports show the support those who resisted the constituted authorities enjoyed in the countryside. In one instance, Josephus speaks of a bandit "who for many years had his home in the mountains."[78] He could hardly have done that without having some base in the local population.

Messianic Claimants

The hope for an anointed ruler was not limited to the literary or scholarly communities, such as those who wrote the Dead Sea Scrolls or the *Psalms of Solomon*. From Josephus we learn that popular messianic figures emerged, claimed significant followings, and learned firsthand Rome's power to put down dangerous movements. The main difference between messianic figures and prophetic movements is that the former reflect stories about Saul and David while the latter recall Moses and Joshua. The messianic figures differ

---

74. Josephus, *Jewish War* II.228; cf. *Jewish Antiquities* XX.113.
75. Josephus, *Jewish War* II.229.
76. Horsley, *Jesus and the Spiral of Violence*, 37–39.
77. Crossan, *Historical Jesus*, 168–87.
78. Josephus, *Jewish War* II.253.

from the brigands and bandits mainly in that they claim for themselves or others claim for them a charismatic authority that transcends that of the brigand. These figures did not emerge because scholars had been searching the scriptures for the time and place that the Messiah might appear but because in popular imagination a particular person fulfilled the expected role of messianic deliverer.

Josephus describes the climate in which messiahs arose, indicating his own negative view of the whole trend:

> Such was the great madness that settled upon the nation because they had no king of their own to restrain the populace by his pre-eminence, and because the foreigners who came among them to suppress the rebellion were themselves a cause of provocation through their arrogance and their greed.[79]

Judas, the son of Hezekiah of Galilee (4 B.C.E.), serves as an example:

> This Judas got together a large number of desperate men at Sepphoris in Galilee and there made an assault on the royal palace, and having seized all the arms that were stored there, he armed every single one of his men and made off with all the property that had been seized there. He became an object of terror to all men by plundering those he came across in his desire for great possessions and his ambition for royal rank, a prize that he expected to obtain not through the practice of virtue but through excessive ill-treatment of others.[80]

A second example follows immediately in Josephus's description:

> Simon, a slave of King Herod but a handsome man, who took pre-eminence by size and bodily strength, . . . was bold enough to place the diadem on his head, and having got together a body of men, he was himself also proclaimed king by them in their madness.[81]

Josephus then describes how he looted and burned the royal palace in Jericho.

To Josephus all such claimants were men of bad character, no different from ordinary bandits. Again, the perspective of common folks likely differed. As Crossan asks, "What was a bandit but an emperor on the make,

---

79. *Jewish Antiquities* XVII.277.
80. *Jewish Antiquities* XVII.271–72.
81. *Jewish Antiquities* XVII.273–74.

what was an emperor but a bandit on the throne?"[82] These messianic claimants kept alive traditions of a popularly chosen king in the context of foreign domination and social confusion.[83]

The great revolt of 66–70 grew out of the economic and social issues that gave rise to bandits, prophets, and messiahs. Like that revolt, they expressed the frustrations of the masses who faced economic pressures and social disruptions. "Landless men, displaced persons and casual labourers who had lost their sources of livelihood, proved an unfailing source for the quarrels and public disturbances that broke out repeatedly."[84] As Stern says, the revolt was not merely the result of the intense desire for independence from Rome. It was also a social revolution within Jewish society. "The great revolt bore all the signs of an inner social upheaval. The social and revolutionary character of the great revolt was particularly manifest among the radical groups which produced messianic figures. . . . In Simeon's view the revolt was not just a war against the Romans but a protest against the social order of Judaea."[85]

The burning of debt records when the revolutionaries took Jerusalem shows clearly that the revolt was not merely "religious," or merely a desire for independence, but that it was spawned by the revolutionary atmosphere caused by economic conditions. It is true that the upper classes sought to prevent the revolt, though they too were highly dissatisfied with Roman procurator Florus (64–66), whom Stern describes as having "behaved like a tyrant in every respect."[86] That dissatisfaction, along with initial success against the Romans, led many moderates among the elite classes to join the rebels. As the war went on, however, radical elements assumed control of the war's direction.[87]

Conclusion

Roman Palestine at the time of Jesus was in a state of social conflict and crisis. John the Baptist and Jesus were not the only charismatic leaders calling for change in the lot of common people and initiating renewal movements to

---

82. Crossan, *Historical Jesus*, 172.
83. Horsley and Hanson, *Bandits, Prophets, and Messiahs,* 130.
84. Stern, "Aspects of Jewish Society," 2:577.
85. Stern, "Aspects of Jewish Society," 2:577.
86. M. Stern, "The Province of Judea," in *The Jewish People in the First Century: Historical Geography, Political History, Social, Cultural, and Religious Life and Institutions,* ed. S. Safrai and M. Stern (Philadelphia: Fortress Press, 1974), 324.
87. Stern, "Aspects of Jewish Society," 2:578–79.

accomplish that change. Radical solutions to the plight of the people were proposed by many others, including those who advocated nonviolent protest and waited for divine intervention, and those more prone to violence. The revolution was a political one against Rome rule, but it was also a social one against those within the Jewish population who exploited the relationship with Rome for their own economic and political advantage.

Jesus' ministry took place within that revolutionary milieu. He can hardly have remained unaffected by it. In fact, his message and activity were largely in response to it. Announcing the kingdom of God in that situation would tell the people of God's concern to change their present that deprived them of happiness and well-being. The issues of poverty, justice, and peace occupy central places in his teachings and in his ministry. Jesus' response to the plight of the poor and to the failure of covenant community to deal with the social situation caused profound disturbances among those who controlled society. They perceived Jesus as dangerous to the system they maintained, and thus they defended it against the threat he posed.

The following chapters will focus on the political content of his actions and teachings, which prompted the ruling authorities to execute him.

CHAPTER TWO

"Crucified Under Pontius Pilate"

Historical as well as theological investigation of Jesus appropriately begins with this article of the Apostles' Creed. The early church faced the theological implications of that fact almost immediately and soon came to include the death of Jesus as central to its gospel. Since Jesus' execution by the Romans is the most secure historical fact about Jesus, any credible interpretation of his work must account for their doing so.

The Gospels present Jesus as recognizing and accepting the necessity of his death; his primary mission is to die. Jesus' way is the way of the cross to such an extent that following Jesus means to take up one's cross. The story of Jesus' baptism anticipates Jesus' death from the beginning: The voice from heaven makes a double allusion to scripture that identifies Jesus as Messiah (Son of God) and Suffering Servant. According to Mark 4:11, the voice says, "You are my Son," an allusion to Psalm 2:7; the voice also tells Jesus he is "the Beloved, with whom I am well pleased," an allusion to Isaiah 42:1. The temptation story in Luke 4:1–13 and Matthew 4:1–11 represents Jesus as rejecting traditional messiahship, leaving as the implied alternative the road of suffering and death associated with the Suffering Servant of God.

Even if theological concerns more than historical reminiscence of Jesus' own intentions inspire the Gospel perspective, that perspective shows the importance of the issue. The theological perspective of the church had had to come to grips with the tragic fact of Jesus' unexpected execution. The trauma of his execution, the experiences that confirmed his continuing life, and missionary work of the early evangelists provide ingredients in the church's view of Jesus.

The Gospel writers were evangelists, more interested in proclaiming the good news about Jesus than in objectively reporting events or probing Jesus' psyche to determine how he felt about his death—or his life. They searched for the meaning of those events that had captured their imagination and their life.

In that sense the Gospel writers share a common perspective with the apostle Paul. On the basis of 2 Corinthians 5:16, some hold the opinion that Paul had no interest in the historical circumstances of Jesus' life and death; all that mattered to him was the fact of Jesus' death and resurrection. Paul's letters suggest that in his evangelical preaching he referred infrequently to Jesus' earthly life, concentrating rather on the bare fact of his crucifixion and on celebrating his resurrection. He finds in those events the creation of a new humanity. Besides these evangelical events, Paul reveals little about Jesus. Only in one passage, of questioned authenticity, does Paul indicate the human agents responsible for Jesus' death. In 1 Thessalonians 2:15 he speaks of the Jews "who killed both the Lord Jesus and the prophets." Otherwise Paul is content to affirm that it was God who gave up God's son for the salvation of those who will believe.

It is an indisputable fact that Jesus was crucified by the Romans, but his death is remembered by those for whom it had significance. The Roman historian Tacitus mentions it only incidentally in connection with another event (a fire in Rome) that was significant to him; Tacitus attributes no significance to the death itself.[1] Jesus' followers remembered it as the key point in their history, as the event that constituted their relationship to God and to one another in the community of believers.

Many modern readers share the latter view. For them, questions concerning historical events and perspectives lying behind the Gospel interpretations of Jesus may seem insignificant or at least swallowed up in the convictions and concerns that motivate discipleship today; or such questions may seem to militate against those convictions and thus should be denied any place in the examination of Jesus. I have stated above why I think it is important to raise historical questions about Jesus, even when they cannot be answered

---

1. Tacitus, *Annals* XV.44.

with complete assurance. Since the crucifixion of Jesus is central both theologically and historically, setting history aside will serve neither interest.

Crucifixion as a Political Execution

Jesus was executed by the Romans with a method of execution reserved for non-Romans condemned for crimes against the state. Jesus' crucifixion thus was a political act and must be accounted for as such.[2] Historical investigation of Jesus begins with that fact and seeks to understand its causes. The primary historical question concerns whether the Roman governor had sufficient political reason for executing Jesus. That question receives three general answers.

1. A popular answer, given by many church people—both clergy and laity—asserts that as a spiritual teacher, Jesus had no interest in social and political issues. He sought to change individuals, called his hearers to love their neighbors and to be moral in personal behavior, but Jesus did not try to change society except through those individuals. He was executed because he offended the Jewish leaders, especially the Pharisees and the Sadducees, by questioning the validity of their interpretation and application of the Torah and their failure to be genuine in their religious observances. Jesus' criticism deeply offended them, leading them to remove their most severe religious critic. They pressured Pontius Pilate into executing an innocent man. If the Romans had any real concerns about him, it was only because they were nervous about his ability to draw a crowd.

2. A more scholarly view also holds that Jesus' primary focus was on the

---

2. Gerhard Schneider, "The Political Charge Against Jesus (Luke 23:2)," *Jesus and the Politics of His Day*, ed. Ernst Bammel and C. F. D. Moule (Cambridge: Cambridge University Press, 1984), 404, asserts that the title on the cross is "the historically unimpeachable point of departure" for historical inquiry. The charge against Jesus can be inferred from this fact. Ernst Bammel, "The *Titulus*," 363–64, in the same volume, agrees that the inscription on the cross "is in all likelihood authentic" but nevertheless doubts its judicial relevance and asserts that it should "not be taken as the 'one solid and stable fact that should be made the starting point of any historical investigation' " (*contra* Paul Winter, *On the Trial of Jesus* [Berlin: de Gruyter, 1961] and Ellis Rivkin, *What Crucified Jesus?*, 109, whom he quotes). See also Bammel's "Crucifixion as a Punishment in Palestine," *The Trial of Jesus*, ed. Ernst Bammel (Naperville, Ill.: Alec R. Allenson, 1970), 162–65. Bammel particularly denies S. G. F. Brandon's assertion in *Jesus and the Zealots: A Study of the Political Factor in Primitive Christianity* (Manchester: Manchester University Press, 1967), 328, that Jesus was condemned for sedition.

transformation of individuals.[3] He was disturbed by the social conditions of his time, and he opposed the rich who exploited the poor. But unlike the revolutionary Zealots, he identified evil in the world not with social or political structures but with the individual; thus not the liberation of the homeland but the transformation of the individual heart was the center of Jesus' approach.[4] For Jesus, only obedience to God and unconditional trust in the goodness of the Father really mattered. Nonetheless Jesus' message was politically and socially explosive because people misunderstood it. If they had not understood it wrongly, they would not have come to him in such numbers.[5] As a charismatic leader, Jesus took a critical attitude toward all political powers, but he was not a demagogue or a provocateur.[6] Jesus separated religion and politics, disrupting the naive view that prevailed in Jesus' day that religion and politics were not only inseparable, they were identical.[7]

3. An increasingly held scholarly view is that Jesus addressed concrete problems and issues of his day, and the way in which he addressed them led to his death by crucifixion.[8] Jesus was not disengaged politically so that his execution was a miscarriage of justice. Quite the contrary. Since Jesus' words and actions called for radical social and political change, the governing authorities had good reason under Roman law to take the sort of action they did. The thesis of this book is that this position contains more historical truth than the other two.

"A Cruel and Disgusting Penalty"

Beyond the statement that Jesus was executed as a claimant to the messianic throne, a would-be "King of the Jews," one can say little of the particular act of executing Jesus. The Gospels do not dwell on the details of actual crucifixion, and it is doubtful that the evangelists had access to eyewitness accounts. Details in the Gospel accounts derive largely from scriptural passages (especially Psalms 22 and 69). A comparison of the words

---

3. I use as an example Martin Hengel. His views are expressed in succinct form in *Victory Over Violence* and *Christ and Power* (Philadelphia: Fortress Press, 1977).

4. Hengel, *Victory Over Violence*, 47–48.

5. Hengel, *Victory Over Violence*, 51–52.

6. Hengel, *Christ and Power*, 20.

7. Hengel, *Victory Over Violence*, 1.

8. Horsley, *Jesus and the Spiral of Violence*; Crossan, *Historical Jesus*, provide the best examples.

of Jesus from the cross contained in the various Gospels shows the differing interpretations of Jesus' attitude. For Mark, Jesus suffers and dies with words of abandonment on his lips. Matthew adds nothing to Mark's account. In Luke, Jesus utters no word of despair but forgives his enemies and confidently promises paradise to others before calmly entrusting his spirit to God. In John, Jesus remains in charge of his own death, which comes only when he has finished the work that his Father gave him to do. All these accounts reflect the writers' interpretations more than their knowledge of the events or of Jesus' precise words or moods as he died.

There is no doubt that Jesus' execution was by crucifixion, which the Roman Cicero described as "a cruel and disgusting penalty."[9] The Romans chose crucifixion as the method of executing those accused of crimes against the state because they believed its extreme cruelty would provide an effective deterrent. "Whenever we crucify the guilty, the most crowded roads are chosen, where the most people can see and be moved by this fear. For penalties relate not so much to retribution as to their exemplary effect," wrote Quintilian.[10] Although Josephus describes the actions of Roman soldiers torturing and crucifying Jewish fugitives during the Jewish War against Rome, in normal situations one would not be crucified without a regular trial.[11]

Questions about Jesus' execution center on the process by which he was tried and condemned. Two major questions must be addressed: Who tried Jesus and on what charges did they convict him? The statement that he was crucified on the charge of treason or sedition may seem to answer both questions. But the Gospel accounts narrate the trial in such ways as to make it unclear whether the charge placed on the cross corresponds to the one for which he was found guilty in the hearings. The Gospel accounts also raise questions about Roman involvement.

The question of charges is directly linked to the question of the courts before which Jesus appeared. The Gospels are not entirely consistent on this point. The following paragraphs summarize the Gospel accounts of the arrest

---

9. Cicero, *Against Verres* II.V.165.

10. Quintilian, *Declamationes* 274, quoted in Martin Hengel, *Crucifixion* (Philadelphia: Fortress Press, 1977), 50.

11. Josephus, *Jewish War* V.449–51: "The soldiers out of rage and hatred amused themselves by nailing their prisoners in different postures; and so great was their number, that space could not be found for the crosses nor crosses for the bodies." Quoted in Hengel, *Crucifixion*, 26.

and trial of Jesus: Mark 14:43–15:15; Matthew 26:47–27:26; Luke 22:47–23:24; John 18:1–19:16.

Gospels in Agreement

All four Gospels agree that Jesus appeared before Pilate, and Pilate bore the responsibility for executing Jesus. All four agree that the religious authorities were involved in the arrest of Jesus. All four agree that Jewish religious authorities handed Jesus over to the Romans. The three Synoptic Gospels agree that the Jewish council (the Sanhedrin) questioned Jesus, while John has Jesus appear before Annas and Caiaphas (high priests) but not before the Sanhedrin itself. All four agree that the Jewish leaders had decided before the arrest took place that Jesus should die. How they reached that decision remains unstated, but the narratives assume that the purpose of the trial was not to decide the fate of Jesus but only to decide the legal basis for carrying out the decision.

All four Gospels portray Pilate as remaining unconvinced after examining Jesus that he deserved the death penalty. All four Gospels contain the story of Pilate's releasing Barabbas rather than Jesus although he preferred to release Jesus. All four Gospels show Pilate actually arguing for Jesus' release while pronouncing him innocent of any crime. Luke only presents a scene in which Pilate sent Jesus to Herod Antipas for a hearing. All four agree that soldiers did the actual crucifixion, though there is some ambiguity about who was in charge of the soldiers. The Synoptics only say Pilate delivered him to be crucified, and then portray the soldiers mocking and crucifying Jesus. John, on the other hand, says Pilate delivered Jesus "to them" (presumably the Jewish authorities who demanded his death), and then reports the soldiers' actions. Both at this point and at the point of Jesus' arrest, John suggests that the soldiers were under the command of the Jewish authorities (John 18:3; 19:2).

Mark and Matthew have the "whole council" (Sanhedrin) meet at night in a vain attempt to garner the necessary testimony against Jesus to warrant the death penalty; on the following morning they met again. Having Jesus appear before "the whole council" (Mark 14:55; Matt. 26:59) suggests that it was a formal hearing. According to Luke, those who arrested Jesus took him to the house of the high priest, where he was mocked and mistreated but not tried on the night of his arrest; when morning came, they led him to the council for trial. According to John, Jesus was taken first to the house of Annas, the father-in-law of the high priest; there he was questioned, presumably by Annas,[12] then sent to Caiaphas. John says nothing about any proceedings or questioning by Caiaphas, but he tells us that "early" in the morning Jesus was led from Caiaphas's house to the Roman praetorium where Pilate questioned him.

The Gospel accounts leave some doubt as to the nature of the charges brought against Jesus during the proceedings. They leave no doubt about the outcome, which has been clearly indicated well in advance. In general, the reader knows that the Jewish leaders have already agreed on the verdict: Jesus must die. But the leaders are portrayed as wanting that verdict to have ample legal justification, and thus they examine Jesus and/or take testimony.

Mark and Matthew report a preliminary unsustained accusation that Jesus threatened the destruction of the Temple, an accusation to which Jesus makes no response. Luke omits this accusation. In all three Synoptics, the conclusive issue concerns Jesus' identity as "Christ" and "Son of God." Jesus' admission and his statement about the Son of Man taking his seat at the right hand of God lead the questioners to conclude that Jesus is guilty of blasphemy (Mark and Matthew) and that he therefore deserves to die. At that point no further testimony is needed. In John, Jesus is asked only "about his disciples and about his teaching" (18:19), and no judicial decision is stated.

In all four Gospels the crucial charge in the hearing before Pilate concerns the claim that Jesus is "king of the Jews." That charge is prefaced in Luke by a more general set of accusations: Jesus has perverted the nation, by prohibiting payment of taxes and by claiming to be king of the Jews (23:2). In John, Jesus' accusers answer Pilate's inquiry by saying that if Jesus did not deserve to die they would not have handed him over (18:30). Pilate tells them to handle the matter themselves, but they protest that they have no authority to impose the death penalty. Pilate's questions then revolve around the issue of kingship; there follow enigmatic statements about kingship and truth.

Questions Remain

This summary of the accounts reveals serious historical questions. While it may be possible to harmonize the four accounts into one consistent one, it seems fruitless to do so. Some of the more significant historical questions include the following:

---

12. John 18:19 says "high priest" but evidently means Annas rather than Caiaphas; see John 18:13 and 24.

1. Does what we know otherwise about Pilate confirm or contradict the character attributed to Pilate in the Gospels? Josephus portrays Pilate as ruthless and tells of his insensitivity to Jewish concerns and his threats and violence against Jews who protested his actions.[13] Would such a person give in to a mob's call for Jesus' crucifixion if he thought Jesus was innocent? Does his concern about the innocence of Jesus and his desire to release Jesus sound plausible in light of his character?

2. The Gospels of Mark and Matthew present formal action by the Jewish Sanhedrin. Judging from Talmudic records, these proceedings would have violated Sanhedrin standards if they in fact occurred as Matthew and Mark narrate them. Many scholars think the violations are so numerous and flagrant that the Gospel accounts cannot be accurate and that there might have been no trial at all by the Sanhedrin, or that, if it did occur, it was not before the "Great Sanhedrin" but before an "Assembly" or "Council."[14] The Great Sanhedrin rested upon and dealt with the Jewish law. Herod had initiated a different sort of council to advise the high priest, who was a political and not a religious appointee. Herod intended that council to reduce the power of the priestly aristocracy. The word used by Mark is simply a general word meaning "council" and should not necessarily be taken to imply the Great Sanhedrin or the authoritative religious court.[15]

3. The Barabbas incident strikes many interpreters as implausible and legendary. Pilate seems to be presented with an alternative: Jesus or Barabbas. How could a person of Pilate's character have been put in such a predicament? Would he have allowed a crowd into his residence during a criminal hearing? Why could he not have granted amnesty to both if he had wanted to? And would he have allowed a dangerous man to go free under pressure from a crowd deliberately stirred up in his presence by the chief priests?

4. Would a claim to be Messiah or Son of God be blasphemous? Blasphemy means reviling or speaking profane or evil things about God. Speaking evil about the Temple, as Jesus did if he threatened its destruction, might be construed as speaking evil of God who inhabits it. But in the context of Mark's report, blasphemy seems to be associated either with the claim to be

---

13. See Josephus, *Jewish Antiquities* XVIII.55–62; *Jewish War* II.169–77.

14. See, for example, Eduard Lohse, *History of the Suffering and Death of Jesus Christ* (Philadelphia: Fortress Press, 1967), especially 79–80; Winter, *On the Trial of Jesus*.

15. For a useful and concise summary of these various views, see Jeffrey G. Sobosan, "The Trial of Jesus," *Journal of Ecumenical Studies* 10 (1973): 80–83. See also Rivkin, *What Crucified Jesus?*, 31–36, 54, 101–2.

Messiah or Son of God or with the assertion that as Son of Man he would be seen to sit at God's right hand. If Son of God were understood in a later Christian sense of divine Savior, it would seem blasphemous, but in Jesus' context it would be a virtual synonym for Messiah. A claim to be either Son of Man or Messiah would not be blasphemous, unless J. C. O'Neill's hypothesis is correct. He believes that Jesus' blasphemy consisted in claiming to be Messiah *before God announced God's choice*. Although it would not be blasphemous to claim to be Messiah per se, "no one should presume to say that he was the Son, the Messiah . . . until God had vindicated his anointed one and given him his appointed throne."[16]

Debate

These questions lead to considerable debate: Was it the Romans or the Jews who bore most responsibility for the condemnation and execution of Jesus? Those who argue for significant Jewish involvement in the death of Jesus have a convincing case. Those who argue that that involvement was for purely political reasons—in other words, that it was only the Jewish aristocracy, in tandem with Roman authority—have a weaker case. Reacting to a long history of Christians accusing Jews of "murdering" Christ, and recognizing in the Gospels a tendency to portray early Christians as politically innocent, some interpreters reduce the Jewish involvement in Jesus' death to near point zero. Some have claimed that Jesus was a Pharisee,[17] or that the friction between Jesus and the Pharisees would not have been serious enough for them to be involved in the proceedings against Jesus. In spite of the fact that many similarities between Jesus and the Pharisees can legitimately be raised, his approach was grounded more in the prophetic tradition than was theirs. Some (many) Pharisees may well have been attracted to Jesus and his message, and may have even become his disciples, but many certainly did not find him acceptable.

Ellis Rivkin argues vigorously that in Jesus' day religious tolerance was such that Jesus' religious views would never have led to his death.[18] While his

---

16. J. C. O'Neill, "The Charge of Blasphemy at Jesus' Trial Before the Sanhedrin," in *The Trial of Jesus*, ed. E. Bammel, 77.

17. See Harvey Falk, *Jesus the Pharisee: A New Look at the Jewishness of Jesus* (New York: Paulist Press, 1985), who places Jesus within the debates between the School of Hillel and the School of Shammai, and argues that Jesus' criticisms were directed at the latter.

18. Rivkin, *What Crucified Jesus?*

conclusion is likely correct, Rivkin overdoes the "live and let live" aspects of first-century Judaism. There were intense struggles within Judaism, and while most of them were rooted in social and economic issues, the tensions involved religious and theological matters as well. The climate was not one of easy tolerance, as both Josephus and the New Testament demonstrate.

The attitude and actions of Paul (and other Jewish leaders) toward Jesus' followers after his death show the intensity of religious debate within Israel. Paul's opposition to the disciples might well have been different from Pharisaic opposition to Jesus, but there must be some continuity in the conflicts and the major contenders. Paul's attitudes may not have been dominant, but they were influential enough for him to be able to execute some of the Jesus people. Nor is it likely that a person like Paul could have operated without the consent of or important support within the Sanhedrin or without the support of other Pharisees. Given Paul's religious convictions, and judging by the lack of engagement with political issues in his letters, it is not likely that Paul's motives were primarily political.

Why Was Jesus Executed?

Jesus delivered his message in the context of tense religious struggle. He drew deeply from the religious heritage of Israel, but he interpreted that heritage in a radically prophetic manner that set him at some odds with all the "parties" of Judaism that we know about from Josephus and others. Rivkin's picture of tolerant Judaism does not seem to match the evidence from Josephus and the New Testament. Jesus himself, like John the Baptist before him, spoke a radical message not conducive to compromise. He challenged the Pharisees on their interpretation of the Torah, particularly their under-standing of purity and their identification of purity with righteousness.[19] He likely rejected the radicalism of revolutionary Zealots[20] and their willingness to use violence as a way of peace and righteousness in society. He might well

---

19. The extent to which the Pharisees were concerned with purity is debated. While Matthew probably exaggerates that concern, it is likely that the Pharisees' wish to see the whole Jewish community practice the purity of the priests led them to place much more emphasis on purity than did Jesus. See Riches, *Jesus and the Transformation of Judaism;* Borg, *Conflict, Holiness, and Politics in the Teachings of Jesus;* and Jacob Neusner, *The Idea of Purity in Ancient Judaism* (Leiden: E. J. Brill, 1973).

20. Horsley's point that the Zealots as a party came into existence later is convincing, but the attitudes that crystallize in the later age were already present in Jesus' time (*Jesus and the Spiral of Violence*).

have dissociated himself from the Essenes, rejecting their withdrawal from society as an abandonment of the people. He rejected the Sadducees' identification of religion with the Temple and its sacrifices. He was uncompromising with any who would dispense with the Israelite concept of justice and *shalom* in favor of the more modern ways introduced by Hellenism and Romanism. Like other prophets before him, Jesus alienated many and angered others with his prophetic message and acts.

Jesus' refusal to compromise in order to build a base of power and support might well have made it impossible for him to achieve his social and religious goals and might even have cost him his life. But Jesus acted on the belief that the only basis for a viable future was the renewal of the covenant that bound all Israel together in one community of faith. His proclamation and his teaching, as well as his actions, were based on that conviction. That sounds highly idealistic, and in a sense it was, but that ideal contained some down-to-earth ingredients that will be articulated in subsequent chapters. For now it is sufficient to emphasize that Jesus' death resulted in part from religious conflicts within the Jewish community.

To argue this way is not to say Jesus' death resulted merely from religious causes, or that the Romans played only a passive part in Jesus' execution. The Romans executed Jesus as a troublemaker because he was making trouble for them.

Those who argue that the Romans were deeply involved in the entire proceeding against Jesus make a convincing case. The high priest was a political appointee under the Romans as he had also been under Herod the Great. In fact David had started that tradition himself. The council itself could well have been a political rather than a religious body, as Ellis Rivkin argues quite persuasively.[21] The charges that Luke notes against Jesus are essentially political charges, and while the verdict rendered is inconclusive regarding the forbidding of payment of taxes to Caesar, and while it is not certainly historically established that Jesus claimed to be king, there is evidence in the Gospels to substantiate both claims. If both charges have any veracity, the charge that Jesus was perverting the nation has some basis in fact. All four Gospels note that Jesus claimed to be king of Israel and that he was executed on that charge. Although the Gospel writers have come to understand "king of Israel" quite differently on the basis of the crucifixion and resurrection of Jesus, they nonetheless think that term appropriate. If the Romans had

---

21. *What Crucified Jesus?*, 27–37, 101, 117.

thought there was any truth to the claim, they would have made short shrift of the claimant, for to them the claim would suggest revolutionary activity against the interests of Rome.

While this reading of double involvement by Jewish and Roman authorities has plausibility on the surface of it, it needs substantiation by a thorough look at the Gospel materials that portray Jesus' words and actions. The remainder of this book, therefore, must continue to weigh such evidence as is available. In this chapter, the evidence from the events closest in context and probably also closest in time will be examined.

Jesus' Entry Into Jerusalem: Mark 11:1–10; Matthew 21:1–9; Luke 19:28–38; John 12:12–19

The Gospels portray Jesus as making a final challenge to Jerusalem in the days immediately preceding his execution, a challenge that eventuated in his arrest and execution. In all four Gospels Jesus' entry into Jerusalem during the Passover festival forms a crucial opening for the other narratives. Matthew and Luke modify Mark's account, while John apparently used the same traditional story but with his own distinctive flavoring. The narratives all reflect the early church's understanding of the event as the decisive coming of the Messiah to Israel, Israel's rejection of the Messiah (sealing Israel's tragic fate), and setting in motion the forces that will bring Jesus to his death.

According to all the Gospel accounts, Jesus went to Jerusalem with the deliberate intention of dying. That purpose dominates Mark's narrative from the beginning and becomes explicit with the "Passion predictions" of Mark 8:31–32; 9:31–32; 10:33–34 (Matthew and Luke follow Mark, with minor changes). Building on the Gospel accounts, Paul's letters, and other early Christian writings, the traditional Christian understanding is that Jesus went to Jerusalem to die so that sins could be forgiven. He did this to fulfill the messianic hopes contained in the Hebrew scriptures. However, the Gospel accounts contain indications of other, more complex reasons. These other reasons include political dimensions that conform much more closely to Jewish messianic ideas.

The four Gospel accounts of Jesus' entry reflect political elements in different ways. Mark is the most restrained of the four (11:1–10). The messianic elements are largely if not entirely absent from his narrative. The shout of the crowd, "Save now! Blessed is the one who comes in the name of the Lord!" derives from a pilgrimage psalm (Ps. 118:26) used by pilgrims coming to Jerusalem for the Feast of Tabernacles and perhaps for the Feast of Dedication. The reference to one "who comes" does not specifically apply to a Messiah; any devout pilgrim would qualify for that epithet. The further refrain, "Blessed is the coming kingdom of our ancestor David!" makes no explicit messianic reference to Jesus, and though it suggests the nearness of a political kingdom, it makes no specific association of Jesus with that kingdom. In keeping with Mark's reticence to have Jesus refer to himself as Messiah, Mark presents the incident as a subdued and implicitly messianic demonstration. Mark also separates the Temple demonstration from the entry, further diffusing the messianic character of the entry, as compared with Luke and Matthew.

Undoubtedly Mark himself understood it (ironically perhaps) as a veiled messianic event that could be grasped only retrospectively (see John 12:16 for a similar view). Mark provides a clue by preceding the entry with the healing of blind Bartimaeus (10:46–52), who for the first and only time in Mark identifies Jesus as "Son of David." In response, the crowds, voicing Jesus' usual admonition to silence, rebuke Bartimaeus, but Jesus calls him forward and uncharacteristically asks him to speak. Their interchange concerns the man's blindness, Jesus' healing, and Jesus' identity, but Jesus does not deny the title or command that it remain unspoken.

Luke has the crowd "rejoice and praise God with a loud voice for all the mighty works [of Jesus] that they had seen, saying, 'Blessed is the King who comes in the name of the Lord! Peace in heaven, and glory in the highest!' " (19:37–38, RSV). The crowd has just "set Jesus upon [the colt]" with words recalling the setting of Solomon upon David's royal mount to initiate his coronation (1 Kings 1:38). This openly messianic demonstration and the crowd's acclamation reflect the tradition of the popularly acclaimed Messiah, just as some of the incidents Josephus records do (see chapter 1 above). That meaning is not lost on the Pharisees in the crowd. They demand that Jesus rebuke the disciples; Jesus refuses the demand, affirming that if the disciples did not make the necessary ovation, "the very stones would cry out" the truth of their testimony. In Luke's sequel in 19:41–44, Jesus proclaims God's lament over the city that did not recognize in his presence God's visitation of Israel (see also 1 Peter 2:12). This sequel provides the best guide to the meaning Luke saw in the incident: The coming of Jesus Messiah is the coming of God's offer of that peace on earth promised in the angels' song at Jesus' birth, but the offer rejected leaves as its deadly corollary the devastation of the nation through war. Luke intensifies the terror of the second visitation (destruction) by the explicit proclamation of the nature of the first visitation:

Faithless Israel shows itself unworthy of the saving visitation of God in the person of the Messiah. Luke thus reflects the early Christian interpretation of the Fall of Jerusalem as a consequence of the rejection of God's messenger, Jesus.[22]

Strangely, Luke does not intend here to emphasize the political dimensions of Jesus' ministry. Jesus is not intending to "restore the kingdom to Israel" (Acts 1:6). Jesus is politically innocent, as Pilate declares and as the Roman soldier testifies (23:47). Nonetheless, Jesus is "king of peace," and as king he enters the city.

Matthew too portrays the entry as the demonstration of the king of Israel, for the crowd says, "Hosanna to the Son of David" (21:9). However, Matthew too plays down the political dimensions of the story, so that the effect is to have the people wonder as Jesus arrives in the city, "Who is this?" The answer is given, "This is the prophet Jesus from Nazareth" (Matt. 21:10–11). Matthew accomplishes this dual task of identifying Jesus as Messiah but subduing the political implications by making particular changes in Mark's account.

First, citing Zechariah 9:9, he has Jesus fulfill the prophecy that "your king is coming to you" (Matt. 21:5). But he omits Zechariah's phrase, "triumphant and victorious is he." He does cite the comment that the arriving king is "humble, and mounted on an donkey, and on a colt, the foal of a donkey."

Second, Matthew takes over Mark's sequence of the request of the sons of Zebedee, the healing of the blind beggar (Matthew does not identify the two blind men as beggars), and the entry into Jerusalem. This sequence joins the announcement of Jesus' kingship with Jesus' rejection of the way of the Gentiles (he does not give positions of prestige and honor but invites to service) and the affirmation of the ministry of compassion (healing the blind men). Matthew makes these themes more evident than Mark by the crowd's explicit affirmation of Jesus' messiahship and by noting Jesus' pity on the blind beggars. The effect of Matthew's narrative is to shift the attention from triumphant messianism to a messianic ministry of taking up the sufferings of the people.

In Matthew the children in the Temple repeat the crowd's identification of Jesus as Messiah (21:15). Again there is resistance, this time to the claim

---

22. See D. L. Tiede, "Weeping for Jerusalem," *Prophecy and History in Luke-Acts* (Philadelphia: Fortress Press, 1980), 65–96, 143–48, for the view that Luke does not turn "the traditions against Israel." Cited in Joseph Fitzmyer, *The Gospel According to Luke X–XXIV,* The Anchor Bible (Garden City, N.Y.: Doubleday & Co., 1985), 1255.

itself, as the chief priests object and Jesus approves. After the children reaffirm Jesus' messiahship, its true meaning is again shown in Jesus' healing of the blind and the lame (21:14). Only the children recognize the presence of the Messiah in Jesus' healing and in his opposition to the authorities. The children thus express the truth that healing of the nation depends on the right worship of God combined with compassion for the people; it does not depend on continuing the status quo in which economic motive, power, and prestige overcome the divine intention for the Temple. The authorities themselves with their vested interests are unable to join in that recognition.

The fact that both Luke and Matthew present a more explicitly political picture of the demonstration might seem to militate against my contention of a tendency away from the political; such is not necessarily the case, however. Even in Mark the demonstration is not politically innocent, but in keeping with Mark's hidden-Messiah theme, the messianic nature of it is evident only in retrospect—or only to the reader, not to the participants themselves. Mark's account contains no warnings by the authorities, because the enigmatic event contained no explicit claims. But all three writers use the event to reinterpret the meaning of messiahship in a way that minimizes it as a political threat. Jesus is Messiah, but he is not the messiah hoped for by zealous nationalists nor feared by the Roman and Jewish authorities. Nonetheless they are right to fear him, for he presents a serious challenge to their authority.

Various assessments have been made of the historical quality of the entry into Jerusalem: (1) A prophecy (Zech. 9:9) made into event, there is nothing historical about the narrative. It derives from the desire to show that Jesus fulfilled scriptures thought by the church to be important or useful in advancing their claim that Jesus was Messiah. (2) It was a spontaneous event that caught Jesus by surprise, not an attempt by him to claim messianic status but an attempt to restrain those messianic hopes that his ministry in Galilee had aroused. He mounted a donkey as a sign of humility, rejecting any temptation to ride a war-horse. (3) Jesus prearranged an openly messianic demonstration, securing a donkey as an appropriate symbol of his messiahship, and no longer maintaining the messianic secret. The narratives themselves do not offer sufficient evidence to decide on the historical quality of the event; it needs to be read in light of the ensuing developments.

The story of Jesus' entry has so obviously been used in church tradition and by the Gospel writers to make points important to their interpretation of Jesus that one cannot safely assert any definitive conclusion regarding its historical character. However, given the nature of Jesus' challenge to his contemporaries and particularly to the governing authorities, given the importance of Jerusalem and Jesus' decision to go there in the face of danger, and given the outcome of that journey, it is plausible that (1) the entry was a memorable occasion; (2) it was seen by Jesus, his friends, and his enemies, as a direct challenge to authority in the name of the kingdom he had proclaimed in Galilee; (3) his challenge was not merely to the religious leadership but to the political authorities as well; (4) his challenge led rather directly to his arrest and execution. The fact that the authorities did not arrest Jesus immediately is not a sufficient argument against this interpretation. The authorities might have been caught off guard, or they might have thought it wiser to bide their time (as Mark implies in 14:2). There is nothing in the narratives that contradicts the implications of Jesus' crucifixion: The political authorities regarded him as dangerous.

Demonstration at the Temple: Mark 11:15–19; Matthew 21:12–17; Luke 19:45–48; Compare John 2:13–22

Setting the entry in the larger context of the narratives of Jesus' final days in Jerusalem provides additional help in understanding the nature of the charges against Jesus.

According to Mark, Jesus went directly to the Temple upon entering Jerusalem. After looking around, he left for Bethany, returning the next day with a disruptive demonstration at the Temple. The location for Jesus' action suggests that he directed his Jerusalem challenge against the high-priestly aristocracy rather than against the Romans, though that distinction is not entirely justifiable. The fact that Jesus went to the Temple and performed there his act of defiance against authority should not be taken to mean his concerns were only religious and not political. Such a conclusion would indicate a misunderstanding of what the Temple meant historically. Carol Myers's comment about the meaning of the Temple as originally established in Solomon's time applies throughout its history:

> It was very much a public building in a political and economic sense. Because ancient Israel, even during the monarchy, was not a secular state, the Temple played an integral role in the organization, legitimation, and administration of the national community.[23]

---

23. Myers, "The Temple," *Harper's Bible Dictionary,* 1022.

With the demise of kingship after the Babylonian destruction of Jerusalem in 586 B.C.E., the restored Temple formed the center of national life, its priests filling the void in political leadership during the Persian rule.[24] Herod's rebuilding and refurbishing the Temple reflected his desire to make his kingdom a worthy part of the Roman Empire. The Hasmonaean combined religious and political authority in the person of the high priest/king. Herod appointed the high priest, a practice the Romans continued during their direct rule in Judea. The Romans looked to the priestly aristocracy to provide internal governance. Secular and religious authority were thus not separate; combined in one group of people, they were integrally related. The seat of that authority was the Temple.

The priestly aristocracy who controlled the Temple enjoyed the prosperity that Roman rule brought for some people. Wilson[25] maintains that the opulence of the Temple shows the unprecedented prosperity of the time. It also provides significant evidence of the social and economic problem: Sadducean priests lived in fine houses at the expense of the peasants and the urban poor (see chapter 1 above). The opulence was not at the expense of the Romans but of the Jews, who were required by Torah and by Roman law to bring a tithe for its support.[26]

The injustice of the situation, perpetrated by the very ones who were responsible for maintaining the ritual expressions of the covenant community, provoked the prophetic conscience of Jesus. The event took place on the eve of the Passover, the festival that more than any other signified God's deliverance of the oppressed and the forging of the covenant community. In attacking the Temple establishment, Jesus challenged the very center of the system that signified the covenant traditions but neglected the social and economic consequences of those traditions.

The Gospels portray the demonstration as a symbolic act of purification. To understand that purification in narrowly religious terms would reduce the encompassing nature of the covenant. Religious purification means also the renewed recognition of the covenant obligations toward the whole of society. Given the conditions in first-century Palestine and the Israelite tradition of enacted prophetic protests (see Jeremiah and Ezekiel), this act was directed against those who held power in Jerusalem. It pronounced God's judgment

---

24. Myers, "The Temple," *Harper's Bible Dictionary*, 1027.
25. Wilson, *Jesus: The Evidence*, 78, 80.
26. Josephus, *Jewish Antiquities* XIV.202–3; Horsley, *Jesus and the Spiral of Violence*, 286–87.

upon them, and it anticipated the coming of the kingdom of justice and peace that the present regime had thwarted through its own selfishness and shortsightedness.[27]

Jesus' actions were a demonstration, not an attempt to gain possession of the Temple. The narratives do not state that any of Jesus' disciples participated with him, though Matthew mentions the response of persons in the crowd. The action was not likely a solitary one, especially if it occurred in the context of a pilgrimage, and especially if it occurred in conjunction with the entry demonstration. Jesus' attack may well have included some minimal use of force or even violence, but it was for purposes of demonstration rather than for takeover. The action was by a group of Galileans, possibly joined by Judeans as well.[28]

The action by Galileans raises the question as to the relationship between the Jews of Galilee and those of Judea. Would the Galileans have been required to pay the tithe to the Temple? Would the Romans have been the ones to enforce that payment? Josephus says Julius Caesar had decreed that the Jews should pay the tithe to Hyrcanus (the Hasmonaean high priest) and his descendants.[29] At that time the decree would have applied to Galilee as well as Judea. The situation did not likely change with the imposition of direct rule on Judea and a change in high priesthood. Thus the Galileans would have been paying tithes to support the Temple as well as taxes to maintain Herodian rule in Galilee; resentment against that situation could have been strong enough for the Galileans to follow Jesus in this demonstration.[30]

As early as the Ptolemies, foreign governments controlling Palestine had recruited Jewish aristocracy to collect taxes and otherwise participate in

27. Horsley, *Jesus and the Spiral of Violence*, 299–300.

28. See Matthew 21:10, which suggests that Jerusalemites might have joined in the action. Stambaugh and Balch, *The New Testament in Its Social Environment*, 94, point out that there were many motivations for pilgrimages to Jerusalem. The spiritual aspect was only one of many; Josephus emphasizes the social and political role of pilgrimage, especially for Galileans. Josephus, *Jewish Antiquities* XVII.149–67, 213–18, places the conflict after the death of Herod the Great in the context of pilgrimage.

29. Probably in 44 B.C.E., according to Ralph Marcus's notes in the Loeb edition of *Jewish Antiquities* XIV.201, p. 554.

30. Freyne, *Galilee, Jesus, and the Gospels*, 135–75, maintains that Galilee was out of the mainstream and not as conflictive as Judea in Jesus' time. If he is correct, there might have been less resentment among the Galileans as a group than among Judeans. Stambaugh and Balch, *The New Testament in Its Social Environment*, 92–94, think Freyne exaggerates the isolation. Even if land tenure had not been as disrupted in Galilee as in Judea, Herod's reign and its aftermath were deeply resented by many, as the case of Judas ben Hezekiah suggests (*Jewish Antiquities* XVII.271–72).

government. "In this way the aristocracy were given a share in the wealth and authority of the state and were open to Hellenistic influence."[31] Such a situation continued in Roman times, so that common people who wished to maintain Jewish ways and avoid Hellenistic influences would look upon the aristocracy as perverters of the nation. The demonstration against the Temple expresses those kinds of frustrations as well as the economic stress of the people. It expressed a declining level of support that ordinary people voluntarily gave to the Temple because of its perceived corruptions.[32]

Even if the Romans were not the direct target of the entry and the Temple demonstrations, they would understand that Jesus' criticism challenged the political and social status quo, not merely the religious activity of the Temple. It is often asserted that if the Romans had so perceived it, they would have reacted immediately and put down the disturbance, rather than waiting until the Jewish authorities proceeded against Jesus. That assertion suggests that Roman authority saw no cause for concern, correctly perceiving that only religious matters were involved and that Jesus had no political motivations or intentions. But we do not know how long Jesus was in Jerusalem before he was arrested, nor do we know what went on between Jewish and Roman authorities as they designed a mechanism to control a potentially dangerous movement. Jesus' actions could easily have triggered Roman reactions that led soon afterward to Jesus' arrest and execution.

The two demonstrations begin a series of confrontations in the Gospel accounts. Through parables and debates, Jesus challenges the Jewish authorities, who determine that he must be removed. Some of the issues dealt with in these exchanges likely derive from continuing debates between the church and the synagogue. In any event, they are not likely to be determined by historical reminiscence. Some of the parables will claim our attention in chapter 5 below. One issue, however, is particularly relevant to the question about Jesus' execution: taxation.

Regarding Tribute to Caesar: Mark 12:13–17; Matthew 22:15–22; Luke 20:20–26

The Markan story regarding payment of taxes to Caesar exemplifies the difficulty of knowing how Jesus stood in relation to the politics of his day.

---

31. Riches, *Jesus and the Transformation of Judaism*, 64.
32. Horsley, *Jesus and the Spiral of Violence*, 287.

"Should we pay taxes to Caesar or not?" represents a difficult political choice. Mark tells us that Jesus' opponents posed the question to trap him. Any reader in the Roman world would know the danger of a negative answer; those familiar with the Palestinian situation would know the hazard of a positive answer. With conflicts within the Jewish community at fever pitch, the question was explosive.

In Mark's presentation, Jesus handles the situation deftly, avoiding difficulty for himself and embarrassing his opponents. Mark shows no overt interest in the political implications of Jesus' response; he ends the episode by stressing the amazement of the bystanders, in a manner similar to the response of those who witnessed Jesus' healing power. Thus, Mark leaves open the possibility that Jesus sees no necessary conflict between being a loyal citizen to Caesar, whose stamp of ownership is on the coin of the realm, and to God, whose stamp (image) is on the human person. Mark's interest centers much more on Jesus' power and his ability to control the situation in which he finds himself. Luke, on the other hand, suggests that Jesus' answer could have been understood to mean that one should not pay taxes, for he later narrates that Jesus' accusers before Pilate charge him with "perverting our nation, forbidding us to pay taxes to the emperor, and saying that he himself is the Messiah, a king" (Luke 23:2).

Since Mark's interest in this political issue is not primarily political, it is not likely that Mark's community originated the story. It more likely comes out of the context of real historical debate, for the issue was one that had a lively relationship to the Jesus movement during its Palestinian origins. The very fact that the question is raised provides evidence that Jesus engaged in political activity and debate. One does not have to argue for the historicity of the stylized question and answer to think that the issue raised was a subject of discussion and debate between Jesus and his hearers. The story brings us then within the context of Jesus' historical ministry and reflects the social, political, economic, and religious issues that made the situation of any renewal movement quite precarious. As a prophet of the coming of God's reign, Jesus' attitude toward Roman taxes would have been a matter of serious concern.

Josephus supplies evidence that the issue of paying Roman taxes[33] had

_____

33. J. A. Sanders, "Tax, Taxes," *Interpreter's Dictionary of the Bible,* 4:521, explains the principal kinds of taxes under the Romans: a "land tax payable in kind or in money, a poll tax, a tax on personal property (Matt. 22:17), export and import customs at seaports and city gates, and in Jerusalem a house tax."

agitated Palestinian politics for some time. A certain Judas from Galilee objected to the Roman census of 6 C.E., scolded as cowards those paying tribute, and encouraged them to revolt, believing that God was the only legitimate ruler of God's people.

> Apparently Judas believed that if God's people insisted on God's rule alone in the land, then God would act to establish that rule on their behalf. Being ideologically motivated, the resistance took no account of the political realities or possibilities of the situation.[34]

The payment of taxes was both an ideological and an economic issue in Jesus' time. Mark's story makes it difficult to know Jesus' attitude toward taxation. In his eagerness to demonstrate Jesus' ability to silence his foes, Mark might have played up the enigmatic character of Jesus' answer, but there is no denying that in its present form it is enigmatic. At least three understandings are possible: (1) One should pay taxes. (2) One should not pay taxes. (3) One should have nothing to do with Caesar's coins.

Jesus' words have understandably been taken to mean that one can without any conflict participate in two realms: Both Caesar and God have legitimate interests, and the two are quite compatible if one keeps one's priorities straight. Money belongs to the secular realm, the human soul belongs to God. So long as one properly attends to the spiritual life, and so long as the secular power does not attempt to usurp or corrupt that life, one can live obediently to the secular realm without guilt or compromise. This interpretation has had a venerable history; it has enabled Western Christians to live as good citizens of all sorts of states, and, except for times of crisis when one realm or the other thought its counterpart was demanding too much, it has worked rather smoothly. Christians have been able to accommodate themselves to the world in ways that have allowed them not to feel guilty toward God or disloyal to the state.

Some see Jesus' major contribution in his advocating such a position. According to Hengel, Jesus separated religion and politics, disrupting the naive view that prevailed in Jesus' day that religion and politics were not only inseparable, they were identical.[35] Jesus opposed the exploitation of the poor by the rich, but, unlike the revolutionary Zealots, he identified evil in the world not with social or political structures but with the individual. Thus not

---

34. Rhoads, *Israel in Revolution: 6–74 C.E.*, 49.
35. Hengel, *Victory Over Violence*, 1.

the liberation of the homeland but the transformation of the individual heart was the center of Jesus' approach.[36] Ellis Rivkin agrees that Jesus separated the religious from the secular but argues that in doing so he followed the precedent already firmly established by the Pharisees.

The problem with this interpretation is that it conflicts with the Judaic tradition. Though the Jews had over several centuries adjusted to living under alien governments—Babylonian, Persian, Hellenistic rulers—such a separation of religion and politics would be at best an expedient, never the ideal. God's kingdom involves God's rule over God's people, not just in part but in the totality of their lives. God rules the people not directly but through a theocratic state. To call for the establishment of God's kingdom is thus to call for a political change.[37] What Hengel and Rivkin see as a change of viewpoint should be understood as a temporary accommodation at most.

In Jesus' day there was a move away from politics by many people. Disillusionment with the politics of the Hasmonaeans, along with religious corruption, had resulted in the rise of sects that "abandoned either nationalist hopes or common life in Jewish towns or cities or both."[38] The Pharisees "moved from politics to piety," just as the Essenes had moved from society and formed communities in the desert. The Essene documents indicate, however, that they did not regard their withdrawal as final. The Pharisees, too, show that giving up on politics was a temporary expedient, as the return of Pharisees to active participation in political life after the destruction of Jerusalem shows.[39]

The next chapters will argue that in his proclamation of the kingdom of God and in his teaching, Jesus was not opting for a "religious" as opposed to a social-political understanding of the covenant community. Therefore the genius of Jesus will have to be found elsewhere than in establishing the principle of separation of church and state.

A second possible interpretation of Jesus' response is that it constitutes an endorsement of the Roman Empire. There is no direct evidence in the Gospels that Jesus opposed Roman rule. He included tax collectors in his groups of special concern. He advocated loving one's enemies, in direct opposition to emerging Zealotism. He renounced the use of violence. He

---

36. Hengel, *Victory Over Violence*, 47–48.

37. Rivkin, *What Crucified Jesus?*

38. Howard Clark Kee, *Christian Origins in Sociological Perspective* (Philadelphia: Westminster Press, 1980), 37.

39. Jacob Neusner makes this point in *From Politics to Piety: The Emergence of Pharisaic Judaism*, 2d ed. (New York: KTAV Publishing House, 1979), 145–47.

advocated compliance with the Roman practice of requisition—even going the second mile when compelled to go one. In light of sayings of this sort, it is conceivable that Jesus regarded the Roman rule as the best available option, having no confidence in the various Jewish factions that would vie for power were Rome not present. The saying on taxes could thus indicate an endorsement of the legitimacy of Caesar's realm and the payment of taxes to that realm as a civic and religious duty.

This interpretation has problems very similar to the previous one. Not only does it conflict with traditional notions of the covenant people of God, with Jesus' popularity with the people, with any messianic claim by or for Jesus, and with his crucifixion. An advocate of Roman legitimacy would hardly have been executed by the Roman procurator. He needed all the help he could get, especially from a charismatic leader.

Thirdly, Jesus' answer could also imply that one should not pay Roman taxes—indeed, that one should have nothing to do with the Romans, even renouncing their coins.[40] The common modern assumption that the coin of the realm belongs to the political authority was not necessarily made by a first-century Jew. What does belong to the Romans? Does political rule? Does the wealth of the land and nation? Does authority to control the lives of God's people? And what belongs to God? As one who read the Psalms, Jesus knew that "the earth is the LORD's and all that is in it, the world, and those who live in it" (24:1). Surely Jesus, like all devout Jews, knew that especially the holy land and its resources belong to God. Thus paying tribute means giving to Caesar what belonged to God. Everything belongs to God, and the symbols of Caesar's usurpations, his coins, should be returned to him. How dare a Jew even possess one of them! Jesus' request for the coin itself intended to embarrass the person who asked the question, by showing how the person had already compromised by possessing it.

Jesus must have made clear during his ministry his attitude toward paying tribute—in that climate he could not have escaped that issue. If he had advocated payment, people would hardly have regarded him as Messiah. The charges against Jesus reported by Luke must have some justification.

Given Jesus' radical demands (see chapter 6 below), with their emphasis upon unalloyed allegiance to God and the kingdom—placing the kingdom

---

40. Horsley, *Jesus and the Spiral of Violence*, 306–7, makes the point that unlike the tradition of interpreting this saying as requiring civil obedience, recent interpreters have recognized that Jesus' ambiguous reply asserts the "absolute and exclusive sovereignty of God."

above primary values such as family, health, etc., Jesus could quite conceivably in that context have meant, "Give Caesar back his coin, and give your undivided allegiance to God so that Caesar and his coins may be removed from God's land." To avoid the trap, Jesus had to respond ironically so that his words could not convict him before the governor, but he still let his point sink in with those who knew what such words really meant.

Horsley makes the valuable point that Jesus not only avoids the intended entrapment but also refocuses the issue to the primary one: Who is Lord?[41] The emphasis throughout Jesus' teaching lies on the absoluteness of one's obligation to God and to God's kingdom. If he here advocates that God's lordship and Caesar's are compatible, it would have to be within the kingdom of God itself. Can that be? Further, if Jesus accepts the payment of taxes, he has fallen into the trap planned for him. But an enigmatic answer that embarrasses those who have found the present situation consistent with God's kingdom, and yet allows Jesus to avoid explicitly condemning their position, serves his purpose well. He has made his political point, pressured his opponents, let everyone know what he means, and still escaped the trap set for him.

Jesus' advocacy of nonviolence does not argue against this view, for noncooperation with the Romans does not necessitate their violent overthrow. His advocacy of going the second mile (Matt. 5:41) would, however, seem to argue against this interpretation, if that saying is authentic and applicable to military requisition. In such a case, Jesus takes a position different from either those who regard cooperation with the Romans as quite acceptable and those who see violent revolution as the only alternative. In subsequent chapters I will argue that that is indeed the position the historical Jesus took.

Conclusion

In this chapter I have attempted to show that there is nothing historically implausible in Jesus' execution by the Romans on the charge of political crimes. His death did not result from Rome's mistaking his religious message for a political one, nor from their failure to understand that his messiahship was spiritual. Rather, both they and the Jewish aristocracy knew quite well that his teaching and his activity posed a serious challenge to their authority

---

41. Horsley, *Jesus and the Spiral of Violence,* 311–13.

and that, if he continued, matters would only become more dangerous. Roman governors knew when to act and how to act to prevent the danger that sedition posed to their rule.

I do not consider that the present chapter has established a "political" Jesus, but I do think it has established a prima facie case. That case must be confirmed in the following chapters through close examination of his words and actions leading up to the climactic events in Jerusalem. To that task we now turn.

CHAPTER THREE

"Seek First God's Kingdom"

Political metaphors relating to kings and kingdoms abound in the Gospel accounts of Jesus' ministry. As the previous chapter has shown, Jesus' final days were filled with claims and hopes as well as fears and threats associated with his being a king. Before Jesus went to Jerusalem, his preaching and teaching in Galilee had centered on the kingdom of God. Thematically his journey to Jerusalem, his activities there, and his execution were consistent with his Galilean activities. The Synoptic Gospels, in contrast to the Gospel of John, all agree that the kingdom of God was at the center not only of Jesus' proclamation but also of his teaching, his healing, even his death and resurrection. The kingdom recurs in all layers of the tradition and in various forms (parables, apocalyptic sayings, ethical sayings, prayers). By the principle of multiple attestation, one has to conclude that the kingdom of God was central to the historical ministry of Jesus.

Jesus set out with a message about the kingdom, its coming, its promises, its demands, its gift. Jesus' ministry centered on the kingdom of God. If that ministry led to his death by execution, then the kingdom must have been a momentous matter with grave implications both for Jesus and for those who put him to death. For it to have resulted in his crucifixion, the kingdom of God must have carried political connotations that the governing authorities in Jerusalem considered dangerous.

Astounding as it may seem, however, neither in the church nor in academic circles has the kingdom of God been assigned the political significance its derivation and its consequences demand. Scholarly debate has largely ignored any overt political dimensions of the kingdom. Two contending polar positions have dominated debate: an individual, interior understanding of kingdom, and an apocalyptic view of a cataclysmic end of the world.

One suspects that the reasons for neglecting the political element in church interpretation relate to the theological need to understand Jesus in universal terms. If Jesus focused on social and political change in Israel, his appeal might diminish as the universal savior the church understands him to be.

The reasons for the neglect in academic circles are more complex. They derive in part from the fact that the academic study of the New Testament emerged within theological seminaries attached to the church. It has thus shared many of the perspectives and aims of the church. Another, and arguably more important, reason is that the variety of kingdom materials in the Gospels and their lack of overt political meanings make a political interpretation a daunting task.

Recent scholarship both in the church and in the academy has begun to take the political dimension of the kingdom more seriously, enlarging the symbolic understanding of the term, and in various ways reintroducing its inherent political dimensions. In this and succeeding chapters, I will argue that the kingdom that Jesus announced as impinging on Roman Palestine had a predominantly social-political meaning.

The Kingdom as Interior

A political interpretation of the kingdom of God has strong competitors with equally good—or better—rootage in the Gospels, church tradition, and scholarship. Those contending views must be given due weight and fair evaluation in relation to a political interpretation.

One of the strongest contenders is the view—actually the cluster of views—that emphasizes the kingdom as an experience or condition within the individual person. In the Gospels Jesus speaks of the kingdom as already present in those who experience God's power over interior forces of evil. After exorcising a demon, Jesus says, "If it is by the Spirit of God that I cast out demons, then the kingdom of God has come to you" (Matt. 12:28=Luke 11:20; compare Luke 10:9, where both hospitality and healing suggest the presence of the kingdom). Again Jesus says, "The kingdom of God is not coming with things that can be observed; nor will they say, 'Look, here it is!' or 'There it is!' For, in fact, the kingdom of God is among you" (Luke 17:20–21).[1] On other occasions Jesus speaks of entering or receiving the kingdom in terms that suggest that the kingdom is already present during his life and ministry (Matt. 5:3; 23:13; Mark 10:15, and parallels).

Although direct textual evidence for the position is meager, it can be argued from scripture broadly that a personal relationship to God means the acceptance of God's rule; God is king where God rules, and thus those who voluntarily come under God's rule participate in God's kingdom. A second-century-B.C.E. writing, *Jubilees*, expresses that idea when it has Abraham pray,

> My God, the Most High God, you alone are God to me. . . .
> and you and your kingdom I have chosen.
> Save me from the hands of evil spirits
> which rule over the thought of the heart of man,
> and do not let them lead me astray from following you, O my God.
>   (12:19–20)[2]

Recitation of the Shema as a confession of faith is spoken of as taking upon oneself "the yoke of the Kingdom of Heaven": "Hear, O Israel: The LORD is our God, the LORD alone. You shall love the LORD your God with all your heart . . . " (Deut. 6:4–5).[3] Jesus' proclamation of God's will and his call for radical obedience to that will also argue for the kingdom as a personal commitment of the self to God.

Adolf Harnack expressed this view in the language of early twentieth-century liberalism:

> The kingdom of God comes by coming to the individual, by entering into his soul. . . . [T]he kingdom . . . is the rule of the holy God in the hearts of individuals. . . . [E]verything that is dramatic in the external and historical sense has vanished; and gone, too, are all the external hopes for the future.

---

1. "Among," "within," and "in the midst of" are all valid translations of the Greek. The translation chosen depends on the perception of the meaning Jesus had in mind. Even though some have argued for the appropriateness of the internal meaning, the consensus is that it refers to the suddenness and immediateness of the eschatological kingdom, as below.

2. James H. Charlesworth, ed., *The Old Testament Pseudepigrapha* (Garden City, N.Y.: Doubleday & Co., 1985), 2:81.

3. In the Mishnah *Berakhoth* II.2, quoted in T. W. Manson, *The Teaching of Jesus* (Cambridge: Cambridge University Press, 1963), 135.

. . . It is not a question of angels and devils, thrones and principalities, but of God and the soul, the soul and its God.[4]

That view continues to find expression in one form or another. C. H. Dodd spoke of God acting to bring salvation decisively into the present, "from the sphere of expectation into that of realized experience."[5] The kingdom of God that has come in Jesus' ministry is the ultimate, decisive act of God in history, and that act takes place within the individual, who is judged but also forgiven in the grace God's presence brings. Rudolf Bultmann's existentialist interpretation shares the view that the kingdom of God is primarily God's rule within individuals. For him, Jesus' preaching the kingdom and his teaching the will of God require that the hearer respond to God's demand for radical obedience. Preaching the kingdom and the teaching of God's will are equivalent in that both necessitate a complete reorientation of the self. In Bultmann's interpretation, then, God's kingdom symbolizes that radical change in the self that is shaped by God's word of address to the individual person.[6]

The belief that the kingdom of God is primarily a personal, internal experience of God's presence does not necessarily negate a political interpretation. As I will argue in chapter 7 below, the experience of God's grace and demands shaped Jesus' prophetic consciousness, which in turn drove him into the social and political arena. So also Bultmann's emphasis on personal transformation and the radical obedience it entails can find expression in various forms of political activity.

Historically speaking, the question is whether Jesus took the approach that God changes individuals and individuals change society according to their new perceptions of what is good, or whether Jesus intended and worked for particular and defined changes in social structures. This question will demand more attention later.

---

4. *What Is Christianity?*, tr. Thomas Bailey Saunders (New York: Harper & Brothers, 1957), 56. The book derives from lectures presented at the University of Berlin in 1899–1900.

5. C. H. Dodd, *The Parables of the Kingdom*, rev. ed. (New York: Charles Scribner's Sons, 1981), 34.

6. Bultmann, *Jesus and the Word*, 129, where his discussion of the relationship between the will of God and the kingdom of God ends with the statement, "This leads us to see *how truly the eschatological message and the preaching of the will of God are to be comprehended as a unity*" (his italics).

The Kingdom as Eschatological

Eschatology means discourse about last things or final events. It can refer to final events in the sense of life after death, the end of the world, or (less ultimately) the end of the present age and the beginning of a new age. The Gospels provide supporting evidence for all three of these understandings.

1. Life after death. Matthew's preference for "kingdom of heaven" rather than "kingdom of God" might reflect this meaning, but it more likely expresses the Jewish reluctance to use God's name. There is no difference in meaning (even Matthew uses the two interchangeably in 19:23–24). Matthew's terminology should not mislead one into thinking that kingdom of God/heaven necessarily refers to an extraworldly realm or to life after death. The choice of terms does not affect the eschatological meanings of kingdom.

The New Testament does provide textual support for understanding the kingdom as the realm or the reality of postmortem life, a view that has had a large place in the Christian tradition. The Gospel of John, particularly in older translations, has lent itself to an otherworldly understanding by having Jesus say to Pilate, "My kingdom is not of this world" (18:36, KJV), which on the surface seems an unequivocal statement against any social and political meanings.[7] Paul adds what would appear to be a clinching statement: "Flesh and blood cannot inherit the kingdom of God, nor does the perishable inherit the imperishable" (1 Cor. 15:50). Many of the remaining New Testament occurrences add strength to the notion that the kingdom is something for the future, equivalent to heaven or life after death (see, for example, 1 Cor. 6:9–10; 15:24; Gal. 5:21; Eph. 5:5; 2 Thess. 1:5; 2 Tim. 4:1, 18). None of these passages strongly suggests the need for transforming the social order.

In the Gospels Jesus speaks of entering the kingdom or receiving the kingdom in ways that suggest that the kingdom is a future reward or gift God has in store for those he deems appropriate to receive it (Matt. 5:20; 7:21; 19:23; 25:34; Mark 9:47; 10:15, 23–25; Luke 18:16–17, 24–25). The Beatitudes in both Luke's and Matthew's versions can be understood to promise a future life in heaven for those who have performed or endured certain things in the present. Storing up treasures in heaven rather than on earth (Matt. 6:19–20) and receiving the rewards for piety from God rather

---

7. Only on the surface, for this statement is another example of John's use of irony. The deeper meaning is that Jesus' kingdom is not "from" this world; it has its authorization/source from God (see John 18:36, NRSV).

than from humans (Matt. 6:1) may suggest that meaning (but see chapter 4 below).

This particular form of otherworldly interpretation has received little attention in modern scholarship. Justifiably, I think, for few of the cited Gospel passages require an otherworldly meaning, and better explanations are available for others. The paucity of clear evidence that kingdom of God refers to life after death may be quite important in understanding the transition between Jesus' self-understanding and the church's understanding of Jesus. The evangelical preaching of the church, exemplified by Paul (as well as Mark and John), centered on Jesus' death as the saving event, which brought the hope of a spiritual salvation within this world and the next. In the context of its evangelical preaching, the church tended to use kingdom as a metaphor for eschatological salvation (=eternal life or life after death).[8] Thus the church transformed the metaphorical content of kingdom of God. It removed the implications for social and political change the term had for Jesus, just as it transformed Jesus into a more spiritual savior. The kingdom has retained some social meaning, but that meaning applies to the community of faith more than to the larger body politic (see 1 Peter 2:9; Rev. 1:6; 5:10).[9]

2. A very different eschatological understanding of the kingdom has received widespread scholarly support in the twentieth century: Jesus' message was apocalyptic. "Apocalyptic" is both a medium and a message. As medium, the term refers to a type of literature in which God reveals a secret message about God's decisive intervention at the end of the world.[10] As a message, apocalyptic expresses confidence that God will overcome the present world disorder and that the righteous will receive God's reward, while the wicked receive punishment.

Focusing on the strong presence of apocalyptic language in the Gospels,

---

8. See, for example, John 3:3, 5; Acts 14:22; 1 Cor. 15:50; Gal. 5:21; Eph. 5:5; 1 Thess. 2:12; 2 Thess. 1:5; James 2:5; 2 Peter 1:11.

9. Not many passages can be adduced from the Epistles to support a social meaning. See 1 Peter 2:9, where the church is a "royal priesthood," suggesting that both king and priest are metaphors for the church. See Col. 1:13, where the kingdom to which believers have been transferred is likely a heavenly kingdom, though it may also exist on earth. Revelation 1:6 and 5:10 provide stronger evidence for the church as the kingdom. These two passages, like 1 Peter 2:9, apply both kingly and priestly metaphors to those who serve God and who "will reign on earth."

10. The Revelation to John in the New Testament and the book of Daniel in the Hebrew scriptures are the best canonical examples of apocalyptic literature. There were many Jewish apocalypses in the period preceding and following Jesus. See James H. Charlesworth, ed., *The Old Testament Pseudepigrapha*, vol. 1.

this interpretation attributes to Jesus the view that the cataclysmic end of the world is at hand. Jesus urges people to prepare so that they may enter the kingdom when it comes. Passages that place the kingdom in the near future may be understood to point to the imminence of the apocalyptic climax. The Beatitudes in both Luke's and Matthew's versions look to the future as the time when the blessings of the kingdom will be received. In Jesus' first proclamation in Mark, "The kingdom of God has come near" (1:15), the kingdom is on the horizon, about to break in upon the hearers in recognizable fashion. In Mark 9:1 Jesus is reported to say, "There are some standing here who will not taste death until they see that the kingdom of God has come with power." Matthew 13:41 (the Son of Man sending out angels), Matthew 13:47 (the parable of the fishnet), Matthew 18:23 (the parable of the king settling accounts), Matthew 22:2 (the parable of the marriage feast), Matthew 24:14 (the apocalyptic war after which the end comes), and Luke 17:21 (the kingdom as suddenly in the midst) all entail apocalyptic eschatology. Beyond the specific passages in which kingdom is mentioned, the urgency with which Jesus approaches his task and sends out his disciples on a similarly urgent mission indicates a view that climactic change is on the horizon.

Albert Schweitzer especially popularized this view and challenged New Testament scholars to accept the apocalyptic interpretation of Jesus regardless of whether it suited them theologically and ethically. Schweitzer maintained that we must let Jesus be what he was—not someone with modern ideas but a first-century Jew who fully shared the apocalyptic outlook of his age. When he spoke of the kingdom, Schweitzer said, Jesus meant the rule of God that is wholly transcendent and supernatural. It is not the evolution of individuals or society into a perfect state. Rather it is the end of history.

As Schweitzer interprets him, apocalyptic expectation dominated Jesus' whole life: He thought that the kingdom would come during his own ministry and that God would reveal him as the Messiah/Son of Man of the coming kingdom. After Jesus sent the disciples out on a preaching tour through Galilee and still the kingdom had not come as Jesus had thought it would, he went to Jerusalem to die to force the coming of the kingdom. Again Jesus was wrong: His death did not precipitate the end of the world; instead of bringing in the apocalyptic kingdom, he showed by his failure to bring it in that his was the wrong form for hope to take.[11]

---

11. According to Schweitzer, what emerged from Jesus' ministry was something quite different from what Jesus had expected: Not the apocalyptic climax but a religion of love was the real result of Jesus' ministry.

Schweitzer's work had enormous impact on the interpretation of Jesus, even among those who resisted its implications. Many believed that if apocalyptic ideas dominated Jesus' thought and action, he would become an irrelevant figure for the modern world. If his work was based on the belief that the world was soon coming to an end, and he was wrong, his work would be without value. Such a radical otherworldliness negates not only a significant social or political meaning but any continuing meaning in an ongoing world. Others, following the lead of Bultmann, have accepted that Jesus' views were apocalyptic and have looked for other than literal meanings of such thought. Bultmann found those meanings in "demythologizing," which means looking for the personal, existential meanings behind the myth of the supernatural kingdom.

Recent study of apocalyptic thought stresses its social function. Apocalyptic outlook arises during times and among groups experiencing great stress. Those who see their world as fundamentally satisfactory do not produce apocalyptic messages. Rather such messages come from the alienated, who feel themselves pressed hard by forces too powerful for them to struggle against successfully. Schweitzer paid too little attention to the social function of apocalyptic. Taking literally the expression of hope for a new world beyond this world, Schweitzer regarded apocalyptic as a way of escaping from an unacceptable present situation. Apocalyptic literature does express pessimism about the present world order and about that order's changing of its own accord. Apocalyptic, however, does not give up on God's relation to the world; it remains confident that God will act in the near future to change the social world. Apocalyptic radically rejects the present structure of worldly power, as it calls in strange language for a restructuring of the present social-political order. Apocalyptic then is grounded in social ethics and is in direct line with prophetic critiques of society. The underlying concern of apocalypses is disorder in this world, which calls for a transcendent solution. That solution is either, as Collins says, cosmic transformation that "fundamentally alters this world, or an otherworldly afterlife."[12] Even the "otherworldly afterlife" reflects a concern about this life in this world.

3. These reflections on Schweitzer's view of apocalyptic lead to a third possible meaning of eschatology: not the end of the world but the end of an era, the end of a political, economic, social, religious system that falls far short of God's will, and the beginning of new order in which God's will comes to

---

12. John J. Collins, "Jewish Apocalypses," *Semeia* 14 (1986): 27.

fruition. The most fully apocalyptic work in Hebrew scripture, the book of Daniel, came from an author who supported the Jewish revolt against the Seleucid rulers around 167 B.C.E. The seer speaks of awesome beasts who terrify and torture, of alien forces who have made God's sanctuary desolate and brought calamity upon Jerusalem. The author prays for renewal of the people, anticipates further anguish, and promises a future resurrection leading to "everlasting life" for some and "everlasting contempt" for others.

Daniel's apocalyptic thought was not otherworldly in the sense of focusing on either life after death or the end of the world. It was concerned with this world and the renewal of God's people, their freedom from oppression, and their future hope. In a similar way, if the apocalyptic language of the Gospels goes back to Jesus, that does not mean Jesus rejected this world and opted for another; it means that he rejected the current situation and sought the renewal of God's people.

The Kingdom as Political

Kingdom of God is a political metaphor, and as I have tried to show above, even if Jesus used it in primarily personal or eschatological senses, those meanings do not negate political implications. But I wish to go further now and argue for more explicit political connections and to explain more fully what I mean by "political."

The strongest indicators of Jesus' political stance occur not in kingdom sayings but in other material: in traditions about Jesus' death (see chapter 2), his ethical teachings (see chapter 4), his parables (see chapter 5), and in units that indicate that Jesus' friends as well as his enemies thought of him in political terms (see chapter 8). Two somewhat stray sayings, although they cannot be relied upon as authentic, offer confirming evidence that some continued long after his death to associate Jesus with a political movement: (1) John 6:14–15 portrays the crowd whom Jesus fed in the wilderness speaking of him as "the prophet who is to come" and seeking to make him king. Whether or not this saying derives from historical reminiscence, it confirms the view that Jesus as a charismatic figure can easily become the center of messianic thought such as that of the popularly acclaimed king of Israelite tradition (see below). (2) In the Acts of the Apostles, the disciples suggest that Jesus is the one to restore the kingdom to Israel (Acts 1:6). This story is consistent with the resurrection story in Luke in which the disciples on the road to Emmaus state the disappointed hope that Jesus was the one to set Israel free (Luke 24:21).

The Q saying of Luke 13:29 (= Matt. 8:11) associates political hope with the kingdom language: "Then people will come from east and west, from north and south, and will eat in the kingdom of God." A second Q saying provides evidence that some viewed the kingdom in political terms, for they tried to take it by force: "The law and the prophets were in effect until John came; since then the good news of the kingdom of God is proclaimed, and everyone tries to enter it by force" (Luke 16:16; compare Matt. 11:12: "From the days of John the Baptist until now the kingdom of heaven has suffered violence, and the violent take it by force"). A third Q saying in Luke's version connects the kingdom with a political form that recalls the days when charismatic "judges" inspired by God's Spirit led the people: Jesus says to the disciples, "I confer on you, just as my Father has conferred on me, a kingdom, so that you may eat and drink at my table in my kingdom, and you will sit on thrones judging the twelve tribes of Israel" (Luke 22:29–30).

The kingdom sayings individually or cumulatively do not establish the claim that the kingdom of God in Jesus' understanding concerns political rule in Israel. The case needs broader support. But the kingdom sayings do offer confirming evidence of the broader base. Setting the issue in the context of kingship and kingdom in Hebrew scripture will enable us to see how Jesus drew upon and reflected dominant Israelite political conceptions.

Background in Hebrew Scriptures

Although "kingdom of God" does not directly occur in Hebrew scripture, the term derives from Hebrew concepts and symbols. God as king provides a frequent metaphorical way of speaking of God's relation to Israel and, by extension, God's relation to the world. The notion of God as king is closely tied to the political world of the ancient Near East in general and Israel in particular. God's rule cannot be equated with any current ruler (not even David), but political rulers ought to express God's rule. Prophets judged rulers by the extent to which the rulers did so.

Kingship in Israel came about only with severe misgivings, for some regarded kingship as a departure from the covenant with Yahweh. Yahweh had guided the people through charismatic leaders and community traditions preserved at key sanctuaries. Kingship became a military necessity in the eleventh century B.C.E., due to the incursion of Philistines. Israel's traditions, however, did not allow investing kingship with the divine prerogatives it enjoyed in some other parts of the ancient Near East, particularly in Egypt. In Israel kingship was theoretically limited, with God ultimately the king.

When the choice was made to have a king, the king (especially represented by David) became a symbol of God's presence and power, for the king was to rule in God's name, according to God's will, to accomplish God's purposes for Israel. One major function of a king was to establish justice, measured by the covenant that bound the people to God and to each other in a community. This view of kingship has as a major consequence that God relates to the people as members of a social order, a community of common interests, and not merely as individuals. God rules through human agents, who are answerable not only to the community but to God.

Such a view could lead to a divinely ordained monarchy and thus to tyranny. For when the king is answerable only to God, he may effectively answer only to himself. But in at least some of the Israelite traditions, God's choice of the ruler was expressed through the people, who recognized in particular individuals the presence and power of God's Spirit. Both Saul and David were such charismatic leaders, whose actions led the people to conclude that God's presence and power were with them. When Saul's actions no longer confirmed God's presence, he was deposed through the same prophetic voice that had enabled the people to accept him originally (1 Sam. 15:26).[13] Thus, this view that the kingdom is really God's has direct implications for social and political activity and organization as well as for understanding the end for which society and politics exist.

Psalm 72 reveals the ideal Israel's king should fulfill. The psalmist prays that God will give the king the qualities of justice, righteousness, and concern for protecting the poor. The psalmist surrounds the petitions for the king's long life, peace, and victory over enemies (vs. 5–11) with prayers that the king will protect the poor, needy, and oppressed (vs. 1–4, 12–14). The psalmist implies that political power has a social purpose—to serve the well-being of the people. Those most vulnerable to exploitation are especially to receive the attention of those entrusted with political power.

Although kings seldom approached the fulfillment of such lofty purposes, prophetic voices judged them by that ideal. In practice, kings in Israel, like those outside Israel, usurped the place of God and became autocratic, answerable only to themselves. Such usurpations and abuses of power were

---

13. The point here is not to affirm the moral quality of Samuel's actions but to stress the point that obedience to God's will is part of the covenantal obligation of the king.

soundly attacked by Israel's prophets, as the example of Elijah's conflict with King Ahab well illustrates (see especially the conflict over Naboth's vineyard in 1 Kings 21).

The image of an ideal king came to be associated primarily with David. The hope for a "messiah" or "anointed one" grew out of the Israelite concept of kingship and the idealized memory of King David. David, the first effective king of Israel, was regarded as most nearly embodying the ideals of kingship in Israel. He thus became the symbol of hope for political restoration during times when foreign powers ruled Israel. God would raise up an anointed one ("messiah") of David's line to deliver the nation from oppression and injustice.

The hope for such a messiah was connected to the concept of a covenant that God had made with David. According to 2 Samuel 7:1–17, after David had securely established himself on the throne and had established Israel's security among the nations, he wanted to build a house (temple) for God. Instead, God said, God would build a house (dynasty) for David. God promised further that David's descendants would sit on David's throne forever (2 Sam. 7:12–16). This promise to David became the basis for hope for a sound government under a "king like David," a hope that kept kingdom and covenant closely related.

Messianic hope intensified in periods of crisis, especially when Israel felt oppressed by alien or usurpacious powers. After Babylon destroyed the Davidic monarchy in 586 B.C.E., hope arose that God would send an anointed one to restore the kingdom and to renew the political as well as the spiritual life of Israel. That hope was long deferred and never fully realized. The Maccabean Revolt did achieve political independence under the Hasmonaeans from 165 to 63 B.C.E., but it failed to establish God's kingdom. Then the Romans took control of Palestine (in 63 B.C.E.).

During the period of Hasmonaean rule and into the first century, hope for a Davidic messiah was often strong. Lamenting that arrogant Gentile foreigners (the Romans) had trampled the Temple (*Psalms of Solomon* 2:2), one author urges God to act in defense of the people, the land, and the Temple:

> See, Lord, and raise up for them their king,
>> the son of David, to rule over your servant Israel
>> in the time known to you, O God.
> Undergird him with the strength to destroy the unrighteous rulers,
>> to purge Jerusalem from gentiles

> who trample her to destruction;
> in wisdom and in righteousness to drive out
> the sinners [Hasmonaean Sadducees?] from the inheritance,
> to smash the arrogance of sinners
>   like a potter's jar;
> To shatter all their substance with an iron rod;
> to destroy the unlawful nations with the word of his mouth;
> At his warning the nations will flee from his presence;
>   and he will condemn sinners by the thoughts of their hearts.
>
> (*Psalms of Solomon* 17:21)[14]

God's kingdom is larger than Israel since God is king of all the earth (a notion both Psalms and the prophets voice). So also the messiah to come is destined to rule not only Israel but the whole world. A first-century apocalypse, the *Testament of Moses,* expresses that hope:

> Then his [God's] kingdom will appear throughout his whole creation.
> Then the devil will have an end.
> Yea, sorrow will be led away with him.
> . . . For God Most High will surge forth,
>   the Eternal One alone.
> In full view will he come to work vengeance on the nations.
> ·
> Then you will be happy, O Israel!
> . . . And God will raise you to the heights.
> ·
> Yea, you will see your enemies on the earth.
>
> (10:1, 7–10)[15]

In this literature, as in the book of Daniel, the kingdom is *from* heaven (that is, from God), not *in* heaven. There is no separation between a spiritual kingdom and an earthly, political kingdom. The expected king will rule in righteousness, according to covenant traditions, bringing peace and justice, renewal and restoration, forgiveness and prosperity to the people of Israel. He will also bring defeat for Israel's enemies.

---

14. Charlesworth, ed., *Old Testament Pseudepigrapha,* 2:667.
15. Charlesworth, ed., *Old Testament Pseudepigrapha,* 1:931–32.

People familiar with such hopes would understand Jesus' announcement of the kingdom of God to mean that God's hoped-for intervention is near. According to *Psalms of Solomon* 17, the king will slay the arrogant with the word of his mouth. That expression could suggest that the righteous king will be more spiritual than military-political.[16] However, "word of his mouth" stands in parallelism with "rod of iron," so that one should not overemphasize the absence of physical force to accomplish the deeds. It is true that, when the victory is complete, the king will rule peacefully and compassionately, even over the nations, provided they "reverently stand before him" (17:34). A possible connection between the messianic kingdom and the Jubilee may be seen in the statement that the king will "distribute them upon the land according to their tribes" (17:28).

As chapter 1 above has shown, Josephus confirms that messianic thought was widespread in Jesus' time and that messianic movements stirred hopes and fears of revolutionary activity. The Gospels portray John the Baptist as announcing the coming of the Messiah, whom the Gospels identify with Jesus. Josephus associates John with political activity (at least in Herod's fears) but does not associate him with messianism as such. The Gospels associate John with messianism but not with overt political activity.[17] The Romans and the ruling Jewish leaders would not likely have distinguished messianic from nonmessianic mass movements, since in their view all such movements were politically dangerous. At any moment a popular charismatic figure could be acclaimed messiah.

Political Interpretation in Recent Scholarship

Recent scholarship has paid increasing attention to the question of Jesus' place within the social and political crises facing Roman Palestine. Tying Jesus' use of kingdom of God to that crisis enables us to see its social and political implications. There are different ways of taking those implications seriously.

1. Jesus might have proposed particular measures to move his society toward closer conformity with norms derived from the covenant standards of

---

16. As Horsley and Hanson argue in *Bandits, Prophets, and Messiahs*, 106.
17. Matthew 3:2 presents John as preaching repentance in light of the coming of the kingdom of heaven, but Matthew does not likely view that as political.

community justice and well-being. John H. Yoder and Sharon Ringe,[18] for example, connect kingdom with the Israelite tradition of Jubilee, "the time when the inequities accumulated through the years are to be crossed off and all God's people will begin again at the same point."[19] The Jubilee theme could go back to Jesus in various ways. (1) Jesus explicitly called for observance of Jubilee, perhaps connected with a specific year. (2) Jesus deliberately used Jubilee concepts but without calling for a general observance in a particular year, as a way of expressing his prophetic call for justice according to covenant norms. (3) Jesus used images associated with Jubilee symbols, though not consciously so. In this last case, the language of Jubilee has become a part of a traditional way of speaking of covenant justice.

Ringe finds multiple attestation of Jubilee themes and concludes, "It appears quite likely that Jubilee images figured in the teachings and ministry of Jesus himself."[20] How it did so is more difficult to determine. Ringe does not think it necessarily the case that Jesus deliberately used Jubilee images to interpret the coming kingdom, or that he identified a particular year as Jubilee year. Ringe implies that Jubilee might too narrowly constrict Jesus and suggests that Jesus' message marks the "experience of humankind at the near boundary of God's reign."[21] In that case, Jubilee would be a symbol but not a concept.

In spite of the tendency to universalize and overly theologize Jesus' message implicit in that last quotation, studies such as Ringe's are important not because they prove the kingdom of God in Jesus' teaching was a particular thing or a particular kind of justice in society. Rather they make the important connection between social condition and religious convictions, with the result that it has become increasingly difficult to maintain that the kingdom of God is either a purely internal, individual experience of God's presence or that it is an otherworldly avoidance of the problems of the present age. Kingdom of God connects closely with concerns for social justice based on covenant traditions. Images and symbols from those traditions continued to have evocative power and normative value in Jesus' world. Jubilee grows out of Israelite faith and tradition, whether or not the Jubilee year was ever strictly observed. It expresses at least prophetically the notion

---

18. John Howard Yoder, *The Politics of Jesus* (Grand Rapids: Wm. B. Eerdmans Publishing Co., 1972); Ringe, *Jesus, Liberation, and the Biblical Jubilee.*
19. Yoder, *Politics of Jesus*, 37.
20. Ringe, *Jesus, Liberation, and the Biblical Jubilee*, 88.
21. Ringe, *Jesus, Liberation, and the Biblical Jubilee*, 88.

that to be Yahweh's people involved operating with a concept of justice for the community as a whole. The analysis of Jesus' teaching in chapter 4 will show that he maintained that connection with norms of covenant justice.

2. Jesus might have recognized the need for social and political change but nonetheless not have proposed any specific remedy, nor even thought the remedy lay in the social and political realm. An intriguing element in much of recent discussion of the kingdom of God is the way various scholars recognize the necessity of relating kingdom of God to the social and political issues of first-century Palestine and then veer away from the serious implication that Jesus wanted radical change in Israelite society, or that he advocated solutions to the economic and social problems of the people. The point is widely accepted in theory[22] that Jesus did not separate religion from politics; yet many maintain that neither in his own practice nor in the practice he urged on others did he focus on any particular social or political change.

This cautious approach guards the universal applicability of Jesus' teaching, since social justice is a universally valid human concern. It also protects the theological concerns of the Christian church by keeping the church at some distance from particular social issues. But it may miss the concreteness both of the problems facing Jesus' society and of his preaching/teaching that addressed those problems. If Jesus thought justice was not adequately being done within the political structures of his day, what did he think would be required to establish justice? Surely justice entails not merely ideals but actions as well.

John Riches provides an outstanding example of recognizing the political and social dimension of Jesus' use of the symbol, kingdom of God, then diffusing the symbol and virtually removing from it any political content. Riches places Jesus' proclamation in the context of various reform and renewal movements in Judaism and seeks for Jesus' distinctiveness. Riches asserts that Jesus chose the kingdom as a symbol because it has a core association and yet was still flexible enough to allow for Jesus' distinctive content. The core meaning was that God was establishing God's rule over humans;[23] what that rule entailed was not determined by the core meaning.

According to Riches, Jesus stripped the symbol of the militarism, ritualism, and particularism it had in Jewish society. Jesus did not connect the kingdom with the absence of foreign rule or with a change in the social or political

---

22. Martin Hengel provides a major exception. See notes 35–36 in chapter 2 above.
23. Riches, *Jesus and the Transformation of Judaism*, 100.

arena. Instead of announcing the kingdom in the context of discussing the plight of Israel under Roman rule, Jesus announced it in the context of his ministry to the dispossessed, the sick, the poor, and the outcast. For Jesus, God's kingdom was interior personal and interpersonal. It brings healing of community relationships, but it does not bring changes in the structures of society, economics, or politics. The forgiveness that God's kingdom brings leads to healing for oneself and to joyful service to others.[24]

Riches thinks that message would appeal to those who lived under the oppressive conditions of Roman rule. He asserts that Galilean farmers, for example, would have had a hard time seeing the relevance to their daily lives of Pharisaic teachings on purity. But somehow Jesus' teaching about God's love and mercy for neighbor and for enemies would have had more apparent relevance. Once they have been transformed by Jesus' message of love and forgiveness, they would view themselves in a new way: not only as oppressed, deprived, and condemned but also as accepted into a new fellowship, forgiven, the objects of love and mercy. This new view would lead to social transformation.[25]

Riches thinks this message would result in opposition and resistance because Jesus went against conventional meanings of the conventional symbol. Some would have resented this unconventional approach and would have regarded it as such a threat to their worldview that they would have turned against Jesus. Riches's assertion implies that it was the oppressed of Galilee, rather than the authorities in Jerusalem, who brought about Jesus' death. That suggestion defies both tradition and history as well as logic.

Riches thus takes us partway in understanding the kingdom. He is correct that it is a symbol with a core of meaning and that Jesus provides his own definition of that core. But in rejecting any political meaning of the term, Riches removes Jesus from the Jewish context in which Riches himself claims to place him. He leaves a weak explanation of both Jesus' popularity and his opposition. Why would anyone execute a preacher of love, mercy, and forgiveness? Riches also drives a wedge between Jesus and Judaism by making Jesus' view so radical that Judaism as a whole rejected him, and thus his followers had no choice but to reject Judaism.[26]

E. P. Sanders, like Riches, connects Jesus with the hope of Jewish restoration. Unlike Riches, Sanders keeps Jesus within that context and does

---

24. Riches, *Jesus and the Transformation of Judaism*, 100–6.
25. Riches, *Jesus and the Transformation of Judaism*, 108–10.
26. Riches, *Jesus and the Transformation of Judaism*, 87.

not conclude that Judaism was unable to contain the radical newness of Jesus. He thinks Jesus' connection to the hope for Jewish restoration is more positive than negative, but we cannot be sure how Jesus intended to achieve his goal or precisely what he meant by kingdom of God. Jesus did not think weapons would be the means, but neither does he use the traditional call for national repentance and return to the law.[27]

Sanders acknowledges that the kingdom implies covenant concepts that deserve more attention than they have received. He cites rabbinic examples that suggest he understands covenant voluntaristically, as one taking upon oneself the yoke of the kingdom by reciting the Shema. I believe Sanders is correct in his recognition of the covenant character of kingdom, but he does not explicitly connect this aspect of kingdom with his second important point, that in Jesus' thought the coming of the kingdom would "result in a recognizable social order."[28] Sanders's words point to the need to explicate what that social order would entail and to look for clues in the Gospels for that meaning.

3. Jesus might have worked for a revolutionary change through direct action, not even ruling out violent means. S. G. F. Brandon is among those who advocate such a position.[29] He uses the generally acknowledged insight that the Gospel writers had good reasons for downplaying Roman opposition to Jesus and the early church and for placing the blame as fully as possible on the shoulders of the Jewish authorities. He develops the following thesis: Jesus expected an imminent kingdom[30] and sought to prepare his fellow Jews for it. Two obstacles to that preparation were the Jewish priestly authorities and the Roman government. The Jewish authorities were an obstacle in that their mode of life was "a scandalous contradiction of his ideal of a holy people, ready and prepared for the coming of God's kingdom. Their power therefore had to be challenged and broken." The Romans were an obstacle in that they maintained the priestly aristocracy in power. Going to Jerusalem at Passover, with his entry demonstration and Temple cleansing, Jesus pre-

---

27. E. P. Sanders, *Jesus and Judaism* (Philadelphia: Fortress Press, 1985), 118–19. For specific criticism of Sanders's point about national repentance, see Bruce Chilton and J. I. H. McDonald, *Jesus and the Ethics of the Kingdom* (Grand Rapids: Wm. B. Eerdmans Publishing Co., 1987), 40–41.

28. Sanders, *Jesus and Judaism*, 146, quoted in Chilton and McDonald, *Jesus and the Ethics of the Kingdom*, 10.

29. Brandon, *Jesus and the Zealots*.

30. Brandon, *Jesus and the Zealots*, 337, acknowledges that the meaning of the kingdom is "undefined."

sented a messianic challenge. Brandon thinks the Zealots might have instigated an insurrection in the city connected with Jesus' attack on the Temple. Jesus was arrested and crucified as a seditionist, along with two bandits[31] who were probably Zealots. Although Jesus was not a Zealot, he had at least one Zealot in his band of disciples, showing that his views were compatible with theirs.[32] In the final result, Jesus' movement converged with the Zealots in those final events in Jerusalem.

Sanders is correct in saying that the kind of treatment given by Brandon "cannot . . . be said to have influenced many."[33] He dismisses Brandon as one who thought "Jesus' action was part of a carefully planned attempt to take the leadership of the country by arms"[34] even though that exaggerates Brandon's view. Sanders's statement reflects a tendency to equate any serious political interest with armed revolution and to dismiss it out of hand on the ground that Jesus could not have been an armed revolutionary.

But much of Brandon's reconstruction does not focus on Zealot armed uprising. Brandon deserves recognition for his serious attempt to place Jesus within the context of his world. Whatever its failings, Brandon's work has the virtue of locating the kingdom metaphor squarely in the political arena. Brandon acknowledges that the meaning of kingdom is "undefined." However, if Jesus proclaimed that Israel should repent in light of the coming of the kingdom, such a message must have involved the destiny of Israel as a nation.

> In other words, the coming of the kingdom of God must have meant the achievement of the prophetic tradition of Israel as the Holy People of Yahweh, vindicated for its faithfulness before the nations of the world, and freed from all mundane hindrance to devote itself wholly to the service of its God. Whether the achievement of this ideal state was located in this world or implied in some cosmic cataclysm is not clear; but it would certainly involve a complete change of the existing world-order, whereby Israel was in bondage to the heathen power of Rome.[35]

---

31. Luke uses Josephus's term for bandit, *lē stai*, for the "thieves" crucified along with Jesus; they were thus revolutionaries.

32. There is "nothing in the principles of Zealotism, as enunciated by Judas of Galilee, that we have definite evidence for knowing that Jesus would have repudiated." Brandon, *Jesus and the Zealots*, 355.

33. Sanders, *Jesus and Judaism*, 68.

34. Sanders, *Jesus and Judaism*, 68.

35. Brandon, *Jesus and the Zealots*, 337.

Much of this statement could be affirmed—and indeed is said—by many of the authors who veer away from its implications.

4. Jesus might have sought a social revolution but stopped short of advocating violence, even though he engaged in direct action to promote the changes he sought.

A fundamental problem that leads many to reject the presence of politics in the ministry of Jesus is the tendency to see politics only in terms of messianism, and to see messianism only in terms of violent political revolution. The resulting position says, since Jesus opposed violence, he did not engage in politics. Since Jesus was nonpolitical, he cannot have been Messiah in the traditional sense; he was Messiah in a more spiritual, transcendental sense. Jesus was inadvertently political, raising political hopes and expectations without intending to. This line of approach assumes that the only alternatives to violent revolution were passive acceptance of the current situation, complicity with the ruling elites, or spiritual renewal. But we know from Josephus that there were many who engaged in various forms of passive resistance. To do so was overtly political but still nonviolent, though it often met with violent responses from the Roman authorities (see chapter 1).

Richard Horsley allows the recognition that the kingdom entailed social change to have a fuller impact. He places Jesus within the conflict that we know from Josephus's account dominated Palestinian society in the first century. By kingdom of God Jesus expresses the active engagement of God's power with the forces threatening God's people. Both individual and social renewal were included in Jesus' expectation that "God was bringing an end to the demonic and political powers dominating his society."[36] The coming of the kingdom means not an all-transforming act but a transformation of relationships—social, political, and economic. The kingdom of God is not a single act but continuing action, entailing a response and participation by the people. The kingdom is not God's intervention to end an abandoned world but God's active participation in a continuing world-transforming process. In that process personal wholeness is an integral part of social renewal; the well-being of persons is integrally related to the well-being of society. Jesus' use of a banquet or feast to symbolize the kingdom, following a widespread

---

36. Horsley, *Jesus and the Spiral of Violence*, 157.

tradition in Israel, suggests the restoration of the people as a new covenant society.[37]

Jesus had confidence that God would act for the salvation of the people. Because of that confidence, he did not need to raise an army to oust the Romans. But the absence of an army signifies less that Jesus thought the Romans irrelevant than that he thought God's action would accomplish that goal and that his part was to prepare the people for God's action. Confident that God was bringing about the necessary political changes, he sought the transformation of society commensurate with God's action. "Jesus was apparently a revolutionary, but not a violent political revolutionary."[38]

Kingdom of God as a Multivalent Symbol

Although some views of how Jesus understood the kingdom of God have more plausibility than others, one does not have to negate all others in order to affirm that one is dominant. "Kingdom" as a symbol may point to a particular thing or concept that it represents, like a "sign" such as the mathematical pi, which has one fixed meaning in all times and places.[39] Or a symbol may have a cluster of interrelated meanings that vary from time to time and place to place.[40] If one regards kingdom as a symbol in the first sense, then one will try to identify the one particular thing that kingdom stands for and reject all others. Candidates for that one thing would include a messianic reign, a transcendental rule of God after the apocalyptic end of the world, a social order expressing a particular standard of justice, or "heaven" as a realm in which God's rule is complete and perfect.

If one regards kingdom as a symbol in the second sense, then there is not one constant, particular thing or concept that kingdom points to. Rather, as Perrin says, kingdom is a symbol that "can *represent* or *evoke* a whole range or series of conceptions or ideas."[41] At the center of the range of meanings kingdom can have are the experience and conviction that God is present and

---

37. Horsley, *Jesus and the Spiral of Violence,* 170, 173.
38. Horsley, *Jesus and the Spiral of Violence,* 326.
39. See Norman Perrin's use of Philip Wheelwright's "steno symbol." Perrin, *Jesus and the Language of the Kingdom: Symbol and Metaphor in New Testament Interpretation* (Philadelphia: Fortress Press, 1976), 29–30.
40. Perrin uses Wheelwright's "tensive" symbol to express this. Perrin, *Jesus and the Language of the Kingdom,* 29–30.
41. Perrin, *Jesus and the Language of the Kingdom,* 33.

powerful, controlling the destiny of God's people. How that presence and power are manifest can be understood in various ways. On the basis of a study of the Aramaic targums (paraphrases of Hebrew scripture) that were read in synagogues in Jesus' day, Bruce Chilton maintains that, for Jesus, kingdom means the "dynamic, personal presence of God . . . his saving, usually future, activity."[42] That description applies to much of the imagery of God as king throughout the Hebrew scriptures. But what God's active presence means changes in different times and historical circumstances: judgment, salvation, eschatological triumph, deliverance of the people, or their punishment, depending on the speaker's perception of the needs of the occasion.

Thus the Gospel writers, living in times quite different from those of Jesus, in circumstances that corresponded very little to his circumstances, could have shared his conviction regarding the presence of God's active power but still conceived of what that power was about to accomplish in quite different ways from Jesus. As they wrote about him in his time, their focus was also on their own time, and their understandings of the kingdom would have permeated their language as they told about him. Kingdom is thus not a stable concept but a symbol that points to certain convictions and possibly evokes different myths.[43]

I believe the political meanings of the symbol are just beginning to receive their deserved attention in historical and theological studies, as well as in ethical reflection. The study of Jesus' teachings and actions in the following chapters will attempt to bring that dimension to the fore in a convincing way. The various views of the kingdom presented in this chapter can be adjudicated fairly only by paying attention to the meaning of Jesus' sayings, parables, and actions. Having attempted to show that Jesus' death requires an explanation of his political involvement, I will now try to show that his words confirm that his death was politically motivated.

---

42. Bruce Chilton, ed., *The Kingdom of God in the Teaching of Jesus* (London: SPCK, 1984), 22.

43. See Perrin, *Jesus and the Language of the Kingdom,* 5.

CHAPTER FOUR

"He Stirs Up the People by Teaching"

The way Jesus addressed concrete problems and issues of his day led the religious and political authorities to execute him as a troublemaker. In this chapter I will argue that although Jesus' reported teachings contain no overt call for revolution, the political and religious authorities correctly perceived that his message posed a threat to the existing order. I intend to show that Jesus' teachings confirm a social-political understanding of the kingdom of God and that they contain underlying elements strongly critical of Israel's social and economic situation under Roman rule. Jesus advocated the cause of the poor and powerless against the wealthy and powerful elites that governed under Roman rule. He shared a perception common in Israel's prophetic heritage that the rich gained their riches at the expense of the poor.[1]

His vision of a covenant society based on norms derived from Israel's social, economic, political, and religious traditions would radically change the conditions of Roman-ruled Palestine. As I have argued in chapter 1 above,

---

1. Both Michael H. Crosby, *House of Disciples: Church, Economics, and Justice in Matthew* (Maryknoll, N.Y.: Orbis Books, 1988), 43, and Bruce J. Malina, *The New Testament World: Insights from Cultural Anthropology* (Atlanta: John Knox Press, 1981), 84, suggest that the notion was widespread in the ancient world that the rich were so because of fraud or extortion or because they had otherwise taken advantage of power.

the Romans did not originate the social and economic order of Palestine; it had roots at least as far back as the Hasmonaean rulers of the second and first centuries B.C.E. But the Romans worsened those rifts in the fabric of society and not only perpetuated but also promoted a system in which the rich were getting richer and the poor poorer. The Romans promoted the same sort of elitist rule in Palestine as in most of their provinces. Jesus announced a kingdom of God that entailed justice and peace, the renewal of social relations, and a renewed commitment to the religious heritage. In doing so, he challenged the continuation of that political system and thus threatened the Roman rulers and their allies among the Jewish aristocracy in Jerusalem.

Omitting the concreteness of Jesus' teachings may have the consequence of transforming them into a universal ethic that can be applied in any situation, but it can also render his teachings nebulous, "spiritual," or otherworldly, and undermine any concrete relation to Jesus' society—or to any other. The desire to relate Jesus' ethic to universal human values or to a contemporary situation can lead the interpreter to miss Jesus' concern for his own time. The real choice is not between a timeless ethic or an ethic related to Jesus' contemporary situation, but between an ethic that engages the social world and one that does not. Because Jesus' teaching was radically contemporary, it can be related to other times and places with appropriate translation and application.

The Beatitudes: Luke 6:20–23; Matthew 5:1–14

The Beatitudes provide a good place to begin a study of Jesus' teaching. The two versions in Luke and Matthew show how Jesus' teachings underwent change as the expanding church faced different situations in different places and times. A comparison of these passages reveals that verbal accuracy was not of primary concern as the church preserved Jesus' teachings. Comparison of Matthew and Luke also shows how the focus of the tradition shifted over time from a social and political toward a more personal and spiritual dimension.

On the surface, Luke's Beatitudes and Matthew's appear to be very different collections of sayings. They differ in three important ways: in regard to the number of Beatitudes, the time of the blessing, and the persons pronounced blessed.

Matthew contains nine statements beginning with "blessed." Both of the last two statements deal with persecution, and thus Matthew's list can be reduced to eight Beatitudes. Four of these parallel those in Luke's version and derive from Q; they are combined with four others that shift the emphasis from social condition to the moral quality of those pronounced blessed. Luke's version contains only four Beatitudes, which he parallels with four "woes" (6:24–26) that express the contrasting consequences for those whose situations are opposite those who are pronounced "blessed."

A second major difference between the two sets of Beatitudes concerns the time when the reward/punishment will be meted out. Luke's version, at least superficially, points to a situation within the present world order when the fortunes of the haves and the have-nots will be reversed. Those now on top will be on the bottom; those on the bottom will be on top. That language suggests a social and political revolution as the means for the reversal promised. However, Luke's language can also suggest the perspective of dualistic apocalyptic literature in which eschatological reward and punishment are a one-time and final rendering of God's verdict on humanity. I have argued above that the distinction between apocalyptic and social-political teaching is false, and that therefore even the apocalyptically phrased promises apply to the present world order. Thus, for Luke, Jesus announces the coming kingdom and its associated well-being for the benefit of those most in need now.

Matthew's version contains language that suggests an otherworldly context for receiving the reward promised. Several phrases in Matthew may point to a heavenly rather than an earthly reward: "Kingdom of heaven" (5:3), "they will see God" (5:8), and "reward is great in heaven" (5:12). The hope of heavenly reward overcomes the fear of death for the obedient ones whose lives conform to the ethical standards of God's kingdom.

I have argued above, however, that often in Matthew "heaven" is a periphrasis for "God." If "kingdom of heaven" means the rule or reign of God and "reward in heaven" means reward from God, then the reward need not be otherworldly. The reward of "seeing God" can refer to that vision of God one has beyond death, in which case it represents an otherworldly hope. Note, however, the example of Job, who "sees" God, or comes to understand more fully the mystery of God, through the worldly struggle of his own suffering (Job 42:5). Neither Matthew nor Luke requires an otherworldly eschatological setting, though either can be consistent with it. But as I have argued in chapter 3 above, apocalyptic language concerns not merely the ultimate fate of persons and nations but the necessity for change in the present, trusting God to bring about that change and living consistently with the anticipated change. Apocalyptic, like prophetic eschatology, issues a call to God's people to live faithfully, in covenant with God and community. Living faithfully alone will enable one to endure the present and the future testing that persons of faith face.

A third apparent difference concerns the identity of the groups pronounced blessed. In Matthew, the emphasis is largely on the character or quality of life of those who receive blessing (meek, humble, pure in heart, etc.). This last distinction has the effect of making Matthew's Beatitudes promises of rewards for those who are morally and ethically upright and who live by the standards that God endorses. In Luke, by contrast, the Beatitudes (along with the woes) emphasize the reversal of conditions. He makes no statement about the moral quality of those who are blessed, but rather emphasizes the conditions of those who are poor, hungry, weeping, and hated. To them Jesus promises a change of objective circumstance. Similarly, those who are presently well off will also experience a reversal of circumstances; to them the reversal is threat rather than promise. This omission of moral quality suggests that there is nothing ethically superior about those who are poor, or nothing wrong with the character of the rich and well off. Rather, problems arise either because the wrong groups are rich and poor, or because of the very fact that wealth and poverty exist in society. Luke implies that those presently deprived will receive a better future merely *because* they are deprived, and those well off will receive a negative future merely *because* they are well off. Justice demands the reversal of conditions. If that is the case, then when the promised reversal occurs, will it necessitate another reversal, and so on? If God is for the poor and against the wealthy, will God not be for the *new* poor and against the *new* wealthy? Such questions show the problem with taking the Beatitudes literally and the necessity of more nuanced interpretation.

Matthew's emphasis on the quality of those blessed may offer a solution to the problem Luke's version presents. For Matthew, it is not merely those who are poor, hungry, mourning, and persecuted who will receive blessing; it is those who combine those objective situations with ethical qualities: the "poor in spirit" (=humble), the meek, the merciful, the pure in heart, those who hunger and thirst for righteousness. This emphasis on quality, both interior and exterior, makes God's promises for the future more rational and acceptable: God is for the pious who are presently suffering because the world sets itself against God and the community of God's people. God promises that such a situation will not endure forever, but in God's unspecified time the reversal will take place.

The differences and similarities between the Lukan and Matthean versions raise questions of source and authenticity of the Beatitudes. Matthew's version stands at the beginning of the "Sermon on the Mount" (Matt. 5:1–7:28), Matthew's compilation of teaching material from Q, Mark, and Matthew's special source. Luke's version stands at the beginning of a shorter sermon (Luke 6:20–49) on "a level place" (Luke 6:17), which derives wholly or in part from Q.[2] Matthew's editorial work on the Q sermon that serves as a basis for both versions is more evident than Luke's, and thus Luke's order and content more nearly represent the Q original. The fact that Q contained the Beatitudes very much as in Luke does not necessarily mean they are authentic. However, the content of the sayings, their appropriateness to the context of Jesus' activity, their conformity with other traditions about Jesus' message, their attestation in early and multiple layers of the tradition argue for their essential authenticity.[3]

The Poor

1. "Blessed are you who are poor, for yours is the kingdom of God" (Luke 6:20). Matthew's version says "poor in spirit," placing more emphasis on spiritual attributes of those blessed. "Blessed" means "happy" or "fortunate," because God's favor rests upon the person. The Beatitudes are not mere comments on the current social world but prophetic words concerning God's coming kingdom. In Matthew's version, those who are assured of God's blessing are the "humble-hearted," those who recognize their need for God and who trust in God for their future hope. Luke's term "poor" can refer to the same reality: those who are poor because they trust in God rather than in their own aggressive self-interests, or those who do not sacrifice their faith in order to get along in a situation dominated by the faithless.

This reflects a strong characteristic of Hebrew faith, in which God vindicates the poor and the needy (see, for example, Psalm 107:39–43). Especially when Seleucid Syrian rulers oppressed Israel during the days just before the Maccabean revolt, "poor" became an almost technical term to describe poor people. Those of humble piety who maintained firm covenant faith in the face of pagan enticements did not fare well. The wealthy, by contrast, cooperated with

---

2. There is debate about whether Luke's "woes" come from Q or whether they are Luke's addition to Q. See John S. Kloppenborg, Q Parallels: Synopsis, Critical Notes, and Concordance (Sonoma, Calif.: Polebridge Press, 1988), 26; John S. Kloppenborg, The Formation of Q: Trajectories in Ancient Wisdom Collections (Philadelphia: Fortress Press, 1987), 172.

3. See Crossan, Historical Jesus, 273, who agrees that all four Lukan Beatitudes "derive from Jesus himself."

the ruling establishment, imbibed its spirit, turned their backs on the covenant traditions, and fared much better as a result. Thus, while Matthew spiritualizes the Beatitudes as a whole, there may be no real difference between Matthew and Luke in this instance. Matthew only makes explicit the spiritual quality that was implicit in the term "poor." The poor in spirit are those who have no haughtiness or pride because of position or possession but rather simply trust in God. Their trust will be rewarded in the coming kingdom.

The Hungry

2. "Blessed are you who are hungry now, for you will be filled" (Luke 6:21). Again, Matthew suggests that the hunger is spiritual: "Blessed are those who hunger and thirst for righteousness, for they will be filled" (5:6). Luke's version leaves no ambiguity: God is for those literally hungry, those who do not have enough food to sustain a full life. God promises them a different future, one in which fullness will replace hunger. Matthew's "righteousness" carries more ambiguity. It can signify (a) vindication or justice for those who are oppressed or wronged, (b) the just conditions that exist when the nation conforms to the will of God, or (c) the ethical quality of those who do God's will (those who are upright). If Matthew's righteousness carries the more social meaning of covenant justice in either of the first two suggested definitions, then Matthew differs little from Luke. If Matthew has the last meaning (ethical qualities) in mind, then he intends to state that personal uprightness is the condition for receiving God's blessing, and he may differ considerably from Luke.

As in the first Beatitude, however, the difference between Matthew and Luke may be more apparent than real, even if the personal meaning of righteousness is correct. Righteousness as a personal ethical term should not be understood individualistically. The upright person must also be concerned with justice in society, not merely possess an interior personal quality of moral integrity. Likewise, those who long for justice in society must also cultivate those personal convictions and actions that promote social well-being. Since poverty and hunger manifest not merely bad luck or hard economic times but also injustice, the upright person must seek a return to the standards of justice expressed in the covenant tradition, according to which any member of the community will have sufficient for life and well-being. God's kingdom entails a return to those conditions so that the hungry and the poor remain so no longer. In Israelite faith, the righteous God is concerned with both the physical and spiritual needs of people.

The Weeping

3. "Blessed are you who weep now, for you will laugh" (Luke 6:21). "Blessed are those who mourn, for they will be comforted" (Matt. 5:4). Matthew's term "mourn" differs little from Luke's, since the two are used in parallelism in Hebrew poetry. Luke's "laugh" may differ, however, from Matthew's "be comforted." Laughter in Hebrew scripture conveys "derision" far more frequently than "joy."[4] Matthew's term then suggests that God's blessing for those who are now mourning will be a comforting or strengthening to enable them to endure, or a favorable outcome which God secures for those who are oppressed (see Isaiah 40). Luke, on the other hand, with his theme of reversal of fortune, has those who are now subjected not only to hardship and oppression but also derision, turning the tables on their foes and holding them in derision when God's blessings come.

Seen against the background of Hebrew scripture, weeping and mourning can indicate either a lamentation over the desolation and ruin of the country or a repentance and turning to God. The first usage occurs in Hosea 4:3: Because of the lack of covenant loyalty[5] expressed in moral living, "the land mourns, and all who live in it languish." The second usage occurs in Joel 2:12, where the prophet urges Judah to return to Yahweh "with all your heart, with fasting, with weeping, and with mourning." This call is followed by the promise that God is gracious and merciful and may yet bless the repentant people. The language of repentance and returning to God does not occur often in Jesus' words;[6] further, the context in the Beatitudes suggests the mourning that expresses consternation over the conditions within the land. Such an attitude would have been appropriate in Jesus' time because of the social conditions, the injustice, the oppression brought on by the political and religious leaders. In that context those who mourn do so because of the conditions of the people in a time when faithlessness characterizes the rulers, but they also look to God for consolation, expecting God to deliver the people from oppression and injustice.

---

4. See, for example, Pss. 2:4; 37:13; 44:14; 52:6; 59:8; 80:6. Psalm 126:2 may be an exception, where the mouth "filled with laughter" is parallel with tongues uttering "shouts of joy."

5. The word here is *hesed*, translated in the RSV as "steadfast love," in the NRSV as "loyalty" in Hosea 4:1.

6. To such an extent that Sanders thinks Jesus did not call for national repentance. Even though I think Sanders is incorrect (see above, chapter 3), Jesus does not often use the formulaic calls to repent even if Mark 1:15 is authentic. Matthew 11:20–21 (=Luke 10:13) may well be authentic, in which case Jesus did call for repentance. The Lukan passages 13:3, 5; 15:7, 10 are more questionable.

Many perceived Israel to be in a chaotic state: The Romans who controlled cared nothing for the traditions of Israel, for covenant faithfulness, or for covenant community. Those Jews who cooperated with them often adopted Hellenistic ways and were considered by the pious to have abandoned their own traditions. Such a situation led the faithful to mourn the condition and to look forward to the time when God would renew all things. Prophets like John the Baptist and Jesus struck responsive chords in the people when they called for a renewal of covenant traditions and promised the reestablishment of God's reign. The people found little hope or comfort in the priestly aristocracy who compromised for their own benefit, in Pharisees whose focus on purity[7] did not provide comfort for the people, or in Zealots too willing to spill blood. Against this background Jesus proclaims the kingdom as consolation, hope, and salvation for Israel. Those who grieve and mourn over the plight of Israel will find occasion for comfort and joy. Isaiah 61:1–3, 8–9 provides a close thematic parallel to all the Beatitudes but especially to this one.

> The spirit of the Lord GOD is upon me,
>   because the LORD has anointed me;
> he has sent me to bring good news to the oppressed,
>   to bind up the brokenhearted,
> to proclaim liberty to the captives,
>   and release to the prisoners;
> to proclaim the year of the LORD's favor,
>   and the day of vengeance of our God;
>   to comfort all who mourn;
> to provide for those who mourn in Zion—
>   to give them a garland instead of ashes,
> the oil of gladness instead of mourning,
>   the mantle of praise instead of a faint spirit.
>
> . . . .
>
> For I the LORD love justice,
>   I hate robbery and wrongdoing;

---

7. To what extent Pharisees concentrated on purity is debated. Neusner, *From Politics to Piety*, 80, believes that the Pharisees did lay great stress on "eating with the right people, specifically those who obeyed the purity laws," and that they held with the "traditions of the elders" about table fellowship, washing hands before meals and other ritual ablutions, and eating the right foods. Neusner thinks these laws applied at ordinary meals, which should be eaten "*as if one were a Temple priest*" (83).

> I will faithfully give them their recompense,
>> and I will make an everlasting covenant with them.
> Their descendants shall be known among the nations,
>> and their offspring among the peoples;
> all who see them shall acknowledge
>> that they are a people whom the LORD has blessed.

The Hated

4. "Blessed are you when people hate you, and when they exclude you, revile you, and defame you on account of the Son of Man. Rejoice in that day and leap for joy, for surely your reward is great in heaven; for that is what their ancestors did to the prophets" (Luke 6:22–23). Matthew corresponds quite closely to Luke in this Beatitude, and like Luke, Matthew puts it last. Matthew precedes it with a variant: "Blessed are those who are persecuted for righteousness' sake, for theirs is the kingdom of heaven" (Matt. 5:10). Matthew changes to the second person plural, which Luke has used throughout. More clearly here than anywhere else in the Beatitudes, Matthew shows dependence on the Q tradition, which probably contained the Beatitudes (and possibly the "woes") very much as Luke has reported them.

"On my account" and "on account of the Son of Man" are interchangeable terms as far as Matthew is concerned; the former is more likely authentic. Luke does not have "persecution" as one of the descriptions of what the disciples may endure. That term describes what Matthew's community has faced, and probably derives from that experience. There is little or no evidence that Jesus' disciples faced persecution early in Jesus' ministry. Luke's phrasing, however, may apply even in Jesus' day, for adherence to his teachings and to his understanding of the Torah might have brought scorn or condemnation. In that sense opposition would be on his account. Further, the example of John the Baptist would have provided a constant reminder to Jesus and his followers of the tenuous position they had in the territory of Herod or in Roman-dominated Judea. At any moment, as events proved, reviling could change into physical danger.

The comparison of Jesus' disciples with the prophets implicitly identifies Jesus also as a prophet. The fate of John the Baptist and other prophets shows that in Jesus' day loyalty to the covenant traditions to which Jesus was committed could be dangerous. Attempts to conform society to those values—by being a prophetic advocate of them—was dangerous. Such people could be regarded as suffering for the kingdom of God. This Q saying reflects the Q document's context of prophetism.[8] Such people, alienated from the dominant powers of their own society, place their hope in God. But while the form of the saying reflects the Q community's experience, Jesus himself must also have reckoned with the possibility of sharing John's fate. That fate shows, as Segundo has said, that "prophetism comes into conflict with *established authority and power*. It threatens the latter and the latter responds with violence, provoking the death of the prophet."[9] Even though the "Passion predictions" (Mark 8:31; 9:31; 10:33–34) represent later reflection on Jesus' execution, there is no reason to doubt that Jesus anticipated a prophet's fate.

So far I have followed the order of Luke's version of the Beatitudes. Matthew's remaining four Beatitudes can more readily be understood as advocating those qualities that those who pursue the kingdom of God should exhibit in their personal, spiritual lives. However, even Matthew's remaining Beatitudes, while they do not have a strong attestation in the sources, may cohere with the more reliably authentic four. Thus they deserve comment.

The Meek

5. "Blessed are the meek, for they will inherit the earth" (Matt. 5:5). The meek are not really different from the poor in spirit understood (as above) to be the humble. A comparison with Psalm 37:9–11 suggests that the meek are those who are committed to the way of Yahweh and who trust that Yahweh protects and succors them. They are promised future well-being in the land God gives them.

> For the wicked shall be cut off;
>> but those who wait for the LORD shall inherit the land.
> Yet a little while, and the wicked will be no more;
>> though you look diligently for their place, they will not be there.
> But the meek shall inherit the land,
>> and delight themselves in abundant prosperity.

---

8. Howard C. Kee, *Jesus in History*, 2d ed. (New York: Harcourt Brace Jovanovich, 1977), 118. See also Theissen's treatment from an organic sociological perspective of the Palestinian Christian community that produced the Q document in *Sociology of Early Palestinian Christianity*, as well as Horsley's conflictive sociological perspective in *Sociology and the Jesus Movement*.

9. Segundo, *Historical Jesus of the Synoptics*, 80.

Inheriting the earth means that the land belongs to them as the land of promise; it does not belong to those presently occupying it unjustly. The promise here corresponds to the promise of the kingdom of heaven in Matthew 5:3: When God rules, the poor will enjoy their inheritance in the land of promise.

The Merciful

6. "Blessed are the merciful, for they will receive mercy" (Matt. 5:7). Matthew again appears to be concerned with spiritual qualities of individuals. But behind Matthew's Greek word there may stand a very Hebraic, covenant concept. *Eleos* ("mercy") and its cognates provide translations for the Hebrew *ḥesed* (and cognates). *Ḥesed* is a major covenant word translated "steadfast love" (often in RSV) or "covenant loyalty." If *ḥesed* stands behind Matthew's *eleēmones,* then Jesus meant that those who have compassionate concern and sympathetic loving-kindness toward others stand faithfully within God's own covenant loyalty and can expect to continue to receive God's blessing. As in the preceding Beatitudes, faithfulness to norms of covenant community are at the forefront of Jesus' meaning.

The Pure

7. "Blessed are the pure in heart, for they will see God" (Matt. 5:8). While purity can imply spiritual or moral perfection, it more likely refers to single-minded devotion to God's will. In saying that "purity of heart is to will one thing," Kierkegaard correctly understands that in Hebrew thinking, the heart is the seat of thought and will more than of emotion. The pure in heart are those who are right with God and whose commitments to God's will lead to right conduct. The pure in heart are therefore those who "love the Lord their God with all their heart." They will what God wills; they seek God's kingdom and God's righteousness on earth as it is in heaven. Their mind and will are set on the renewal of Israel in accord with the rule of God. It is they who will "see" God in God's manifestations within the covenant community.

The Peacemakers

8. "Blessed are the peacemakers, for they will be called children of God" (Matt. 5:9). The Greek word for peace (*eirēnē*) means an absence of hostile conflict, including but not limited to armed warfare. The word more likely used by Jesus is the Hebrew *shalom* (or its Aramaic equivalent), which means not only the absence of strife but also the well-being of persons within

community. Wholeness, health, prosperity, security, and spiritual well-being are all included. Those who establish well-being and harmony in society are the ones whose actions correspond closely enough to God's actions that they can be called God's children.

Jesus' notion of *shalom* and the way to achieve it differed from that of major groups within Israel. As opposed to those who pursued peace through violence (such as those who later emerged as the revolutionary Zealot party), Jesus did not advocate violence, even if his confrontation with the authorities provoked violent reactions. As opposed to those of the Jewish aristocracy who thought social well-being was consistent with the status quo, and who thus cooperated with the Romans in maintaining it, Jesus saw the need for fundamental changes. As opposed to those who identified the well-being of the covenant society with the maintenance of purity, as some within the Pharisaic school thought, Jesus placed priority on compassion.[10] As opposed to those who sought their own peace in a small community separated from society, such as the Essenes, Jesus sought the peace of the larger society by engaging its most strategic institutions and groups: the Temple and its associated ruling elites, the synagogue and its influential teachers. The renewed *shalom* he sought would require institutional change, brought about either by those who currently controlled the institutions of the covenant community or by their replacements.

The Beatitudes, like all Jesus' ethical teaching, should properly be seen in the context of his announcement that God's kingdom is breaking in upon people. Jesus announces that reality as good news. In Matthew's version, the Beatitudes implicitly call for a response. As in the Bible generally, Jesus announces God's impending actions so that the hearers will know and respond to the reality of God. Both Matthew and Luke reflect the general biblical connection between God's action and human response. Because God is acting to establish God's sovereign rule of love over Israel, all should respond by loving God and fellow members of the covenant community. The faithful should exhibit the qualities of life that correspond to God's will for all. By addressing promises to those in poor straits regardless of moral quality, Luke's version does not as clearly imply the need to respond in faith to God's action. But even it implies the call by warning that God's actions will turn the existing order upside down. Thus, those who want to be on the right side of

---

10. See Marcus Borg, *Jesus: A New Vision: Spirit, Culture, and the Life of Discipleship* (San Francisco: Harper & Row, 1987).

God will change their own situation accordingly. They will give away all that they have in order to join the poor in receiving God's promises.

In Matthew's version, Jesus calls the hearers to adopt the attitudes and actions described in the Beatitudes; in Luke's version, Jesus does not so much call his hearers to become poor, mourning, etc., as he implicitly addresses society's elites who have the power to change present structures. Insofar as Luke's Beatitudes present a call to the oppressed, the call is to remain faithful and to look for God's justice to change the situation in which they find themselves. They are not so much a call to revolution by the oppressed as a call to trust in the goodness of God even when that faith does not offer evident success. The waiting and trusting, however, do not mean passivity, as Josephus's examples of nonviolent demonstrations show. At the same time the Beatitudes are invitations into the kingdom, and (especially in Matthew) they are in part descriptions of the way in which citizens of God's coming kingdom should conduct themselves.

Behind Matthew and Luke, we can believe Jesus spoke to his own contemporaries of the social change God's impending kingdom will bring. He did not advocate their patient waiting for heaven as a time to redress the ills people suffered in the present. The Marxist complaint that the Beatitudes provide an opiate for the people to prevent their revolt against oppression finds no justification in the historical Jesus. It may find justification in what Christian piety has made of his teachings. Jesus addressed the poor, the hungry, the discouraged, and the persecuted with the message that God is on their side, supporting them in their struggle, and that God's just will focuses on their relief. Because people opposed to God are currently in charge, God's kingdom is not now fully present, and God's will is not now being fully done. But it will not remain so. To God's oppressed people Jesus promises participation in God's kingdom, where they all experience happiness and satisfaction because of the establishment of God's rule in the world.

These promises include both "physical" and "spiritual" aspects. The Beatitudes form a revolutionary messianic proclamation of the reversal coming when God's righteous rule will eliminate the oppressive social conditions. Jesus admonished his hearers to pattern life in the here and now according to God's will. The one who sees God's action establishing the kingdom is challenged to manifest a character consistent with that kingdom.

It has often been stated that Jesus had no "program" of a social or political nature by which he sought to remove the deep-rooted evils and injustices of society.[11] That assertion partly applies to the Beatitudes, but it is not correct to say that the Beatitudes have no social or political relevance. Even if those who see in Jesus' proclamation a call for instituting the Jubilee are not fully correct, the Beatitudes call for a renewal of those social values derived from covenant traditions. While this cannot be called a program, it provides the basis for society to change from what it is to something that brings those traditions into historical reality.

The Beatitudes preserve the unmistakable and authentic voice of Jesus that the kingdom involves social as well as personal transformation.

The "Antitheses": Matthew 5:21–48

The connection between committed character and ethical action is contained in the section of Matthew's Sermon on the Mount that follows the Beatitudes. Often referred to as "the Antitheses," this section stresses that action without internal commitment to God's will does not suffice. Matthew firmly insists on this point again in 7:15–27, where he warns that profession without practice leads to doom. Although the connection between the antitheses and the need for social and economic change is not prominent, it can be seen to underlie the sayings.

The preface to this section (Matt. 5:17–20) affirms the validity of Torah and states Jesus' intention not to abolish but to fulfill it.[12] The preface has the effect of keeping the following sayings from being really antithetical.[13] There is nothing in Luke that corresponds to the passage as such, but Luke (16:17) has a saying closely correlated with Matthew 5:18: "It is easier for heaven and earth to pass away, than for one stroke of a letter in the law to be dropped." This Q[14] saying, then, has Jesus affirm the continuing validity of the Torah, even though in Q Jesus does not tell his disciples to teach the Torah as he does in Matthew.

---

11. For examples, see Francis W. Beare, *The Gospel According to Matthew: Translation, Introduction, and Commentary* (Peabody, Mass.: Hendrickson Publishers, 1981), 127, and Martin Hengel, *Victory Over Violence,* 1.

12. Hengel, *Christ and Power,* 17, certainly overstates Jesus' conflict with Judaism (as opposed to the powerful elites within Judaism) when he says that Jesus "makes a direct attack on the center of the Jewish theocracy's power, the Torah." Neither here nor elsewhere does Jesus make an attack on the Torah.

13. W. D. Davies and Dale C. Allison, *A Critical and Exegetical Commentary on the Gospel According to Saint Matthew,* International Critical Commentary (Edinburgh: T. & T. Clark, 1988), 1:481.

14. See Kloppenborg, *Q Parallels,* 180.

This preface (5:17–20) and the following statements (5:21–48) express Jesus' attitude toward the Torah in two different and seemingly contradictory ways. The preface emphasizes the necessity of *doing* what is commanded. But in the following statements the emphasis falls more upon the internal quality of the person than on the exterior act. The presence of both these characteristics can mean that Matthew is inconsistent. He might have inherited Jesus' sayings that emphasize the internal quality, while Matthew himself wanted to emphasize obedience in action. The two may not be contradictory, however, if related in this way: Matthew wants an obedience in actions that spring from an obedient heart. Such an attitude is not unlike that of Jeremiah, who spoke of the new covenant written on the heart, in which obedience to God's commands is certainly present in the faithful person's action, but that obedience proceeds from the committed heart (=will) and is not merely outward conformity to external commands.

But apart from Matthew's practice, did Jesus look to the Torah as a way of understanding God's will for the present? The Q saying provides good evidence of what one would expect to be the case: As a teacher Jesus debated points of interpretation of Hebrew scripture. The interpretation and right application of scriptures were vigorously debated in Jesus' society, and as a loyal member of the covenant community, whom many regarded as a teacher, Jesus undoubtedly took part in those debates. There is no significant evidence that he thought scripture was to be abandoned in favor of his own understanding of God's will. Jesus' actions and words lead to the conclusion that he looked to Torah as well as the prophets for his vision of what the covenant community should be and how it should structure itself. The words here about his fulfilling scripture should be taken to mean that he intended to keep rather than to deny scripture. The idea that Jesus fulfilled what scripture foretold about himself represents the church's understanding of the relationship of Jesus to scripture rather than Jesus' own thought.

Verse 20 suggests that an intention to keep scripture rigorously provides no adequate guarantee that the covenant community will in fact fulfill God's will. Both the Essenes and the Pharisees intensified the Torah with that intention. The Essenes did so by withdrawing into a community totally governed by its interpretation of Torah. The Pharisees derived from the Torah a standard of purity by which the people as a whole could become a nation of priests. In Jesus' view, neither intensification of the Torah provided a real hope for the people. Jesus derived from the Torah and the prophets a standard for social justice. Without justice, attempts to bring in God's kingdom by purity or by piety were futile.

The so-called "antitheses"[15] stress that understanding of Torah. These sayings relate Jesus' teachings to what was said "to those of old." "What was said" should be understood as a divine passive equaling "what God said to them." If Jesus contradicted what was said, then he was setting himself up against God as well as Moses. But nothing Jesus says here contradicts the Torah, even though it goes beyond the Torah and intensifies the demands found there. Parallels to Jesus' sayings occur in other Jewish sources.[16] Since Jesus does not contradict the older sayings, "statement" describes Jesus' sayings better than the term "antithesis" does. Translators should not emphasize the "but" in Jesus' statements. Matthew does not have Jesus use the strongly adversative conjunction *plēn* but the continuous conjunction *de*, which like its Hebrew equivalent can mean "and" as well as "but." Jesus thus says, "You have heard it said . . . and I say to you."

The first two statements quote the Decalogue (the Ten Commandments; compare Matt. 5:21, 27, with Ex. 20:13,14). Another reflects the Decalogue in part (compare Matt. 5:33 with Ex. 20:16, or possibly 20:7) but does not directly quote it. Another quotes from the Torah (compare Matt. 5:38 and Ex. 21:24; Lev. 24:20; and Deut. 19:21); another refers to the Torah but does not directly quote it (compare Matt. 5:31 and Deut. 24:1). Another is partly taken from the Torah but adds something not found in the Torah ("hate your enemy") (compare Matt. 5:43 and Lev. 19:18).

The statements call for a total integration of life. The all-encompassing will of God provides the basis of thought, motive, will, desire, feeling, and action. Jesus understood the Torah to point to that all-encompassing will of God, even though the statements suggest the commands of Torah do not express fully what God intends for either the interior or the exterior life. Matthew contrasts Jesus' teaching with the "righteousness of the Pharisees." Although Matthew exaggerates Jesus' conflict with the Pharisees, and possibly also the degree of casuistry they employed, Jesus approaches God's will in a different manner. Case law tends to set out an elaborate and extensive, but still limited,

---

15. "Antithesis" suggests that Jesus is contradicting previous admonitions/commandments. But not all he says is contradictory; some is supplementary, some is intensification, some is interpretation of older statements. See Pinchas Lapide, *The Sermon on the Mount: Utopia or Program for Action?*, tr. Arlene Swidler (Maryknoll, N.Y.: Orbis Books, 1986), 44–45. See also Crosby, *House of Disciples*, 182, and Davies and Allison, *Matthew*, 597.

16. Ulrich Luz, *Matthew 1–7: A Commentary*, tr. Wilhelm C. Linss (Minneapolis: Augsburg, 1989), 279.

obligation under the Torah. Jesus grounds his teaching on the will of God that stands behind Torah and finds partial expression in Torah. He draws upon notions of creation to construct an even more complete expression of God's will that contains an infinite obligation. Jesus supports his statement on divorce by referring to God's intent in creation (Mark 10:2–9). The appeal to universal humanity implied in Matthew 5:43–47 and the appeals to nature in Matthew 6:26–33 suggest a similar grounding in creation. In going behind the Torah to God's creation revealed through Torah, Jesus calls for an attitude that cannot be prescribed by law, no matter how detailed that law might be. Commands and obedience to commands are subject to calculation, while no one can calculate all that God's complete will entails.

When Jesus places anger along with murder (Matt. 5:21–22) as equally contrary to God's will, failure to fulfill God's will is no longer subject to the same calculus as before. One can measure an external act of murder but not the motivations and subconscious attitudes that lead to it. Placing internal attitudes along with outward actions means that no one escapes a negative verdict when facing judgment.

The statement on adultery (Matt. 5:27–28) also asserts an internal rather than an external criterion for understanding the will of God. Acts of adultery can be calculated and measured; the lust that leads to acts cannot be. The will of God behind the Torah comes to fulfillment only when intention as well as action expresses righteousness.

Matthew's version of the statement on divorce moves away from that standard: "except on the ground of unchastity" (5:32). The exception reflects the difficulty that such a comprehensive and noncalculable standard posed for a community that sought to find in Jesus' teachings a rule for its life. To be analogous with the other statements, the saying on divorce should refer to the internal quality of the marriage relation rather than the inadmissibility of divorce on any grounds except one. The divorce saying more analogous to the adultery statement occurs in Mark 10:1–12: "From the beginning of creation, 'God made them male and female' " (v. 6). Here Jesus asserts the full intention of God expressed in creation in contrast to what Moses allowed due to the hardness of the human heart and the consequent inability to fulfill God's will. In the Markan saying, the bond between husband and wife that God intends must exist not merely in the legal form of marriage but in the internal quality of the relationship. Matthew's version is more casuistic than Mark's and thus more suited to use in a community's rules of discipline. Matthew's version therefore represents a secondary development, and Mark's (though also with the secondary addition of Mark 10:12[17]) more nearly expresses Jesus' creative interpretation.

The saying on oath taking (Matt. 5:33–37) teaches one to be so aware of the presence of God that one is fully truthful and does not hide deceit by calculated words. "You have heard that it was said to those of ancient times, 'You shall not swear falsely, but carry out the vows you have made to the Lord.' But I say to you, Do not swear at all. . . . Let your word be 'Yes, Yes' or 'No, No.' " Although some interpreters have taken this saying as a prohibition against oath taking,[18] this saying is best regarded as a "memorable way of requiring total honesty in every situation."[19]

The issue here does not concern formal oath taking (as in courts). Nor does it contribute anything to historical or religious understanding to say that Jesus intends to reject the swearing practiced daily by the Jews of his day.[20] It is more likely that Jesus intends to teach an honesty that is transparent and that he rejects any notion that degrees of honesty or dishonesty may be acceptable depending on the circumstances. Beyond that general point, one must ask whether this statement has any direct bearing on any specific social issue of Jesus' day.

Prophetic voices suggest that the statement on swearing does relate to a significant social-political issue. In Hosea 4:2 "swearing" along with adultery, murder, stealing, lying, and bloodshed are signs that there is no knowledge of God in the land. Other prophetic passages connect false swearing with other ethical failings that compromise concern for social justice. Jeremiah 4:2 calls for swearing in God's name in truth, justice, and uprightness. In Jeremiah 7 the people are accused of using the Temple as a talisman against trouble (v. 4: "the temple of the Lord, the temple of the Lord") while oppressing the alien, the

---

17. The reference to a woman divorcing her husband reflects a Roman setting since Jewish law had no such provision while Roman law did.

18. According to Josephus, the Essenes prohibited oath taking (*Jewish War* II.135: "Any word of theirs has more force than an oath; swearing they avoid, regarding it as worse than perjury, for they say that one who is not believed without an appeal to God stands condemned already." But in II.139, Josephus speaks of candidates for membership being made to "swear tremendous oaths" to practice piety, observe justice, and do not wrong, etc.). See Gerald Friedlander, *The Jewish Sources of the Sermon on the Mount* (New York: KTAV Publishing House, 1969), 63. Friedlander also cites Philo's assertion that innate honesty is preferable to oaths.

19. Davies and Allison, *Matthew*, 535.

20. J. Schneider, "*omnyō*," *Theological Dictionary of the New Testament*, ed. Gerhard Friedrich, tr. and ed. Geoffrey W. Bromiley (Grand Rapids: Wm. B. Eerdmans Publishing Co., 1967), 5:178, correctly rejects that oft-repeated suggestion.

widow, and the orphan, shedding innocent blood, stealing, committing murder and adultery, and swearing falsely (Jer. 7:3–9). Swearing "as the Lord lives" without heeding God's call to ethical righteousness opens one to judgment, according to Hosea 4:15. Malachi 3:5 similarly connects swearing falsely with oppression and injustice: God will "draw near . . . for judgment; I will be swift to bear witness against the sorcerers, against the adulterers, against those who swear falsely, against those who oppress the hired workers in their wages, the widow and the orphan, against those who thrust aside the alien, and do not fear me."

The connection among swearing, Temple, and social justice bears resemblance to Jesus' concerns in this context. Although there are no direct clues as to specific forms of oath taking involved, the use of oaths in making loans, disposing of lands, and conducting other financial matters allowed the powerful to take advantage of the poor and powerless. Forms of oath taking that violated the openness and honesty of the covenant community of justice would in Jesus' eyes be contrary to God's will expressed in the Torah.

Matthew's next saying concerns retaliation and resistance: "You have heard that it was said, 'An eye for an eye and a tooth for a tooth.' But I say to you, Do not resist an evildoer. But if anyone strikes you on the right cheek, turn the other also" (Matt. 5:38–39). Luke contains neither the saying from the Torah on retaliation nor Jesus' command against resistance, but Luke does have Jesus' instructions against retaliation (Luke 6:29–30). Further, Luke puts in one continuous paragraph (probably following Q's order) much of what Matthew places in this "antithesis" and the next one (compare Matt. 5:38–48 and Luke 6:27–36).

Jesus forbids insisting on rights to such an extent that one desires to render "justified" injury on others. Jesus renounces the use of reciprocity in human relations, either negative or positive. Doing good to those who do good or evil to those who do evil, while understandable as a human action, violates the basis on which God acts. Thus, those who would be God's people should eschew returning in kind what they receive from others and imitate the actions of God, who does good to the good and evil alike. "Do to others as you would have them do to you" (Luke 6:31; Matt. 7:12) negates reciprocity.

The command "Do not resist an evildoer" (Matt. 5:39) can have three meanings: Do not resist an evil person, the evil one (Satan), or the evil act or thing. The resistance forbidden does not include all kinds of opposition to evil. Moral resistance, some forms of political resistance, even some expressions of physical force could be allowed. The resistance forbidden is that through a courtroom or on a battlefield. In the context of Jesus' day, it likely has the meaning of not resisting in battle. Going a forced mile and beyond (an admonition which Luke does not include) could apply to the Roman right to requisition the services of occupied peoples for transportation; going two miles exceeds what is legally required. The saying therefore could oppose revolutionary violence even in the cause of liberation from Rome. It less likely opposes nonviolent resistance of the sort that Jesus' actions in Jerusalem represent.

Matthew follows the statement on nonresistance with a related saying on love of neighbor: "You have heard that it was said, 'You shall love your neighbor and hate your enemy.' But I say to you, Love your enemies, and pray for those who persecute you" (Matt. 5:43–44). This saying, too, denies the appropriateness of reciprocity in determining what to do. It demands that response to others be based on the love one receives from God and not on categorizing others or their actions. The command to love the enemy has generally been taken to indicate Jesus' lack of sympathy for, or even strong disagreement with, those who sought revolutionary liberation through armed resistance. Davies and Allison say that Jesus "would undoubtedly have thought of the Romans in Palestine [as the enemies one is to love]. . . . So far from fomenting hatred and wreaking vengeance upon the occupying forces, Jesus was asking his hearers to display a spirit of love and tolerance (cf. 5.41)."[21]

Horsley, though not putting Jesus in the camp of armed resisters to Rome, thinks this saying more likely belongs to the sphere of community relations and refers to "personal enemies"; the enemy in question is not Rome at all but the enemy who is also in some sense neighbor.[22] In Horsley's view, the issue in this section is neither nonviolence (certainly not in a social or political sense) nor nonresistance to evil. Nonretaliation comes closer, but even that derives from Matthew's use of the lex talionis and probably does not go back to Jesus.

Jesus rejected any zealous attitude that would build peace through conflict, or see the sword as a means of salvation and peace, or establish the kingdom by killing, or build human community through the politics of hate and conflict, or suppress others so that one's own narrow vision of life might prevail. Jesus believed that those who live by the sword will also die by the sword. The sword cannot produce life; it can only produce death. The pursuit of power, prestige, and glory lead to the pursuit of power, prestige, and glory, and not to the kingdom of God. To build a social order on egoism and violence is to build it on

---

21. Davies and Allison, *Matthew*, 1:551.
22. Horsley, *Jesus and the Spiral of Violence*, 266.

sand. To build it on obedience to the prophetic word is to build it on an enduring rock.

Whether these sayings apply to the context of interpersonal and communal relations or to the repression or persecution by Romans or Jewish collaborators, they address a community facing economic and social conflict, and generally call for reconciliation on the basis of covenant traditions of caring concern for one another rather than selfish or narrow concern for one's own particular situation. Jesus called people to face difficult and harsh times without resorting to conflict and competition. He called for a response different from "natural" human inclination. He asked people neither to accept the status quo under the Romans nor to acquiesce in an unjust situation, but rather he reminded them of mutual obligations that alone can enable community to survive conflict and bring about change. He likely addressed a peasant audience prone to the sort of internal conflict represented in the parable of the day laborers (see the next chapter on this parable), and he urged them to find a basis for cooperation and mutual support on the basis of their shared heritage as a covenant community.

To any rational person in Jesus' day, a successful revolt against Rome would seem a human impossibility. Even those who thought a revolt might be accomplished looked to God to bring it about. Jesus' teachings, calling for a renewed community of concern among the covenant people, were aimed at the amelioration of the present desperate situation, where community fragmentation made those ills all the more dire in their impact on persons and families. Even if the Romans were not there, the fragmentation of the people would make harmonious, just, and prosperous community life impossible. In keeping with the prophetic view that God protects and liberates the just community, Jesus thought that the renewal of community would prompt God's own action to take care of the Romans. Reestablishing covenant community is a precondition for God's action on their behalf.

The final summarizing sentence, especially in its Lukan form, supports this interpretation of the "antitheses": "Be merciful, just as your Father is merciful" (Luke 6:36; compare Matt. 5:48). Matthew's term, "perfect" (=whole, complete),[23] harks back to the preface to these statements (Matt. 5:17–20), contrasting the behavior Jesus required with that required by the Pharisees. Luke's term "merciful" is therefore more likely authentic. "Merciful" carries a

---

23. Cf. Deut. 18:13. *Tamim* = perfect, blameless, sincere. NRSV translates *tamim* in this instance as "completely loyal."

connotation recalling Matthew's Beatitudes (Matt. 5:7). Mercy (=*hesed*), as argued above, is a covenant word, meaning "covenant loyalty" or "covenant love." By it Jesus appeals to the standards of the covenant as a basis for renewing the community. The mercy that God has toward the people must be the basis for a renewal of their care for each other. Even if Matthew's "perfect" should be the more authentic reading, its meaning of completeness or integrity could have a similar social implication: God's people are expected to express in their corporate life the integrity and maturity that reflect the character of God and God's dealings with Israel.

Jesus is thus not instituting new legal rulings to govern interpersonal relations but focusing upon the interpersonal relations themselves within the covenant community. He regards God's will for interpersonal relations as impossible to calculate on the basis of casuistic laws but as necessary for the well-being of the people. Jesus' words are "illustrations or 'focal instances' of a certain spirit or orientation towards one's life circumstances."[24] Jesus calls for incorporating God's will into one's interior life; that act at the same time incorporates the neighbor within one's self, so that neighbor is loved as the self is loved. Neighbors are to be treated neither as enemies nor as those with whom one's relations are governed by formal requirements, but those to whom one relates according to the community's transformed covenantal relationship with God.

On Anxiety: Luke 12:22–31; Matthew 6:25–34

Jesus' call for radical obedience to covenant norms of social justice would meet with opposition from those who were concerned for their own personal security and who identified that security with their privileged social and economic situation. Giving up the privileged status and renewing society so that the poor share more equitably in the benefits of social wealth would jeopardize their own secure and comfortable place. Jesus challenges such people to trust in God, who is able to provide for all needs. In Jesus' view no other security is possible; the desire to achieve any other security drives humans to act inhumanly. No one, Jesus says, can have two gods (Luke 16:13; Matt. 6:24). On

---

24. Richard A. Horsley, *Jesus and the Spiral of Violence*, 265, quoting Robert Tannehill, "The 'Focal Instance' as a Form of New Testament Speech: A Study of Matthew 5:39b–42," *Journal of Religion* 50 (1970): 377–82. Horsley argues that nothing in the Sermon on the Mount, especially in the Antitheses, could be applied directly in conduct; they are not commands.

the basis of monotheism, the central tenet of Israel's faith, Jesus calls for radical trust in the one God. God is neither money, nor economic power, nor a commodity to be stored in barns or vaults. Jesus advocated trust in God rather than in material success as a way to gain security. The world God has given is fundamentally good. God's goodness and God's justice can be trusted to provide all that the faithful community needs, if those in the community have the faith to relinquish personal aggrandizement or possessions in order to enhance the well-being of all. Jesus does not advocate Essenic withdrawal from the world in ascetic abandonment. The world with its beauty, its promise of life, its generous supplying of all that is needed is God's and thus is not to be despised. That trust can provide the freedom for radical commitment, freedom from posturing or pretense, freedom from compulsion to hoard as a means of security, freedom from the tyranny of hate and enmity, and freedom from the powerlessness that fear and anxiety generate.

God is the one who calls persons into human community, into loving relations with others, into the acceptance of covenant relatedness and a common fate. Trust in the God who is trustworthy provides the means to relieve anxiety about life and security. "Do not worry about your life. . . . Your heavenly Father knows that you need all these things. [Instead,] strive first for the kingdom of God, . . . and all these things will be given to you as well" (Matt. 6:25, 32–33; Luke 12:22, 30–31).

If Jesus' admonition applies only to the poor, it could deserve the Marxist accusation that it intends to divert the attention of the poor from the desperateness of their condition. But if Jesus spoke to the wealthy and secure as well as to the poor, the implications would be quite different. His words could provide the basis for a community that trusts in God, cares for each other, and follows covenant justice. In this case, they offer the basis for renewal and hope.

Jesus as Teacher: A Summary

1. Jesus' teaching is God-centered, not Christ-centered. Jesus points to God's concerns, God's blessings, God's will, God's grace as the basis for ethical action. He does not point to himself, appeal to the presence of a Messiah or the expectation of the Messiah who can bring the teaching into reality. Nor does he claim to be the embodiment of what he teaches. Instead, he points to God, whose covenant faithfulness provides the model for the covenant faithfulness of the community. The character of God provides a

model for human character.[25] God's goodness, God's parental care, and God's justice provide the norm for human ethical conduct.

2. Jesus' teaching presupposes the covenant traditions that have ideally provided the foundation for Israel's common life in the past. It does not matter that historically Israel has never fully lived up to the standards demanded of a covenant community. Jesus does not point back to a time when the ideal was actualized. Rather he points forward to God's kingdom and the shape that kingdom would take within the covenant community. He does not even regard the Torah as a full expression of what God intends for that community. Even though he does not contradict the Torah, he looks beyond it for the more comprehensive understanding of God's will toward which it points.

3. Jesus' ethic is an ethic of repentance.[26] Even if Mark's statement (in 1:15) connecting the announcement of the impending kingdom of God with a demand for repentance does not go back to Jesus himself, still Jesus' preaching implies repentance. Renunciation of self, the reaffirmation of God's will as the basis for community, love of God and neighbor, and the call for radical obedience all express the need for repentance. Repentance involves a change not merely of mind but also of attitude, intention, will, and conduct. Both actions and attitudes are included in the changes that repentance demands.

4. Jesus' ethic represents a radical revisioning of society. He offered a vision more than a program. The condition of Israel in a revolutionary situation deeply disturbed him. Those conditions included social and religious divisions, many impoverished people, lack of cohesion around the basic values of covenant society, and lack of committed and decisive leadership at the very moment when Israel faced an acute political and religious crisis. Whether Jesus offered any specific program for accomplishing the revolutionary change he advocated cannot now be determined. He might have called for observance of Jubilee, but it is I think more likely that his teachings were less programmatic than foundational. He proclaimed the necessity and possibility of new social relations through the recognition of

---

25. Chilton and McDonald, *Jesus and the Ethics of the Kingdom*, 37.
26. Wolfgang Schrage, *The Ethics of the New Testament*, tr. David E. Green (Philadelphia: Fortress Press, 1988), 41–42. Sanders, *Jesus and Judaism*, 119, does not think Jesus called for national repentance but does not rule out a call for individual repentance.

God's gift. He offered a standard by which programs may be judged, the standard of a just society centered on covenant with God. His standard accepted that God was concerned for the social well-being of the people. He was especially concerned for those who are relegated to the margins—the poor, the sick, the victims of poverty, injustice, ignorance, and repression. Jesus combined consoling words for the victims with calls to obedience and trust for both victim and oppressor. He promised a better day, which would come through God's intervention. Jesus' teaching calls for the implementation of his radical vision of a society of covenant justice.

5. Jesus did not give rules for behavior or practical wisdom about how to live. Rather Jesus taught his ethic by proclamation. Jesus proclaimed the kingdom of God that was dawning, and he called for repentance. In the same way he proclaimed what God's will for society was and called people to accept wholeheartedly and to do uncomplainingly God's will in the here and now—not just because the end is at hand and one faces judgment but because God's will provides the basis for a just society. Jesus' proclamation of the kingdom and his proclamation of God's will are one and the same. They both demand that the people see their common life under God, that they repent—change their mind—about what makes their life good, and that they affirm God's sovereignty over their common life, thus renouncing their own individual autonomy.

Such teaching does not provide an ethical system, but it provides a visionary basis for reconstructing the social order and individual life within it.

6. Jesus' ethic was based on scripture, as was Jewish ethics generally. His vision of a renewed covenant community grew out of his knowledge of scripture and his radical engagement with his own time. He viewed scripture not as rules but as revelation, a window through which one sees God's will. He was not a literalist, nor did he teach his followers to be. But he took with utmost seriousness the vision of a people of God, bound together by a past, sharing a common future, and thus necessarily bound together in the present with its threats and promises.

7. Jesus' ethic is worldly in the sense that it engages the present world as the arena of faithful life. Jesus does not invite his followers to cultivate their own individual or communal piety in isolation from present social conflict. Nor does he advocate the cultivation of one's inward relation to God in preparation for future life. His eschatology had more to do with the future of God's people as an earthly society than with the afterlife of individuals. Neither did Jesus advocate mystical experience as the way to realize God's

presence in human life. Even though the Gospel of John has been interpreted as focusing on Jesus' mystical relation with God ("The Father and I are one," John 10:30), such mysticism is almost totally lacking in the Synoptic Gospels; it does not likely go back to the historical Jesus.[27]

Instead of mystical or pietistic or otherworldly, Jesus' ethic is this-worldly and interpersonal. It is within the context of worldly responsibilities that the faithful are to be obedient and to incarnate in ordinary life the vision of life that Jesus offers. It is for that reason that the emphasis falls upon deeds performed in faithful obedience to God's will within the social, economic, and political context.

8. Jesus' ethic is not a new case-specific law. Rather it is largely parabolic, illustrating by concrete example the quality of relations with God and with others. Jesus offered examples of right and wrong behavior, which do not merely tell one what to do in a specific instance but engender an attitude toward oneself and one's circumstances within society. To take the specific examples as laws can lead to reducing the all-encompassing nature of his teachings and to confining his teachings to carefully circumscribed areas given in the illustrations. For example, the admonition to turn the other cheek presents an attitude to be adopted, not an action to be imitated.

9. The dual commandment of love summarizes Jesus' ethic. Love provides the foundation for the covenant community, and in that sense it is the fulfillment of what the law and the prophets taught. In the context of covenant community, love is more a matter of will than of emotion, deriving from the meaning of God's love for Israel. "God loved Israel" not primarily in an emotional sense but in a sense of "election" or "choosing." God's choice was not conditioned by Israel's response, as though their present or future righteousness could cause God to love Israel. But God's choice does call forth response from the people. Without that response the covenant relationship is not established. As God's love means "choosing" Israel, so Israel's love for God means "choosing" God, letting God be God for Israel.

Similarly, being part of God's people requires hearing God's electing call and responding in trust and commitment. Love for neighbor means choosing the particular neighbor, that is, choosing to live in a covenant relation with the neighbor, as a person to whom one is inseparably related.

The commandments to love are addressed to a community—to Israel—

---

27. Even in John's use, the meaning may be less mystical and/or ontological than a reflection of Jesus' obedience to the will of God.

and are to be implemented in a society of justice. But they are also personal, whether expressed in the singular or in the plural. The individual is neither to abrogate personal responsibility to impersonal society, nor to assume that the individual act alone is sufficient. Both individual will and social decision are to express concern for the welfare of the neighbor in the covenant community of persons. In Israel's covenant thought, love of neighbor provides a test of love for God, though it does not substitute for it. The command to love God may be expressed in the form of a particular neighbor's need, but it must also be expressed in the community's broader quest for social justice. Jesus' ethical teaching as a whole can be seen as specific exposition of this general stance, interpreted in light of the Israelite concept of covenant community.

10. Jesus' ethic builds on the notion of grace, but grace is not cheap. The kingdom is God's gift, but that gift lays claim to the whole of life in the most radical way. Matthew captures this dimension of Jesus' teaching by having the Sermon on the Mount begin with promise and end with promise, and having those promises bracket a call for radical commitment expressing itself in obedient practice. The promise of the kingdom then contains the conditional "if": The kingdom is yours if you will receive it. The kingdom opens those who receive it to transforming grace, demanding the utmost of those who allow it to work in their individual and community life. In keeping with this radical notion of transforming grace, judgment is ultimately based on deeds, though the promise is based on grace. In putting it so, Matthew has undoubtedly captured an element of Jesus' authentic prophetic voice. The voice of a prophet announces both God's grace and God's righteous will, portrays both in the starkest terms, and makes no allowances through casuistic argument for escaping the demand and promise of radical transformation. Even though Matthew has partially adjusted the radical prophetic voice into a practical code of conduct, he has nonetheless retained the sharp expression of the uncompromising demand of God.

11. Jesus' ethical teaching can tell us something about Jesus' understanding of himself. Since Jesus proclaims that one should live in complete, radical obedience to the will of God, we may assume that Jesus attempted to live that way. Since Jesus' ethical teaching means that one should elevate concern for social well-being above concern for oneself, we may assume that Jesus lived that way. The narratives about Jesus confirm that assumption.

Can we go further? Does Jesus' teaching reveal that he regarded himself as having an authority greater than that of other proclaimers of God's will? Some affirm that it does. They argue that in the antitheses Jesus assumes an authority greater than that of Moses, showing that he regarded himself as

Messiah, since according to the Jewish understanding only the Messiah would have an authority greater than that of Moses. If one could be sure that the antitheses ("I say unto you") are authentic, that point might be established, but one cannot be absolutely sure of that. Even without these words, however, Jesus does go beyond what Moses said. That might mean he thought of himself as greater than Moses. Or it might mean Jesus drew out the implications of what Moses said rather than replacing Moses. Deuteronomy 18:15, 18 speaks of a new prophet "like Moses" who will speak God's word with authority. Jesus saw himself as one upon whom the Spirit of God had come. With that credential that came from God, Jesus speaks authoritatively as a prophet of God's word and God's will. In Jewish expectation "the prophet" will be even greater than Moses; for those who preserved the earliest traditions about Jesus, he fulfilled that role, going beyond what Moses said, and completing the Torah by expressing more completely the intention of God partially expressed in it.

Conclusion

In interpreting Jesus' ethic I have placed more emphasis on the community than on the individual, not to deny the importance of the individual but to emphasize the Hebraic notion that individuals exist in communities and for community. Even though early Judaism came to recognize the individual more than had ancient Israel, I believe modern interpreters, imbued with Western individualism, have too frequently missed the strong emphasis on covenant community that was still alive in the prophetic tradition. Jesus reinvigorated the notion of community as the arena of God's concerned action.

In Jesus' teaching the individual is both more and less important than in modern individualistic thinking. The individual is less important in that the world does not revolve around the good of the isolated individual, salvation does not consist merely in the future life of individuals, and justice is not merely justice for the individual. The individual is more important in Jesus' teaching in that the community is judged in terms of what happens to persons within it, to each and to all. In Jesus' teaching, God cares for each one even more than each one cares for himself or herself; the well-being of none, not even the "least of these" is to be ignored. But there is an inclusiveness in Jesus' understanding of God's relation to people that indicates that the individual finds salvation (wholeness) not as an individual but in relationship. The whole is not complete without the parts. Israel is not whole as long as parts are missing or deprived of full participation.

Emphasis on community also raises a vexing question concerning Jesus' relation to the Gentile world. Was Jesus exclusively focused on Israel and its renewal? Or did he himself direct his attention to the Gentile world? This question cannot have the attention here it deserves, but a perspective on it is necessary for understanding the meaning of Jesus' ethic. There are some anti-Gentile sayings attributed to Jesus especially in Matthew's Gospel: They heap up empty words in prayer (Matt. 6:7), they anxiously seek material things (Matt. 6:32), and they "lord it over" others (Mark 10:42=Matt. 20:25=Luke 22:25). Jesus also initially rejects the request of the Gentile woman that he cast the demon out of her daughter (Mark 7:24–30), and he tells his disciples to go only to the "lost sheep of the house of Israel" (Matt. 10:6). Some of this anti-Gentile bias probably derives from the community that preserved the traditions Matthew has inherited.

Even if Jesus regarded his mission as primarily to Israel, he does not seem to have been motivated by the anti-Gentile bias reflected in the Dead Sea Scrolls or by the idea that the essential problems of the people were due to Roman occupation. Even if love of enemy applies to fellow Israelites or fellow villagers and not to the Romans, Jesus' attitude in general contains more openness to than rejection of those who differ in thought, attitude, or action. We know from Paul that the Jew-Gentile issue troubled the church for some time after Jesus. That fact suggests that Jesus never declared himself unambiguously on the issue.

At least some of Jesus' followers began almost immediately after his death to include Gentiles within the covenant community. That inclusion caused conflict and controversy in the early church. Probability lies in the assertion that such an attitude derived from Jesus himself, though that assertion is not fully demonstrable.

Regardless of how Jesus himself regarded the Gentiles, he did not reject his Jewishness; neither did he ape Hellenistic ways. His fraternizing with people whom some would label "sinners" may have provided the basis for the openness that some of his followers demonstrated toward Gentiles. Jesus' commitment to God's will and to the covenantal basis for community life was held along with a perception that such a community could be open to all people. Thus Jesus provided a basis for an inclusive community of caring. Paul and others correctly perceived the universal implications of Jesus' message: The whole of God's people is not just Israel but humankind. The particularly Jewish aspects of Jesus' ministry and teaching made possible a universal understanding of their implications.

CHAPTER FIVE

"With Many Such Parables He Spoke"

Reflecting Jesus' most original teaching, the parables contain very little that is overtly political, but they confirm a concept of the kingdom of God that entails social and political as well as personal renewal.[1] This chapter will argue that the parables not only reflect the social conditions of first-century Palestine as a backdrop for spiritual teaching, but that the parables intentionally engage the social, economic, and political issues of the day. The parables appeal to an underclass and challenge the status quo and its authorities, for they portray the poor, the outsiders, and the "sinners" more favorably than the well-to-do, the insiders, and the "righteous." They hold up a mirror to existing social relations, and call the hearers to reassess the current structures of community life, by reflecting the economic conditions of agriculture and commerce, the relationships of patrons and clients, absentee landlords and

---

1. Douglas E. Oakman, John R. Donahue, and Bernard Brandon Scott especially help to open up parables to the sort of interpretation advocated here: Oakman by specifically relating parables of growth to the agricultural situation of Jesus' day; Donahue by a sensitive reading of the varied dimensions of parable, though Donahue himself stops short of the explicit political application that his insights warrant; Scott by careful analysis of "originating structure" and social context. See Oakman, *Jesus and the Economic Questions of His Day*; Donahue, *The Gospel in Parable: Metaphor, Narrative, and Theology in the Synoptic Gospels* (Philadelphia: Fortress Press, 1988); Scott, *Hear Then the Parable: A Commentary on the Parables of Jesus* (Minneapolis: Fortress Press, 1989).

tenants. As a mirror can both reveal the truth and create a wish for something better, Jesus' parables contain a reflection of existing conditions under Roman rule, while they also create a vision of renewed relationships among the people and advocate a new way of seeing society, the self, and others so that God's rule can transform social relationships.

Authenticity of Parables

General skepticism about the authenticity of the Gospel tradition does not apply as fully to the parable as to other parts of the tradition about Jesus. Many scholars think the parables offer the best hope of recovering Jesus' historical message. There is much about them we cannot know with certainty: whether Jesus actually told all the parables attributed to him, the original wording of particular parables, the original context in which they were spoken, or the meaning each one conveyed.[2] Yet there remains a confidence that we can gain probable answers to these questions, and gain genuine knowledge about Jesus through the parables.[3]

A critical approach that will yield information about Jesus and his message must reckon with the fact that parables underwent change as they were used in the life of the early church. One example will illustrate that point and the difficulty it poses. In Matthew 24:42–25:46, a block of parables deals with the crisis that the return of the Son of Man creates. Phrases indicating that the expected return has been delayed—"My master is delayed" (Matt. 24:48) and "the bridegroom was delayed" (Matt. 25:5)—reveal that the failure of Christ's expected return caused problems. It is doubtful that Jesus spoke of his own return, or that he thought of himself as the apocalyptic Son of Man who would return; it is even more doubtful that he dealt with the problem of his "delay" in returning. All this could suggest that these parables do not go back to Jesus. However, the theme of urgency and crisis they contain is appropriate

---

2. Sanders, *Jesus and Judaism*, 320. Earlier Sanders expressed doubt that the parables concerning the self-righteousness of the Pharisees goes back to Jesus: "I think that he had his mind on other things than the interior religious attitudes of the righteous. The parables are about God, who seeks and saves sinners, not primarily about elder sons, who resent them" (281).

3. Scott, *Hear Then the Parable*, 63. I agree with Scott that the burden of proof lies with those who deny the general authenticity of the parables. Reasons for this judgment include the sparsity of evidence for the similar use of parable in the Judaism of Jesus' day and the early Christian neglect of the parables except in the Synoptic accounts of Jesus.

to Jesus' message. Thus it is quite possible that parables Jesus told relating to the crises of his time have been modified to deal with later crises that the church faced after Jesus was no longer present.

The number of parables (and sayings) containing a sense of urgency and crisis is quite large. These parables convey the message that a critical moment is here and that all must be ready to act decisively or else they will miss the moment and its promise of salvation.[4] The particular nature of the crisis, however, has shifted. The social crisis of Jesus' time gave way to other crises in the life of the church, especially the crises of Jesus' death, the destruction of Jerusalem, and the failure of Jesus to return as expected. The parables reveal the consequences of these crises as they reflect the questions posed by the changing situation of the church, and they urge that the church maintain its faithfulness during an indeterminable period of waiting.

Jesus interpreted the coming of God's kingdom as a crisis for Israel. It entailed the renewal of Israel in all dimensions of its community life, it demanded a radical response, and it provided hope to those in distress. Jesus' parables would have expressed those themes. They later came to express the themes as they had been modified through the experience of the church.

This chapter will focus on the social and political dimensions of Jesus' parables. I do not claim that all the parables deal with social and political issues—certainly not only with those subjects. I do not intend to dispute messages interpreters find in the parables for contemporary readers. I will focus only on what the parables tell us about the social context of Jesus' ministry and the way the parables address the issues of Jesus' society.

To be fair to readers, I must make as plain as possible how my approach and interpretation relate to some current emphases in parable investigation. First, some ground clearing can be done by stating some ways in which I do not intend to approach parables.

1. I will not treat parables primarily as "religious" or "spiritual" teaching, having to do with the individual relationship between God and humans. Popular reading tends to regard parables as "earthly stories with heavenly meanings," as illustrations of personal spiritual life, concerned with the relationship between God and humans or with the moral obligations of individual Christians. Much past scholarly work on the parables followed the sort of spiritual interpretation reflected in Harnack's statement that the

---

4. See Joachim Jeremias, *The Parables of Jesus*, rev. ed., tr. S. H. Hooke (New York: Charles Scribner's Sons, 1963), who calls special attention to this theme.

parables concern "God and the soul, the soul and its God."[5] Current scholarship would not put the matter in Harnack's terms, but much of it does concentrate on the relation between the individual and transcendent reality. But the parables no more than the rest of Jesus' teaching make a distinction between spiritual life and secular life. The parables do not offer advice on how to enrich one's life of piety, how to cultivate the inner spirit, or how to find God in one's closet.

Jesus sees that "[human] destiny is at stake in . . . ordinary, creaturely existence, domestic, economic and social."[6] The parables focus on ordinary life. They are earthly stories with earthly meanings, pointing to Jesus' convictions about his own social world. It is in the ordinary world that ordinary people experience God's presence or absence. The point of contact between God and humans is the "everyday world of human experience."[7] The parables present God as acting in this world, shaping it to God's own ends through the decisions of those who hear and receive God's word spoken through the prophet Jesus.

2. I will not treat the parables primarily as "wisdom" teaching.[8] Wisdom appeals to what is common to all humans more than to the experience of particular humans with their individual problems and hopes.[9] Jesus' parables strike responsive chords in people in varying circumstances because of the power of the narratives with which he addressed the concrete issues of his own time.

3. I will not treat the parables as primarily theological. Some interpreters speak of parables as confronting the hearers with a radical challenge to understand themselves in a fundamentally different way. They regard parables as metaphors that point to transcendent reality. While that is true, it

---

5. Harnack makes this statement in rejecting Schweitzer's apocalyptic interpretation of Jesus.

6. As Amos Wilder maintains in *The Language of the Gospel: Early Christian Rhetoric* (New York: Harper & Row, 1964), 82. Cited by Donahue, *Gospel in Parable*, 14.

7. Donahue, *Gospel in Parable*, 16.

8. Scott, *Hear Then the Parable*, 65, correctly suspects that those parables that portray "common wisdom" are not as likely to be authentic as those that provide a distinctive "voice."

9. In the late nineteenth century Adolf Jülicher transformed the interpretation of parables by rejecting the allegorical meanings that traditional interpretation usually gave them. Jülicher treated parables as human wisdom; they make a single point with the widest possible meaning. By rejecting the church's christological interpretation, Jülicher opened the possibility for a more historical approach, but his contention that parables be given the widest possible application moved interpretation away from a real engagement with the social and political issues of Jesus' world.

may mislead. Donahue correctly says that "Jesus . . . spoke a language of the familiar and concrete which touched people in their everyday lives but which pointed beyond itself and summoned people to see everyday life as the carrier of self-transcendence."[10] Such theological language has the advantage of pointing the hearer to the need to look at the personal self that transcends the particular occasion the parable presents: What shapes that self, to what is it committed, how does it understand its relation to God and neighbor? This approach can show how parables challenge the hearers to new discoveries about themselves and their world, about the demands of God upon the self and world.

The danger in escalating the theological language used in interpreting parables is that it can cause the interpreter to miss the concrete connections that Jesus made to the everyday world. David Stern warns that literary critics such as Paul Ricoeur often allegorize the parables in a new way, presenting a veiled Christian theology.[11] Stern argues that such interpretation imports into the text meanings the parables never intended. Jesus told parables, like the later rabbis told *meshalim,* for the purpose of impressing certain views on the hearers regarding the situation at hand.[12]

4. I will not treat the parables as evidence for Jesus' understanding himself as the Christ. Some parables as we have them do suggest that Jesus interpreted what would happen to him in the future: his death, resurrection, or return ("second coming"). All such elements in the parables belong not to the historical Jesus but to the church.

5. I will not treat the parables as artistic creations, though I do not deny their artistry. The value of a literary approach lies in discerning the way metaphor and paradox function with the narrative, and thus how the parable makes an existential impact on the hearer, regardless of the social situation in which the hearer stands. The risk in such interpretations is that in regarding the present function of parables, the historical meaning may be swallowed up. Jesus' parables are concrete and their effect powerful, as Donahue

---

10. Some scholars distinguish between simile and metaphor, and see many of Jesus' parables as metaphors. Donahue points out in *The Gospel in Parable,* 8, that such interpretation finds a *logos* rather than concrete teaching in parables.

11. David Stern, "Jesus' Parables from the Perspective of Rabbinic Literature: The Example of the Wicked Husbandmen," in *Parable and Story in Judaism and Christianity,* ed. Clemens Thoma and Michael Wyschogrod (New York: Paulist Press, 1989), 56–58.

12. Stern, "Jesus' Parables," 58–59.

reminds us, not primarily because of their literary quality[13] but because they capture the historical moment in which Jesus lived, they reflect the life to which he was committed in that moment, and they challenge the hearers with the danger and opportunity provided by that moment.

Approaching the Parables as Social Commentary and Criticism

In what follows, I will use the parables to investigate the social and political context of Jesus' teachings and his message within that context, for I believe the parables provide insight into that particular world and that they reveal Jesus' concrete hopes and criticisms of those who participate in it.

I will treat the parables as *instruments* Jesus used to convey his message. They proclaim his interpretation of the will of God for Israel in its time of crisis. They hold up the present experience and situation of the people so that they can see in different ways things very familiar to them, look with a new vision at the personal and social crises facing them, and act in new ways to build community in accord with their covenant traditions.

The exact meaning of individual parables may escape us in many instances. The parables are enigmatic for various reasons: (1) In retelling them the church often lost the original context and provided a new context, obscuring the original intent of a parable. (2) Jesus intended some parables to be oblique, in order, as C. H. Dodd put it, to leave "the mind in sufficient doubt about its precise application to tease it into active thought,"[14] or to cause the hearer to ponder a situation to gain insight. (3) Some parables might have been deliberately obscure because in the political context it would have been dangerous to be more direct.[15]

---

13. Donahue, *Gospel in Parable,* 11.

14. Dodd, *Parables of the Kingdom,* 4.
15. Oakman suggests that the conflictive situation of Jesus' ministry best explains the indirect and multileveled meaning of parables. Using a perception from social science that "revolutionary" activities and utterances may be sublimated under other forms than political revolution or nonpolitical reform, Oakman maintains that only by being enigmatic could Jesus "have conducted his mission for even a short time" (Oakman, *Jesus and the Economic Questions of His Day,* 103). James Breech *The Silence of Jesus: The Authentic Voice of the Historical Man* (Philadelphia: Fortress Press, 1983), 11–14, adds a less convincing reason when he suggests as a fundamental tenet the notion that if Jesus was elusive it was because the reality to which he referred escapes our grasp. Breech's Jesus thus becomes a philosopher expounding elusive realities.

In approaching the parables, I will follow certain guidelines. (1) When parables exhibit evidence of the church's allegorical and christological treatment, those dimensions will not be regarded as authentic. (2) The applications given to parables in the introductory verses (such as Luke 15:1–2) and in the applications (such as Matt. 25:29–30) belong to the church and were not part of the original parable.[16] (3) Reflections of Palestinian social life in Jesus' time provide evidence for authenticity. (4) Criticism of Palestinian social and political structures and concern for the historical well-being of Israel establish a presumption of essential authenticity. (5) Reconstructing the exact wording of parables is less important and less possible than establishing an "originating structure."[17]

Any attempt to relate parables to the particular social situation of Jesus faces a difficult task. The hypothetical nature of any attempt at re-creating their context provides a strong argument against connecting the interpretation of parables to the specific questions, dilemmas, and conflicts of Jesus' own day. Since we cannot regard as authentic the context provided by the Gospel writers, and since the reconstruction of any other context is inevitably hypothetical, the interpreter of parables might do well to avoid any particular context.[18] But as problematic as the task is, it must be undertaken in order to avoid separating Jesus from his own history. When interpreters separate him from the Judaism of his day, he no longer seems what he fundamentally was, a prophet addressing concrete social issues. Instead he appears to be a philosopher or a theologian speaking universal wisdom, or the founder of a new religion opposed to Judaism.

While precise historical occasions for particular parables cannot be established, the social and political setting can be. By reflecting that setting, by describing typical situations and typical persons, and by speaking directly to that situation, the parables reveal Jesus' critique of it. Even though the social criticism is oblique more often than direct, the dynamics of the narratives show where Jesus' sympathies lie: with the poor, the outsiders, and the "sinners." The parables implicitly challenge the status quo and its accepted authorities.

Many of the parables have their setting within the economic and political world of Galilee and Judea, not that of Hellenistic-Roman cities. Political rule

---

16. Scott, *Hear Then the Parable*, 17.
17. Scott, *Hear Then the Parable*, passim.
18. As Breech thinks, *Silence of Jesus*, 8–9, seemingly in criticism of Jeremias's approach.

is exercised by kings and their slaves. The social classes portrayed are "the very rich and the poor, the king and the peasant."[19]

Few parables deal with explicitly religious activities or themes; rather, they deal with activities and scenes from common life. That fact means not only that parables take something from ordinary life to illustrate some moral or spiritual truth; the connection between the spiritual and the worldly is even closer than that explanation suggests. The parables point to the fact that it is within ordinary life in the world, as one relates to one's fellow human beings, that one reveals one's character and expresses one's religious commitments. One's relationship to God is not separable from the life of sowing and harvest, of business and investments. Even those parables that portray future judgment focus upon present time, the present world, and present obedience or disobedience as the basis for judgment. The obedient person must live within the kingdom of God whose standards the parables reveal.

The parables express Jesus' prophetic critique of his own particular society.[20] Just as Nathan spoke to David through parable in order to say, "You are the man!" (2 Sam. 12:7), so Jesus used parables to illuminate the flaws in his society and in those who determined its course. The parables thus are not merely innocent stories about God in relation to individual humans (as they are often regarded in popular piety); nor are they about a human self disconnected from particular locations (as they can become in overly theological language). Rather, they proclaim God's will in relation to a particular human society whose members they confront with standards of justice that challenge that society to change.

Parables of the Kingdom

Jesus' central message concerned the kingdom of God, and his parables served as his distinctive medium for conveying it. The interpreter's understanding of the kingdom will therefore heavily influence the interpretation of parables. If one views the kingdom in apocalyptic terms (Schweitzer), the metaphor of "harvest" will suggest the imminent apocalyptic end. If one believes the kingdom has already arrived (Dodd), the harvesttime is now. If

---

19. Stambaugh and Balch, *New Testament in Its Social Environment,* 89.
20. Jeremias, *Parables of Jesus,* 124, sees Jesus' parables as weapons in his battle. While Jeremias exaggerates the conflict with the Pharisees (as do the Gospel writers), he is correct in seeing the parables as weapons.

one thinks the kingdom is both present and future (Jeremias), the parables will reveal the grace and the judgment of the inaugurated kingdom. If one thinks of the kingdom as a symbol for inner transformation (Bultmann and Perrin), the parables will be seen as metaphors effecting that transformation. These examples show the importance of connecting an interpretation of kingdom to the interpretation of parables; they also serve as a warning that one may not simply be deriving one's view of the kingdom from the parables but instead may be imposing it upon them.

I have argued above that Jesus used kingdom of God primarily as a symbol of God's renewal of Israel, and as a symbol of what Israel must undergo to avoid catastrophe. The church, with a more apocalyptic outlook than Jesus had, looked for the return of Jesus as the Son of Man coming on the clouds to inaugurate final judgment. Thus, the kingdom as Jesus expressed it in parable has to be distinguished from the modifications the church made.

In what follows, I will be looking especially for the social meaning of the kingdom of God in the parables. The social and economic conditions described in chapter 1 above provide the background for Jesus' parables. The alienations caused by the structure of the economy are manifest in several parables dealing with agricultural and patron-client themes. My interpretations of parables will take for granted the following propositions about the economy. (1) Independent peasant farmers were under severe pressure in the Hellenistic-Roman period. (2) The norms and standards of the Torah regarding land use had eroded, but they had not disappeared from the consciousness of the people, especially the rural people. (3) Common people regarded the wealthy with the suspicion that they had compromised covenant standards for their own benefit. (4) Peasant farmers resented absentee landlords who controlled much of the land. (5) Stewards of such landlords, whether Jew or Gentile, would be resented by those they employed. (6) Peasants were bound to the soil and had little real option but to remain as they were. (7) Many peasants were landless.

Day Laborers in the Vineyard: Matthew 20:1–16

Matthew alone contains this parable, which he puts in the context of other stories pointing to the eschatological judgment, where God's decisions overturn human expectations. Matthew's unit begins with the story of the rich young man (19:16–30), sayings on the difficulty of entering the kingdom (19:23–30), this parable, the third prediction of Jesus' suffering (20:17–19), and the request of James's and John's mother (20:20–28). The surrounding stories provide an occasion to present the theme of reversal: the first will be last, the last will be first (Matt. 19:30; 20:26–28). In addition, the same sort of reversal is implied by the preceding story of Jesus blessing the children (19:13–15). Matthew uses the parable to present his warning against exalting oneself over others and to offer a critique of those who distrust or dislike God's generosity to those who are relatively undeserving.

The first workers agree on a contract: a denarius for a day's work. The owner fulfills the contract, but they are disappointed nonetheless. The other groups of workers have no contract. They work by invitation and trust, and although their response is not given, they are apparently satisfied with the result. However, the absence of their response indicates that they are not the real focus of the parable; rather, the parable is more concerned with those who came first and labored longest and who consequently have conflict with the householder.

In terms of Matthew's own theology, the point has to do with the relationship between God and humans. Joyous participation in God's kingdom, with trust that the outcome will depend more on the generosity of the "householder" than on the amount of work by the laborer, is preferable to a mere contractual relationship that easily breeds resentment against those who seem to deserve less. For Matthew, then, the parable is an allegory: The householder is God, who is generous beyond human expectation; the first laborers are the longer-term servants (either Israel, or perhaps the first disciples, or the first converts into the church); the other laborers are the latecomers into the church (either the Gentiles, or more recent converts), whose shorter length of service would seem to deserve less generous blessing.[21]

What is the original meaning of the parable?[22] Does it take something from the world of householders and workers in order to comment on something else? It has usually been so interpreted, beginning at least with Matthew. In Matthew's context, it probably relates to the resentment some Christian-Jewish members felt over admission of Gentiles: Why should Gentile

---

21. For fuller treatment along this line, see Daniel Patte, *The Gospel According to Matthew: A Structural Commentary on Matthew's Faith* (Philadelphia: Fortress Press, 1987), 274–78.

22. Even though it has only single attestation, the parable without Matthew's interpretive additions is largely authentic. See Robert W. Funk, Bernard Brandon Scott, and James R. Butts, *The Parables of Jesus: Red Letter Edition* (Sonoma, Calif.: Polebridge Press, 1988), 33: "The upsetting and disturbing end is characteristic of the parables of Jesus."

newcomers receive the same treatment the Jewish members of the covenant community receive, when the latter have labored long with small reward?

If Jesus intended a similar meaning, the groups would be different, but the point would be the same: the resentment of the "righteous" over Jesus' treatment of "sinners" (those whose conduct did not meet the standards of purity demanded by piety). The Gospels frequently attribute that attitude to the Pharisees. Even though the Gospels exaggerate Jesus' conflict with the Pharisees, they likely reflect a historical reality. Those who specialized in piety and purity (not necessarily to be identified with Pharisees as a group)[23] resented Jesus' fraternization with the sinners and the affirmation that God's promises were especially for them.[24]

Jeremias helped set the stage for an interpretation that emphasized Jesus' conflict with Pharisees. He also provides a christological interpretation:

> God is depicted as acting like an employer who has compassion for the unemployed and their families. He gives to publicans and sinners a share, all undeserved, in his Kingdom. So will he deal with them on the Last Day. That, says Jesus, is what he is like; and because he is like that, so am I; since I am acting under his orders and in his stead. Will you then murmur against God's goodness? That is the core of Jesus' vindication of the Gospel.[25]

The Parable as Reflection of Palestinian Conditions

Setting this parable in the historical context of Jesus' ministry provides an avenue for understanding its social and political content, and leads one away

---

23. See Ellis Rivkin, "Defining the Pharisees: The Tannaitic Sources," *Hebrew Union College Annual* 40–41 (1969–70):205. I am indebted to Karl Plank for sharing his unpublished paper, "Ellis Rivkin and the Study of Pharisaism: An Interpretation and Assessment."

24. J. C. Fenton, *The Gospel of St. Matthew,* The Pelican Gospel Commentaries (Baltimore: Penguin Books, 1963), 319. See also Dodd, *Parables of the Kingdom,* 94–95, and Jeremias, *Parables of Jesus,* 33–38, 136–139. Fenton represents the approach taken by many interpreters since Dodd and Jeremias distinguished the meaning of parables in Jesus' situation from that of the Gospel writers:

> The setting in the ministry of Jesus is probably his controversy with the Pharisees over his treatment of the tax collectors and sinners: He admits them to his fellowship, he eats and drinks with them, he invites them into the kingdom, because God who has sent him is generous with his forgiveness and mercy; those who complain in the parable are the Pharisees, who, like the older brother in the Lukan parable of the prodigal son, claim more from the Father because of their good works.

25. Jeremias, *Parables of Jesus,* 139.

from interpretations that emphasize antagonism between Jesus and Phari-saism (or Judaism) or Jesus' unique revelation of God. As Jeremias correctly says, the "parable is set in a period over which broods the spectre of unemployment."[26] This parable corroborates other available evidence of large estates worked by a plentiful supply of day laborers and of the client-patron model of relations assumed as the economic background of parables.[27] The dependency and inequality that prevailed in the Roman world (see, for example, Luke 17:7–9) are taken for granted here. The position of servant and master are predefined by that system.

The client-patron system resulted from many economic forces at work in Palestinian society as early as the Hasmonaean period, exacerbated by Herod and by direct Roman rule: high taxes resulting in debt for many peasants, loss of land due to debt, disruption, or confiscation. The client-patron system disrupted the traditional pattern of patriarchal families and villages, where ancestral land tenure helped cushion the impact of economic hardship on the poor. Roman domination broke down this patriarchal structure. Peasant families ridden by debt could no longer rely on protection by the head of the family. Thus, loss of ancestral lands, debt-slavery, and unemployment were common experiences of those on the margins.[28] The practices of sabbatical year and Jubilee could have provided relief for families, had they been fully implemented.

Neither in this parable nor elsewhere is there any explicit comment on the client-patron relationship. Indeed, that relationship sometimes provides a model for the relationship of God to humans, a fact that suggests the early church was not uncomfortable with the client-patron system, even though Jesus himself might have regarded it as contrary to covenant norms.[29]

The laborers in this parable have no regular work; they depend on the varying needs of potential employers. Although no comment is made on the economic impact of their unemployment on themselves or their dependents, the hearers of the parable would be very much aware of that impact. Nothing

26. Jeremias, *Parables of Jesus,* 139.
27. Scott, *Hear Then the Parable,* 207, comments on the patron-client parables and states that Jesus, unlike rabbinic parallels, implies a subversion of that structure. Scott draws upon an anthropological study by S. Einstadt and L. Roniger, "Patron-Client Relations," *Comparative Studies in Society and History* 22 (1980): 42–77.
28. Horsley, *Jesus and the Spiral of Violence,* 232–33.
29. Some parables using this model have to do with an absentee master coming (again) and thus seem to reflect Parousia expectation of the early church rather than Jesus' own time. See Scott, *Hear Then the Parable,* 207–8.

is said about how they came to their present situation, but many of the hearers would know such people, for their number was quite large in Roman Palestine.

Only the householder himself comments on his character. He refers to his generosity. He may be unusual in his persistent trips to the marketplace looking for workers, but the parable does not state whether his motivation derives from his concern to provide employment or his desire to pursue his harvest with dispatch. No one contradicts his claim to be a generous person, though a positive self-image in a parable is not always confirmed by the parable itself (see, for example, the parable of the Pharisee and the tax-collector, where God's perspective contradicts self-images).

The tension among the workers reveals the intention of telling the story. They are set against each other, worker against worker. Jealousy and resentment dominate their attitude. None of them criticized the householder or the system under which they work until the householder paid a full day's wage to the late workers first. The workers' conflict with the householder grew out of their jealousy toward each other due to what the householder (and perhaps the workers themselves) regarded as his generosity.

The workers have little control over their own economic lives. A denarius would hardly buy daily bread for a worker's family, even on the days when someone hired them to work. Reduced to squabbling among themselves, some were resentful over the meager wages paid to the latecomers instead of being glad that a neighbor family might eat bread that night. In making his payment to the latecomers, the householder is more generous than he has to be, perhaps more generous than most, but his generosity does not match the need of the workers for regular jobs and dependable income.

What is Jesus' point in holding up this system through narrative? The householder's raising the issue of "justice" provides a clue to the parable's interpretation. The workers themselves do not use the term, but they do question the householder's actions. The workers are at the mercy ("justice") of the owner. Even though some owners may be "generous," the system has robbed workers of their dignity and humanity. They appeal not for justice but for fairness, by complaining that the householder has made the latecomers "equal" to the early comers. They do not question the justice of the system under which they work, but only the way the householder has acted within the system. Accepting the system and seeing it violated puts the workers at odds with each other, showing that the problem is not merely in the controllers of society or those who benefit most from that control. It is also in the workers, who respond to each other with the kind of complaint that is not unusual in oppressed situations. In desperate times, they misdirect their resentment toward their fellow sufferers, as though the unfairness was their fault.

The householder's protest that he was not doing any injustice (Matt. 20:13: "wrong" in RSV, NRSV) invites further attention. He fulfilled his agreement with them and did not commit any unjust act such as reducing or withholding wages. So long as he did no unjust act, the householder believes, his justice allows doing as he pleases with what is his. No question is raised as to how householder and worker arrived at their present economic situations; no question is raised as to whether or not the agreed-on wage was "just." Absent such reflection, his going beyond the contract price for some of the laborers expressed generosity. But if one regarded either the system itself or the original wage unjust, then his apparent generosity would evaporate.[30]

The original workers, too, implicitly appeal for justice. To them it is not just to give equal pay for unequal work. Breech says the workers who complain want a system that prevents the outrage to their sense of justice.[31] On this reading this parable illustrates Perkins's assertion that parables cause the hearers to recognize that the kingdom transforms the taken-for-granted arrangements that people have.[32] The householder violates those arrangements, thus causing consternation among the workers. Implicitly in both these interpretations the householder's action and attitude reflect that of God, and the workers must renounce their attitudes. The fact that "vineyard" and "vineyard owner" or keeper are transparent symbols for Israel and God supports this view.[33]

That interpretation reaches its high point in Bornkamm's statement that Jesus offered a new vision of the relationship between God and humans, no longer that of contract, of work and reward, but a vision of father and son, a vision that the laborers have not come to share. In a statement that Riches quotes approvingly, Bornkamm maintains that the householder, the father of the family,

> breaks through all boundaries of civil order and justice. No scales of remuneration could ever be set up on these principles. Thus the notion of

---

30. See Donahue, *Gospel in Parable*, 70–85, on the sense of justice in Matthew.

31. *Silence of Jesus*, 153: The workers "want everything to be controlled by a system that prevents anyone from benefiting unexpectedly from someone else's spontaneous gift." They want this system to control everyone else because they distrust everyone else. "They do not want there to be bonds between people; they want systems to control people" (155).

32. Pheme Perkins, *Hearing the Parables of Jesus* (New York: Paulist Press, 1981), 4.

33. See three other vineyard-related stories: the barren fig tree; the two sons; and the wicked tenants, for examples; cf. Isa. 5:1–5.

rewards which was so carefully worked into the narrative is rejected because precisely by contrast with all human concepts of reward and achievement, of justice and fairness, God's sovereignty is to be demonstrated by his goodness (Matt. 20:15f.). This then is the meaning of God's kingdom (20:1): *God's mercy knows no bounds.*[34]

Breech modifies that theological interpretation and applies the parable to the problem of human-human relations: The laborers want the contractual arrangement to continue because they do not trust each other, and they want a dependable system that allows no one to gain an unfair advantage.[35] They determine what is right by comparing themselves with others; the householder, on the other hand, acts with freedom to decide for himself what is right. He will not allow them to judge what he has done, for only he himself can determine the validity of his actions.[36]

Breech thus gives the parable a universally applicable meaning. As an effective literary work, it provides a stimulus to reflection and existential awareness, and it invites personal change. For Breech, it would not matter whether Jesus told it in Palestine or another philosophically astute observer of human behavior told it in some other cultural setting. Unlike Bornkamm and Riches, he correctly applies the parable to human-human relations, but they are more correct than he in looking for an application within Jesus' own historical context.

The parable is about human relationships fundamentally, relationships that are in disarray because of the reality of their present lives and the attitudes that present conditions foster in those who are the victims. The marginalized laborers have been so molded by the system under which they jointly suffer that they can see only threats in their fellow sufferers. Until the hearers can see with clarity what the set of relationships taken for granted in the parable amounts to, they cannot see what is happening to society.

The householder is not a bad person, but he is in a position to determine the lives of others who must live out of his goodness and generosity rather than out of their own productivity, which has been taken away by the current economic situation. The householder is similar to the "kings of the Gentiles"

---

34. Quoted from G. Bornkamm, "Der Lohngedanke im Neuen Testament," *Studien zu Antike und Urchristentum* (Munich: Kaiser, 1970), 116–18, in Riches, *Jesus and the Transformation of Judaism*, 152–53.

35. Breech, *Silence of Jesus*, 152–55.

36. Breech, *Silence of Jesus*, 149, sees the householder as a paradigm of the human freedom in which both John the Baptist and Jesus lived (28).

and "those in authority" who are called "benefactors" (Luke 22:25). He also resembles the rich man who combines piety and wealth and who rejects the call to radical obedience that entails giving up possessions for the benefit of the poor (Mark 10:17–23). According to the Gospel tradition, Jesus condemned those who live in that fashion, and he challenged them to change.

The workers are not evil people either, but because of the precariousness of their own situation they cannot enter sympathetically into the plight of others who are also on the margins, nor can they accept their fellow day laborers as their allies in a common struggle for a system of economic and social life more in keeping with covenant standards of justice. They too have internalized the values of the social-economic arrangements that came to dominate Israelite society in the Hellenistic period.

Jesus challenges those values in this parable. According to all three Synoptics, he directly rejects such a model of relationships in his visionary reconstruction of society ("But it is not so among you," Mark 10:43; Luke 22:26; Matt. 20:26). As it stands in Matthew's parable, the challenge is not direct, and Matthew's relatively affluent society probably would not recognize it. Nonetheless the parable deliberately holds up social relations to the close scrutiny of those who have eyes to see.

Those who look for God's kingdom, both among the poor and among the wealthy, need to be aware of the ways the present arrangement contradicts covenant norms. The wealthy need to recognize their own responsibility to go beyond generous acts to reestablish a system of covenant justice; the poor need to recognize their natural allies and be more sensitive to the factors that hinder covenant justice.[37] Neither may blame the outsiders—Rome—for the absence of those standards as long as they themselves do not recognize or accept them.

Prophetic connections between vineyards and renewal of Israel confirm that such an interpretation is not fictional. Isaiah uses "vineyard" to speak of the renewal of the people after the Assyrian attack (Isa. 37:30). In language reminiscent of the Sabbath year described in Leviticus 25:2–7, Isaiah promises that the people will plant vineyards and eat their fruit. Again Isaiah 65:21 promises planting vineyards and eating their fruit in the time of renewal. In contrast to this promise, in Jesus' parable the laborers are

---

37. Donahue suggests that the parable is not about the servants but does not completely follow Jeremias's suggestion that it is about "the good employer" (Donahue, *Gospel in Parable*, 81: "The grumbling workers, while not the main characters in the parable, provide the dramatic foil for the interpretation ").

harvesting where they did not plant, reaping a harvest they will not eat. Similar use of the symbol of vineyards occurs in Jeremiah 31:2–6, Ezekiel 28:26, and Amos 9:14. Ezekiel combines that promise of living safely on their own soil, where they plant vineyards and build houses, with the prospect of judgment on their neighbors who have treated the Israelites with contempt.[38]

The picture the parable presents directly contradicts God's promises for the future of Israel. A landowner with hired servants who only on lucky days earn enough for bread, no matter how benevolent that landowner may appear in his unjust context, stands opposed to the visions of prophetic renewal promised to Israel. That vision contains promise of landowners who enjoy the fruits of their own labors, live in their own houses, and sing and dance at harvest rather than fight among themselves and accuse their "benevolent" masters of injustice. For those who know the prophetic hopes and who long for their fulfillment in times of occupation and exploitation, it is not necessary to point out the contrasts; they would be evident merely in the telling of the story.[39]

---

38. Jeremiah 31:2–6 contains a hope of restoration, again symbolized by the planting of vineyards and enjoying the fruit. The following verses depict the joy of the people, who will sing aloud over the Lord's goodness, over the grain, the wine, the oil: "Their life shall become like a watered garden, and they shall never languish again" (31:12). God will comfort them, "and my people shall be satisfied with my bounty" (31:14).

In Ezekiel, too, the building of houses and the planting of vineyards is promised to the restored people: "They shall live in safety in it [their own soil], and shall build houses and plant vineyards. They shall live in safety, when I execute judgments upon all their neighbors who have treated them with contempt. And they shall know that I am the LORD their God" (28:26).

Amos 9:14–15 contains the same sort of promise:

> I will restore the fortunes of my people Israel,
>   and they shall rebuild the ruined cities and inhabit them;
> they shall plant vineyards and drink their wine,
>   and they shall make gardens and eat their fruit.
> I will plant them upon their land,
>   and they shall never again be plucked up
>   out of the land that I have given them,
>   says the LORD your God.

39. Segundo, *Historical Jesus of the Synoptic Gospels*, 126–27, relates this parable to Jubilee year when "ownership and freedom were . . . shared out equally. . . . It made no difference how people had worked or administered their goods. Every fifty years people would recover their basic human possibilities."

Parable of the Independent and Confident Farmer: Mark 4:26–29; compare *Gospel of Thomas* 21:4[40]

This brief, enigmatic parable found only in Mark (and partially in Thomas)[41] contrasts with that of the day laborers. Rather than speaking of a landowner with hired servants, the parable reflects the world of the independent peasant farmer, who in patience and confidence sows seed, observes its mysterious growth into a harvest, and then reaps the reward. Mark says such a process illustrates the kingdom of God.

Mark does not reveal his understanding of what the parable conveys about the kingdom. He provides neither explanation nor sufficient context to give a clear clue. Two phrases within the parable suggest an interpretation. "He does not know how" conveys mystery and connects with Mark's frequently expressed motif of secrecy. "Of itself" (*automatē*) may also reveal Mark's understanding. The kingdom as Mark understands it is beyond both human knowledge and human doing. The kingdom comes as inevitably as harvest follows planting, but its mysteriousness is not reduced by that certainty.

Interpreters have sought to resolve some of the mystery by focusing on different elements in the parable. Focusing on *growth* as the central metaphor, some have thought the parable presents a kingdom that Jesus' ministry has inaugurated and that will continue to grow through history. Focusing on *harvest* (a metaphor for judgment), others have thought the parable points to a future kingdom. Focusing on the *inactivity* of the farmer during the time of growth, others have thought the parable points to the fact that God rather than humans brings the kingdom.

Too little attention has been paid to a simpler element in the parable: As a symbol for the kingdom stands a farmer who operates in the ancient manner, neither an absentee landlord nor a day laborer, but one who sows, plants, and harvests on his own plot of land, with confidence that God's promises come to fulfillment through those very acts.

The farming scene in this parable differs dramatically from that of the

---

40. For this and other references to parables in Thomas, see Robert W. Funk, *New Gospel Parallels,* Vol. 2: *John and the Other Gospels* (Philadelphia: Fortress Press, 1985).

41. Its absence from Matthew and Luke could indicate that their editions of Mark did not have it, or they might have regarded it as offering nothing not already contained in other seed/harvest parables. Its presence (partially) in Thomas provides it with dual attestation in primary layers of tradition (see Crossan, *Historical Jesus,* 439). Its narrative content fits a Palestinian context, though it could fit other contexts as well. I regard it as authentic because it coheres with Jesus' other sayings relating to agricultural economy.

laborers in the vineyard. The type of agricultural economy is quite different. Instead of a landholder with the means to employ many day laborers, we have a peasant farmer who evidently owns his own land and does his own work. Instead of the resentment accompanying a harvest conducted by day laborers for a "generous" householder, we have the implied joy of the farmer reaping a harvest that comes naturally as a result of his working according to God's promises. Though brief, the parable of the confident farmer points to the joy known to the vanishing number of small, independent farmers. In contrast stands a system that is supplanting it. In neither case is the system directly commented upon, which could mean it is inconsequential, as most interpreters suggest by their inattention to it. But such indirection might be purposeful and even necessary in Jesus' political context.

One can imagine what the effect might be on rural people if they should hear this parable and the parable of the day laborers in the same address. We cannot, of course, reconstruct the original form or the original context, but inasmuch as many of Jesus' parables relate to agricultural economy, the interpreter should pay special attention to the use of negative and positive images of that economy. Which of the images would Jesus' hearers have regarded positively, as being consistent with the use of God-given land? The continued observance of Sabbath year shows that such questions had not lost their relevance in Jesus' day. This parable would remind those who knew such prophecies as Isaiah 37:30–31 that during a fallow year (such as Sabbath year or Jubilee) the people will eat only what grows of its own accord; the following year they will again sow, reap, plant vineyards, and eat their fruit; and "the surviving remnant of Judah shall again take root downward, and bear fruit upward."

Oakman suggests connections with prophetic tradition by focusing on the absence of labor: "What would a harvest without labor imply for those who perhaps labored mightily (mostly for others) and for only a bare subsistence, or for those without access to land and secure food reserves?"[42]

Would not hearers of Jesus' parable have noticed the pregnant silence about agricultural work? For them, the parable spoke volumes about the coming [order] of God that would take into account their physical needs, in contrast to

---

42. Oakman, *Jesus and the Economic Questions of His Day,* 111. He cites instances from Papias as well as *1 Enoch* 10:19 and *2 Baruch* 29:5 to suggest that at the end of time there will be great blessing and peace and abundance (112). Cf. also Rev. 21:4: *oute ponos*, "no toil" (NRSV translates "no pain"), reversing the situation created by human alienation in Gen. 3:17–19.

the present [order] which did not. . . . The harvest comes to meet material
need. It is a real harvest . . . not a cipher for theologians' speculations about
time and eternity.[43]

As intriguing as Oakman's comments are, "of itself" does not deny the
farmer's ordinary and necessary tasks of planting and harvesting, without
which there would be no yield to be enjoyed. "By itself" takes place after
planting and before harvest, and means "the coming of the harvest is
assured," not that human agency is irrelevant. As Schrage comments, "The
parable is not antisynergistic, anti-Zealot, or even quietistic." The word
automatē means "unfathomably, miraculously, without visible cause."[44]

Even if the parable originally did not intend to comment on the agricultural economy, it nevertheless reflects the situation that would have been
considered ideal in Israel's past. The response of peasant hearers to this
parable would be as positive as their response to the parable concerning day
laborers would have been negative.[45]

Parable of the Sower: Mark 4:1–9; Matthew 13:1–9; Luke 8:4–8; *Gospel of Thomas* 9

Occurring in all three Synoptics and the *Gospel of Thomas*,[46] the parable in
all its versions tells of a yield of grain in spite of the loss incurred by the farmer.
The Synoptics' allegorical interpretation reflects the church language about
the proclamation of the Gospel;[47] the explanation can hardly be original. The
parable circulated without that interpretation, as Thomas demonstrates. The
details of the parable themselves may presuppose the allegorical interpretation,
but all the versions suggest an original structure containing three episodes of
failure and one of success.[48] This parable, Matthew's parable of the weeds (Matt.
13:24–30), and Mark's parable of the confident farmer (Mark 4:26–29) all

43. Oakman, *Jesus and the Economic Questions of His Day,* 114.
44. Schrage, *Ethics of the New Testament,* 21.
45. Chilton and McDonald, *Jesus and the Ethics of the Kingdom,* 18ff., provide a sensitive
reading of this parable: The parable portrays interaction of man, seed, and earth, all elements
from common life. The harvest is a product of all three. The man benefits from that interaction,
and is the final actor in securing the product of it for himself. "Hopeful action and enacted hope
characterize the parable" (24). The parable never focuses just on hope or on action alone. "The
creative interface between the two is of the essence of the Kingdom which is presented."
46. And perhaps in *1 Clement* 24:5.
47. Jeremias, *Parables of Jesus,* 77–78.
48. Funk and Smith, *Gospel of Mark* , 90.

contain the process of sowing and reaping, and may all derive from a single original.[49] They have all undergone development in keeping with the interests of the church and the Gospel writers.

The belief that a one-hundredfold harvest would be abnormally large has provided the basis for applying this parable to Jesus' eschatology. An unexpectedly large harvest suggests that the eschatological kingdom will exceed human expectation. By pointing to that unusually large harvest, Jesus encouraged his disciples, when their efforts seemed wasted, to trust that God would bring their efforts to fulfillment.[50] Scott offers evidence that contradicts the basis for that interpretation. He cites Roman naturalist and historian Pliny to the effect that thirtyfold to one-hundredfold would be an ordinary harvest.[51] The point could still be to encourage trust in God's goodness, but the fulfillment would not consist in eschatological superabundance.

Scott's reckoning makes a thirtyfold yield small but within normal range, the sort of yield one might expect when farming marginal land. The farmer's difficulties are more than one would expect on good land. In a time of a shortage of land, farmers bring all available land under cultivation, risking a small yield as preferable to no yield at all.[52] In that situation, even an ordinary harvest requires a miraculous growth. Peasant hearers would respond sympathetically to a farmer trying to wrest a living from a difficult patch of land.[53] They would rejoice in the production of an adequately good harvest. Much that is crucial to success or failure is beyond the control of the sower. Sowing is inevitably done in trust and hope, and the outcome is never sure. Yet the farmer cannot be deterred by that fact. He must trust the soil and the seed, regardless of their limitations, and fundamentally he must trust God. That trust finds its reward, and the harvest is plentiful enough to confirm his hope.

This parable, like others concerning sowing and harvesting, implies confident acceptance of God's gift of land to the covenant people, as well as God's presence in their use of that land. Just as a good farmer does not neglect to plant out of fear of a failed harvest, so those invited to participate in the

---

49. Funk and Smith, *Gospel of Mark,* 91, regard it as essentially authentic, as does Crossan, *Historical Jesus,* 437.

50. Jeremias, *Parables of Jesus,* 150–51.

51. *Hear Then the Parable,* 357. Scott thinks the ordinariness of the harvest, in contrast to fantastic harvests in some eschatological expectation, makes the parable's point: "In failure and everydayness lies the miracle of God's activity. . . . The kingdom does not need the moral perfection of Torah nor the apocalyptic solution of overwhelming harvest" (361–62).

52. Oakman, *Jesus and the Economic Questions of His Day,* 104–7.

53. Oakman, *Jesus and the Economic Questions of His Day,* 107.

coming kingdom within God's land should not neglect to do so out of fear
that their hope will be disappointed.

Jeremias ties this hope to the eschatological fulfillment of Jesus' ministry.[54]
My interpretation places it more in the context of the call to renewal of the
social and communal life of God's people. That renewal is symbolized by the
farmer who works his own land and enjoys his own harvest, in the same way
the independent and confident farmer of Mark 4:26–29 does. Those who
participate in this process face difficulties and setbacks, they know the limits
beyond which they do not control events, but they know one can participate
in confidence and trust, using those techniques that confirm and do not
contradict the ends being sought. The result finally rests in God's hands and
therefore will be good.

Parable of Wheat and Weeds:
Matthew 13:24–30; *Gospel of Thomas* 57[55]

Matthew uses this parable as an allegory of eschatological judgment.[56]
Both eschatology and judgment correspond to Matthean concerns. Matthew
frequently uses them to express his theme of warning that judgment is
coming, and his parallel theme of patient waiting for God's judgment to deal
with sinners. These themes therefore belong to Matthew and not to the
original parable. Without them the parable provides another example of
farming practices consistent with a Palestinian setting. Interpreters who
recognize that the original parable was not an allegory may nonetheless
continue to provide allegorical meanings. But the parable does not concern
God's judgment or God's patience with sinners.[57] It deals with farmers and

---

54. Jeremias, *Parables of Jesus,* 149–51.

55. I agree with the Jesus Seminar that the allegory we have in Matthew is not authentic.
See Funk, Scott, and Butts, *Parables of Jesus: Red Letter Edition,* 65. However, if one assumes the
approach taken by Oakman and followed here, the likelihood of there being an authentic
parable in the background of the allegory may be greater.

56. As he did the parable of the fishnet (Matt. 13:47–50). William G. Morrice, "The
Parable of the Dragnet and The Gospel of Thomas," *Expository Times* 85 (June 1984): 271,
believes that *Thomas* 8, which omits eschatological judgment, shows that Matthew added that
theme to the parable of the fishnet under the influence of his interpretation of the parable of
the weeds (Matt. 13:36–43).

57. Jeremias, *Parables of Jesus,* 81–85, rejects the sort of allegorical interpretation given in
Matt. 13:36–43 but nevertheless gives the parable a similar allegorical interpretation that
enjoins patience in waiting for "the time of separation." He believes the parable is "eschatological in character" (see 225–26).

farming, and, as Oakman argues, it provides a social criticism, especially directed toward the landowning class.[58]

The narrative tells of a landowner who is wealthy enough to cultivate land with the use of servants. However, he does not know much about farming conditions and practices in Palestine. Whether the assertion that an enemy sowed weed seeds in his fields represents a narrative fact or his perception of what has happened, the man misunderstands what he is dealing with. "Darnel" (zizania) was a common grass that could ruin a wheat harvest. If left until the harvest, as this farmer intends to do, it would be very difficult to separate from the wheat. Since zizania is toxic, the farmer's strategy could lead to tragedy. His decision to wait is, therefore, not in keeping with good agricultural practice. The man thus provides not an example of God's wisdom in judgment but a negative example. By not attending to darnel earlier, he harvests a crop that is dangerous.[59]

What could lead to this situation? One explanation is that the man is not an experienced Palestinian farmer. Possibly he is one of those to whom land has been leased by the Herods or the Romans, or one who has acquired land through astute lending practices. Jesus' hearers would know of such people, whose success at gaining land was greater than their knowledge of how to use it. The parable, then, provides not only humor at the expense of the ignorant farmer, but also a social critique of the patterns of land tenure developed during the period immediately prior to Jesus' lifetime.[60]

Parable of the Rich Fool: Luke 12:13–21

Agricultural life also provides the setting for this parable. Like the parable of the workers in the vineyard, it portrays an alienation associated with the practice of farming. Luke's introduction provides clues to Luke's interpretation, though one cannot assume that his interpretation corresponds to the original intent. The first clue derives from the request that Jesus intervene in a dispute over inheritance. We are not told enough to know the validity of the claim. The parable does not deal directly with it but diverts attention away from it as almost

---

58. Oakman, *Jesus and the Economic Questions of His Day*, 123, says the "parable is socio-critical over against the landowning class."

59. Oakman, *Jesus and the Economic Questions of His Day*, 114–15.

60. Oakman, *Jesus and the Economic Questions of His Day*, 124–28, thinks the parable of the mustard seed (Matt. 13:31–32; Luke 13:18–19) may have a similar point, since mustard (in some of its domesticated and wild varieties) is potentially dangerous to the garden.

irrelevant. However, such disputes were quite common in Jesus' time, particularly as Hellenistic ways eroded covenant standards. Whether Luke knew a tradition that involved Jesus in such disputes cannot be determined from this introduction, but if Jesus concerned himself with questions of economic justice, people likely put these kinds of questions to him.

The second clue to Luke's understanding is found in Jesus' implicit rejection of the role of "judge or divider" and the warning against covetousness. Usually this warning is taken to refer to the covetousness of the one who is asking for Jesus' assistance. This understanding then leads to the conclusion that Jesus considers material concerns irrelevant; the man should forget his claim and go on with more important spiritual matters. However, the *de* ("but" in v. 14 and "and" in v. 15) merely continues the narrative and does not imply negation. Thus, the covetousness condemned may belong to the brother who possesses the land, rather than or in addition to that of the brother who wants to possess it. The rich fool may portray possessor-brother, implying that unjustly accumulating property jeopardizes his place in the life God offers God's people.

The setting is likely to be Luke's own, as is verse 15, for both contain one of Luke's major themes: covetousness and false treasures. The interpretation of the parable thus should depend only on the parable itself and not on Luke's interpretation. One cannot find sufficient reason to attribute the parable to any particular setting in the life of Jesus.

Fitzmyer's comment that the attitude of Jesus reflected in Luke 12:51–53, where Jesus speaks of bringing not peace but division, explains why Jesus would not get involved in family disputes. Presumably Fitzmyer means that Jesus, aware that his preaching caused family tension and wanting to avoid that tension, refused to become embroiled in family inheritance disputes. However, the saying (Luke 12:51–53) could indicate that Jesus did get involved in such disputes over ownership and use of land, resulting in an increase in family tensions. Prophetically calling attention to failure to follow community attitudes and practices required by the Torah was part of Jesus' public ministry, and he did not refuse to do so in order to avoid conflict. Whether within or without families, Jesus' words would have challenged those who controlled the land by methods not consistent with covenant justice.

Is Luke correct in seeing covetousness as the main problem of the successful farmer? The man is not at first sight covetous, unless amassing his wealth was possible only by effectively coveting what legitimately belongs to others in the covenant community. The man's mistaken notion that his life *does* consist in the abundance of possessions leads to covetous behavior. The fool in the parable is insensitive, selfish, and oblivious to any rightful claims of anyone else. Especially if he has held on to land beyond the time allowed by the Sabbath and Jubilee laws, his actions could be deemed covetous. Fitzmyer refers to his "superficial self-confidence," implying that the most urgent problem is the lack of recognition of God's reality and claim upon him. While that is accurate, the "I" language also betrays ignorance of the way God's claims on the individual are made within the context of community.

The man not only relies upon himself rather than upon God; he also lives by the egoistic code typical of the Hellenized social group that tends to see the individual in isolation from community. "Eat, drink, and be merry" expresses that same egoism. The man is radically individualistic; his speech acknowledges no person, human or divine, except himself. He has lost any concept of covenant community. He implicitly denies any notion that he owes God for his life and wealth. Crops, barns, and comfort have replaced God, neighbor, and justice.

The man's inability to take it with him is an implied part of his problem of ordering his life. That moralizing conclusion ("so it is with those who store up treasures for themselves but are not rich toward God," Luke 12:21) is likely Luke's own. The parable likely ended with God's address to the man: "This very night your life is being demanded of you. And the things you have prepared, whose will they be?" The man (and Jesus' hearers) is left to ponder the question of inheritance. What does he leave behind, and to whom does he leave it? In his "I" monologue, he has mentioned neither family nor community. Thus, he has forgotten the basic premise that binds a covenant community together: The future of that community and the happiness of those who participate in it must be prime considerations in the way one orders one's own life. Amassing lands and living by self-indulgence negate one's own future as it negates the future of God's people.

The parable portrays the man as a fool but not as a consciously bad person. He shows no overt hostility to anyone, no awareness that he has harmed anyone, no judgment against himself at all. In fact, that is precisely the problem: He thinks of life in complete isolation from the communal responsibilities that life in a covenant community entail. He does not express any thanksgiving to God who provides the increase; he does not reflect on the needs of anyone other than himself. Even his own needs and wants are expressed in terms of self-indulgence: "my crops . . . my grain . . . my barns."

If the man did not live in alienation from God and from covenant community, he could see that he already has storage in the mouths of the needy.[61]

Presumably he already had more than enough for himself, for he was
described as rich. The desire to have even more and to think only of how to
preserve it all for himself is clearly excessive, with no apparent motive other
than to accumulate for the sake of accumulation.[62] If Luke intended to
connect the parable with the next two paragraphs (Luke 12:22–34) about the
danger of being anxious about life, clothing, and food, he suggests the fool is
anxious in spite of his apparent security. He stands in striking contrast to the
carefree existence indicated by the birds and the lilies. A security gained by
accumulation is revealed as specious when he is confronted with the same
demand that God makes of every human being. God requires the self.[63] In
order to be rich toward God, according to Luke's moral application, he would
need to acknowledge dependency on God and exercise responsibility toward
the covenant community by the right use of what God has entrusted to
him.

Parable of Wicked Tenants: Mark 12:1–12; Matthew 21:33–46; Luke 20:9–19; *Gospel of Thomas* 65

Matthew and Luke follow Mark in placing this parable in the context of
Jesus' disputes with the Jerusalem authorities. The parable follows Jesus'
entry into Jerusalem, the demonstration in the Temple, his cursing of the fig
tree, and his questioning by the authorities. It precedes disputes and hostile
questions concerning payment of taxes to Caesar, resurrection, interpretation
of Torah, and the identity of the Messiah, as well as his strong condemnation
of the Pharisees. All three Synoptic Gospels emphasize the theme of conflict
between Jesus as the true Messiah and the rejection of that Messiah by Israel's
authorities. The parable intensifies the conflict by deliberately provoking a
hostile response from an already hostile audience: "When they realized that

---

61. Kenneth E. Bailey, *Through Peasant Eyes: More Lucan Parables, Their Culture and Style*
(Grand Rapids: Wm. B. Eerdmans Publishing Co., 1980), 64, credits Ambrose with this
statement.

62. Bailey, *Through Peasant Eyes*, 63–66, says the parable introduces the idea of "loan"—
the man discovers his soul to be on loan. Not even his soul belongs to the one who has
emphasized "my crops . . . my grain . . . my barns."

63. Whether this demand is individual eschatological, universal eschatological, or individual existential makes no difference here.

he had told this parable against them, they wanted to arrest him, but they feared the crowd" (Mark 12:12; compare Luke 20:19 and Matt. 21:46).

Mark's version is highly christological and allegorical, though it lacks some important elements of Mark's Christology, especially any reference to the exaltation or resurrection of the "son." Drawing upon Isaiah 5, Mark understands the vineyard to be Israel, the owner God, the servants the prophets, and the son Jesus. Unlike Isaiah 5, the vineyard is not destroyed for its failure; rather, its keepers (=Israel's leaders) are destroyed and the vineyard is given to others (Jesus' disciples? the church?).

Matthew's version is also christological and allegorical. Matthew more than Mark concentrates on the "fruits" of the vineyard (Matt. 21:34, 41, 43; compare Mark 12:2), in keeping with Matthew's insistence elsewhere that faithfulness must be expressed in deeds, or else negative eschatological judgment will fall upon those who profess faith.[64] Matthew heightens the judgment against the "chief priests and the Pharisees" by having the hearers of the parable pronounce judgment on themselves, as well as by including their perception that the parable was directed at them (compare Mark 12:9 and Matt. 21:41), similar to the way the crowd at the trial of Jesus calls God's judgment upon themselves (Matt. 27:25).

Except for not having a clear allusion to Isaiah 5 at the beginning, Luke's version is much closer to Mark's than is Matthew's. In keeping with Luke's understanding that the return of Jesus is not near at hand, he has the absentee landlord gone "for a long time." Where Matthew has the listeners pronounce judgment on the tenants, Luke has them recoil from the judgment pronounced by Jesus: "Heaven forbid!" (Luke 20:16).

The authenticity of the parable as it stands is extremely doubtful[65]: (1) The behavior of the characters is not true to life. (2) Jesus is represented as knowing of his death in advance. (3) Jesus knows of the destruction of Jerusalem in advance. (4) The open messianic claim implied in the parable seems improbable, as does (5) the exclusion of the Jews and the mission to the Gentiles who replace them. The parable, especially with the citation of Psalm 118, presupposes the resurrection; within the parable itself the son's death is avenged but not reversed. If an authentic parable stands behind the allegory, it would probably be closer to the shorter (and more realistic) version found in the *Gospel of Thomas*.

---

64. Scott, *Hear Then the Parable*, 242.
65. See D. E. Nineham, *The Gospel of St. Mark* (Baltimore: Penguin Books, 1963), 309.

While many scholars have doubted that one can reconstruct an original parable behind the allegory, Scott provides a credible reconstruction. In many ways closer to the version in the *Gospel of Thomas* than to that in the Synoptics, Scott's reconstruction contains the following elements: planting a vineyard, letting it out, departure, sending two servants and then a son, killing the son to gain the inheritance.[66] In the context of Jesus' telling, it would occur to no one that the son in the story was Jesus, but in light of the tradition of his death and resurrection, the original parable has been transformed into an allegory about God's dealings with Israel (especially with its leaders) up to and including God's sending of the Messiah Jesus, whose death and resurrection provide the salvation event.

The meaning of the reconstructed original is difficult to determine. Scott says, "The parable frustrates not only allegory but also any effort to make sense of it!"[67] It is not clear whose side the reader is to be on. If one omits the *Gospel of Thomas*'s identification of the owner as a "good" man, it is not entirely clear that the hearers' sympathy would be with the owner. Is this a case of successful murder, resulting from a justifiable revolt against an illegitimate owner? If the man planted the vineyard (and not merely owned it), it might seem the tenants are in the wrong, but if, instead of "planting," the man "owned" the vineyard, as in *Thomas*,[68] the owner has no more legitimate claim than many who possessed land in Roman Palestine. In that case, the actions of the attendants would receive the approval of Jesus' hearers. Then the story would unfold in a realistic manner, as Crossan thinks the *Thomas* version does, for numerous peasants were inclined to rebel against absentee landlords.[69] *Thomas*'s version is without the punishment theme; it is thus a story of successful murder by those who took necessary action to gain possession of the vineyard. Jesus may be referring to a situation (possible or real) in his own time.[70]

My interpretation is similar to Segundo's. He thinks the Synoptics correctly attribute to the "leaders" the perception that Jesus told the parable

---

66. Scott, *Hear Then the Parable*, 248–51.

67. Scott, *Hear Then the Parable*, 252.

68. Scott, *Hear Then the Parable*, prefers "planted," for that would explain the way the parable comes to reflect Isaiah 5 (246–47).

69. John Dominic Crossan, *In Parables: The Challenge of the Historical Jesus* (New York: Harper & Row, 1973), 94.

70. As Crossan suggests in *In Parables*, 94.

against them.[71] It was, but not as an allegory condemning them for their treatment of him. Jesus told it against the system of absentee landlords that prevailed under Roman rule.

Does this mean that Jesus advocated violent rebellion, or even murder, against those who maintained the system of land tenure that betrayed covenant norms? Not necessarily. The actions of the tenants led to a kind of justice denied by the system, and in that sense the sympathy may have been with the tenants, who have some justification for their action. Could the tenants have prevailed, and did their attempt at takeover have any legal basis? The answer to both questions is probably no. Such actions would be born out of frustration more than out of real hope or legality, but they show the extremes to which frustrated justice can drive a person in desperate times. The parable then would have been told not to arouse the kind of rebellion represented in it but to show a logical outcome of the system in place.

Thomas 66 alludes to Psalm 118:22, which the early church frequently applied to Jesus: "The stone that the builders rejected has become the chief cornerstone."[72] The Synoptics actually quote the psalm here and point to the resurrected Jesus as the "stone" on which God builds a new foundation. The christological implication is clearer in the Synoptic versions than in *Thomas*, who comes closer to understanding the psalm on its own terms. The psalmist gives thanks to God for God's goodness, expressed to the psalmist when he had been surrounded by "all nations" (Gentiles) and that enabled the psalmist to overcome threatening enemies (Ps. 118:10–11). God has delivered the psalmist, who anticipates entering "gates of righteousness" (justice) and giving thanks to God (118:19). By leaving this meaning intact, *Thomas's* allusion suggests the possibility that the parable originally concerned a return to the covenant justice Jesus advocated, standards that had lapsed in the emulation of Hellenistic ways. The reference to Psalm 118 took on a different meaning after its use in Christian tradition to speak of Jesus' rejection by Israel and his acceptance by God. After the identification of Jesus with the rejected stone, any references or allusions to the psalm would have lost their social meaning in preference for the christological one.

---

71. Segundo, *Historical Jesus of the Synoptics,* 127: "Dismantling the mechanism of oppression they use, [Jesus] accuses them of nothing less than wanting to *take possession* of Israel for their own advantage."

72. For example, in addition to the use in this parable, see Acts 4:11; 1 Peter 2:7; and Eph. 2:20.

The strongest argument against my interpretation may derive from the fact that Isaiah 5 so identifies the metaphor of vineyard with Israel (and thus the owner with God) that that meaning would be automatic and transparent.[73] Horsley sees the vineyard as a standing metaphor for "land and/or inheritance of Israel" and asserts that the hearers would understand the wicked tenants who are to be destroyed as the priestly aristocracy.[74] The prophets offer precedent for this interpretation. According to Isaiah 3:14,

> The LORD enters into judgment
>   with the elders and princes of his people:
> It is you who have devoured the vineyard,
>   the spoil of the poor is in your houses.

Amos differs from Isaiah in that he does not name the rich, but he asserts a similar condemnation, which he directs at the rich:

> Therefore because you trample on the poor
>   and take from them levies of grain,
> you have built houses of hewn stone,
>   but you shall not live in them;
> you have planted pleasant vineyards,
>   but you shall not drink their wine.
>   (Amos 5:11)

Amos does not say the "pleasant vineyards" will be taken away from the rich, nor that they got them dishonestly, but such are the implications of Amos's general message.

While that thought is consistent with my interpretation of Jesus, I think this parable addresses the issue from another angle. Vineyard provides a symbol of hope in several passages, and the picture that expresses that hope consists of the people planting vineyards and enjoying their fruit:

> They shall build houses and inhabit them;
>   they shall plant vineyards and eat their fruit.
>   (Isa. 65:21)

---

73. Scott, *Hear Then the Parable,* 251, suggests that the metaphor is not as transparent as is often thought.

74. Horsley, *Jesus and the Spiral of Violence,* 305–6.

Again you shall plant vineyards
  on the mountains of Samaria;
the planters shall plant,
  and shall enjoy the fruit.

(Jer. 31:5)

For thus says the LORD of hosts, the God of Israel: Houses and fields and vineyards shall again be bought in this land (Jer. 32:15).

They shall live in safety in it, and shall build houses and plant vineyards. They shall live in safety, when I execute judgments upon all their neighbors who have treated them with contempt. And they shall know that I am the LORD their God (Ezek. 28:26).

I will restore the fortunes of my people Israel,
  and they shall rebuild the ruined cities and inhabit them;
they shall plant vineyards and drink their wine,
  and they shall make gardens and eat their fruit.

(Amos 9:14)

But they shall all sit under their own vine and under their own fig trees,
  and no one shall make them afraid;
for the mouth of the LORD of hosts has spoken.

(Micah 4:4)

For there shall be a sowing of peace; the vine shall yield its fruit, the ground shall give its increase, and the skies shall give their dew; and I will cause the remnant of this people to possess all these things (Zech. 8:12).

Thomas 65 does not support the identification usually made between the parable and Isaiah 5. It lacks the parts of the narrative that explicitly make the connection with Isaiah (that is, Mark 12:1). The connection would more likely have been made after the absentee landlord has been identified with Christ. In Isaiah, the owner of the vineyard is not absent but is present in the tower, watching in frustration as the vineyard yields wild grapes in spite of his care and attention.

The image of absentee landowner is used in a positive way in the early Christian tradition, but only in the parables. In Jesus' time, that image would have been a negative one. Jesus' "departure" and expected return came to be associated with the image, which consequently became positive. Since Jesus himself did not speak of his departure and return, the absentee landlord image in his parables has not yet become a positive one. If the image is negative, then the tenants rather than the absentee landlord would have gained the sympathy of Jesus' hearers.

Parable of the Unforgiving Servant: Matthew 18:23–35

This parable receives a mark of probable authenticity from Crossan, even though it has a single attestation.[75] There seems to me no insuperable difficulty in accepting its essential authenticity if one removes three elements: (1) Matthew's introduction connecting the parable with the question of frequency of forgiveness; (2) the conclusion expressing Matthew's aversion to cheap grace; and (3) Matthew's identification of the king with God. The original parable deals with a severe economic problem in Roman Palestine: debt. Matthew takes indebtedness as a symbol of sin, though it can also simply be indebtedness. The parable reflects a hierarchical social structure, with a king, an important servant, a lesser servant, and other servants. Matthew often transforms masters or high-ranking persons into kings (see, for example, the parable of the banquet, Matt. 22:1–10 in comparison with Luke 14:16–24). As in rabbinic parables,[76] the king represents God for Matthew; for him the whole parable is about God's forgiveness and the necessity of allowing that forgiveness to make one forgiving. Matthew makes that point unmistakably clear with his moral in verse 35: God will not finally forgive "if you do not forgive your brother or sister from your heart."

The parable as Matthew has it conveys a disturbingly inconsistent message. God's forgiveness is unmerited and beyond calculation. The size of the first servant's debt, which equals Herod's annual income, far exceeds his ability to pay unless he is a major tax contractor. By comparison, the second debt is comparatively small, representing the equivalent of one hundred days' wages for a laborer. Although difficult for a person with lesser responsibilities than the first servant had, it could be repaid. The comparison intends to make the point that God forgives regardless of the enormity of the debt, while it should be relatively easy for humans to forgive each other. But in the end, the king (God) retracts the forgiveness because subsequent behavior proves forgiveness to be undeserved. The parable as Matthew uses it thus makes a

75. Crossan, *Historical Jesus,* 448.
76. Scott, *Hear Then the Parable,* 207.

typically Matthean point: God extends grace (and forgiveness) freely, but that grace must transform the recipient; if it does not, God's judgment still impends and threatens destruction of grace's intended recipient.

Since Matthew's theology is so evident in the parable, one should look for clues to earlier meanings. If we change the king-servant relationship into its more likely original master-servant, and if we separate the positive view of that relationship derived from the expected "return of the master" when all will be resolved, we are in a Gentile world of patron-client relationships. Relationships of that system, like those of absentee landlord–tenants, were contradictory to norms of covenant life. Jesus' teachings explicitly reject hierarchical social structures (see Mark 10:42–44).

Jesus' audience would recognize Gentile ways in the servant's falling down and worshiping as he begs the master for mercy. "Groveling before a master, 'worshiping him,' is something no Jew would ever do."[77] While the Torah allowed for selling oneself into slavery for indebtedness (with a six-year limit), the first servant's treatment of a fellow servant would outrage the hearer. The unexpected kindness of the king, matched by the unexpected harshness of the first servant, confuses the hearer. Especially if one assumes that the king/master is a Gentile, and the servants are Jews, the outrage is even greater: Gentiles show more mercy toward Jews than Jews toward each other. The shock to the hearer would increase with the king's retracting of forgiveness. Now one can find nothing to rely on. The whim of the king provides forgiveness, and the whim of the king takes it away; everything is random, with no reliable standards for social relationships.[78] The standards of covenant community, in which love of neighbor can provide equity and hope, have vanished.

The fellow servants appeal to the king because those standards have been violated. They report the behavior to the king, prompting a punishment as harsh as the king's earlier action had been merciful. That action comes because fellow servants demand it. They belong to the Jewish world, but they observe a system alien to covenant norms. Instead of the servant's being sold for six years (appropriate if he is Jewish, according to Ex. 21:2 and Deut. 15:12–18), he is jailed until he pays the now impossible debt.

Gentile ways, then, not only bring repression of covenant standards; they

---

77. Scott, *Hear Then the Parable*, 275.
78. Scott, *Hear Then the Parable*, 278, makes a similar point.

draw the Jews into the alien world, so that they themselves act contrary to their own best norms.

The Parable of the Dishonest Steward: Luke 16:1–8

Luke does not provide a clearly defined narrative or thematic context for this parable. Following the parable of the prodigal, it reflects that parable's theme of wasteful spending (Luke 16:1). The sayings following the parable concern right use of possessions (Luke 16:9–15), signaling the way Luke understood it.

A surface reading will understand the parable to provide a negative example, as a way to encourage the personal quality of responsibility as opposed to narrow self-interested use of what one has received. The steward shows no sense of responsibility for managing the estate for the benefit of his employer. Nor does he show any remorse for that mismanagement; he concerns himself only about his own future. Talking like a victim,[79] he puts the responsibility on the rich man: "My master is taking the position away from me" (v. 3). The steward, recognizing himself as too weak to dig and too proud to beg, looks for a way to turn the situation to his own advantage. He astutely attempts to create an indebtedness to him so that his master's debtors will accept him later and provide for him. He is a parasite. He wants to live off of others and not work for himself.

When regarded as a mirror of social-economic relations, the parable makes a different impact. Its perspective is that of the lower classes, and it takes a poke at the upper classes. "In the world of Galilean peasants, rich masters play the expected role of despots, and the master in this story may be an absentee landlord, a common phenomenon in Galilee."[80] The steward manages the estate of such a person, with full power to conduct his business, including "the renting of plots of ground to tenant-farmers, the making of loans against a harvest, the liquidation of debts, the keeping of accounts of all such transactions."[81] The notes he holds, which he changes in order to make friends for himself, correspond to the loans made against future crops. The amounts would be stated in terms of so much produce. Stating debts in terms

---

79. Breech, *Silence of Jesus,* 106.
80. Scott, *Hear Then the Parable,* 260.
81. Fitzmyer, *Luke,* 1097.

of oil and wheat provided a way of hiding interest on loans.[82] Since the debts were calculated in terms of the future crop, the loans would bypass laws against usury.[83] The amounts owed were substantial, suggesting either that the debtors were not peasants,[84] or that the debts had accumulated over considerable time.

In this parable, the rich landlord has not been transformed into a metaphor for God. Neither in the beginning nor in the ending of the story does this one act like God. The values of the landlord and his treatment of the steward are opposed to values of the kingdom. From the standpoint of peasant hearers, the master and his servant deserve each other; if the peasants derive some benefit from the antagonistic relation that develops between lord and servant, that may be the only benefit the peasants derive from the system the lord and servant both cooperate to maintain.

Were the debtors also guilty of "injustice"? Derrett cites rabbinic evidence that since taking interest was against Torah, one could avoid paying it without violating conscience.[85] However, one does not need to guard the honor of the rogue. No doubt his personal qualities are despicable, but that is not the whole story. He is a functionary in a system that creates persons of his character because it invites abuse. The parable thus demonstrates systemic as well as personal failure. Given the circumstances, self-interest too easily takes precedence over all other considerations. Concern for community and loyalty to the norms that make community possible have eroded to such an extent that only self-preservation matters. No doubt the steward is a conniving man, but is he any more a "parasite" than the remote owner for whom he works? He at least knows that he must reestablish relations within the only possible community for him.

---

82. J. Duncan M. Derrett, "Fresh Light on Luke XVI," *New Testament Studies* 7 (1960–61): 208–9: "Our steward, then, lending at interest to Jews, was morally a transgressor, but legally secure, so long as his contracts hid the fact that the loan was usurious."

83. Fitzmyer, *Luke*, 1097–98, documents such practices.

84. Jeremias, *Parables of Jesus*, 181, thinks the debtors were merchants or substantial tenants. He calculates that some 800 gallons of olive oil would require more than 140 olive trees, and 100 *kors* of wheat would be the yield of some 100 acres. Fitzmyer, *Luke*, 1100–1101, makes a similar calculation of amount but does not attempt to calculate the amount of property needed to produce it. Derrett, "Fresh Light on Luke XVI," 213, suggests that the amount of wheat is more than 1,000 bushels. A *kor* is equal to 10–12 bushels, according to Bauer-Arndt-Gingrich.

85. Derrett, "Fresh Light on Luke XVI," 208.

In this sense, the steward is a picaresque hero.[86] However, the master's final commendation may represent his taking back into service one who proves he has the capacity to be so cunning. If so, the debtors would be left without the economic services of the one who had temporarily planned to come over to their side. They gained a temporary relief but no long-term advantage, for the steward's intention was no conversion; as soon as his perceived self-interest changed, so would his actions and "allegiance."

At most the peasant hearers could only partially see the steward as one of themselves. Since he was too lazy to work and too proud to beg, he could not really participate in their life. Such hearers would immediately be warned not to expect too much from such a person, even if his crisis has momentarily pushed him toward their camp. He proves by his actions that he still belongs to the world of the master, not to that of the peasants who might have had some benefit from his "unjust" behavior.

Would a peasant audience have understood his behavior to be unjust? Scott thinks so:

> The comedy has a barbed end: the action was unjust. The story ends by leaving the hearer in an uncomfortable position. The hearer has supported immorality by sanctioning the rogue's deceiving the master. . . . The hearer has witnessed and condoned injustice.[87]

That seems a doubtful conclusion. One can imagine Jesus' hearers laughing at the suggestion that the master is capable of defining justice. Only those who thought the exploitive system of client-patron was just would agree with the notion that they have been tricked in the narrative into making a moral error of endorsing injustice. The master's claim to be a victim could easily provoke the hearer to reflect on the issue of justice, but the hearer would hardly sympathize with the master's facetious claim. Or, the hearer might even think the steward had finally acted justly by canceling the usury built into the loan.[88] Derrett distinguishes between the "law of man" and the "law of God" in this regard. According to the one, the man acted unjustly, depriving the master of something owed to him (assuming the master would have part of the interest added to the loan). According to the other, the man acted justly, restoring what

---

86. Dan Otto Via, Jr., *The Parables: Their Literary and Existential Dimension* (Philadelphia: Fortress Press, 1967), 158–60.
87. Scott, *Hear Then the Parable*, 264, 265.
88. Derrett, "Fresh Light on Luke XVI," 209.

contractually had been unjustly taken away from the debtor.[89] In this instance, the steward can do both what is right and what is popular.[90] The question remains whether he will return to his master's service, or whether he will continue with the new friends he has made by relinquishing "unrighteous mammon."

Parable of the Talents: Matthew 25:14–30; Parable of the Pounds: Luke 19:11–27

Luke and Matthew provide different contexts, both of which maintain a focus on the end time, which they probably received from Q.[91] Matthew includes this parable along with others relating to the return of Christ (Matt. 24). By adding "enter into the joy of your master" (v. 23), as well as by placing the parable within a group emphasizing Christ's return, Matthew shows his interest in the benefits of that return. Luke places the parable following the Zacchaeus incident, with its proclamation, "Today salvation has come to this house" (Luke 19:9). Luke suggests that Jesus' hearers thought his statement (along with their being near Jerusalem) implied that "the kingdom of God was to appear immediately" (Luke 19:11). The parable then responds by speaking of a nobleman who went to a "distant country," hinting that the end is some time off. Both Luke and Matthew, then, understand the parable to refer to the departure and return of Christ. For both Matthew and Luke, faithful service until the return of Christ is the main teaching of the parable. Failure to perform faithful service to the absent master will result in loss of opportunity, even loss of place within the master's service (in Matthew, hell may be the punishment; see 25:30).

If Luke's version comes from Q, Luke's changes[92] occur primarily in verses 12, 14, 15, 27, where the man is a nobleman who goes away to get royal power. Curiously the image of departure is both positive and negative. The negativity centers on the conflict between the nobleman and the citizens who hate him and who send an embassy to thwart his goal (reminiscent of the accession of Archelaus to rule in Judea in 4 B.C.E.). The positive element derives from the

---

89. Derrett, "Fresh Light on Luke XVI," 210.
90. Derrett, "Fresh Light on Luke XVI," 217–18.
91. For a summary of positions regarding the Q origin of both versions, see Kloppenborg, *Q Parallels*, 200.
92. For a discussion of what the Q parable might have been and what Luke's and Matthew's additions might have been, see Fitzmyer, *Luke*, 1230–31.

(secondary) identification with Jesus and the promise that, though he is going to Jerusalem where death awaits, he will also be "taken up" (9:51) and given a kingdom. Luke makes the eschatological return of Christ evident by placing the parable in the context of disputing those who think the kingdom is to appear immediately (19:11). The parable confirms Luke's general view that though Jesus will return, it will be in the indeterminable future, allowing time for the church's faithful service. Luke's insertion of the allusion to Archelaus deflects the eschatological theme but does not erase it.

The evangelists' interests are secondary, reflecting the situation of communities at some remove from Jesus' own circumstance. Other likely secondary elements include Matthew 25:29 (Luke 19:26), which, while it fits the story thematically, was a floating saying found in several places (Mark 4:25; Matt. 13:12; Luke 8:18; *Gospel of Thomas* 41). The fact that Luke and Matthew both have it here can indicate that they found the saying in Q, but even so it is likely secondary.

The ending, except for the final verse in each Gospel, must come from Q. It was part of Q's eschatological preaching, emphasizing the necessity of the faithful use of what one has received in trust. Both Matthew and Luke have the master order others to take away from the unadventurous person and to give to the most adventurous. Both have the saying about taking away from the one who has nothing. Then they diverge: Luke emphasizes the punishment of those who opposed the king-to-be. Matthew emphasizes a favorite theme of "outer darkness." The differences between numbers of servants and amounts of money in Matthew and Luke make little or no difference to the interpretation.

The meaning of the parable should be sought internally and not derived from the additions or from the settings Matthew and Luke (or Q) provide. Internal evidence strongly suggests that the parable did not originally point to the relation of God or Christ to the believers. Interpreters often present the master in a positive light. He generously entrusts his property to the servants, makes no inordinate demands upon them in advance, and generously rewards those who have been successful. None of those actions raises any problems for casual readers in a Western, Christian, capitalist society.

A more careful reading reveals disturbing elements in the parable. We see in the parable the same system as in the parable of the laborers in the vineyard: large estates with many servants and an absentee landholder. The absent master is called a "hard" or "severe" man, a description no one contradicts. The description fits the master's treatment of the "wicked servant." How Luke and Matthew could let that characterization stand when they saw Christ as the master is puzzling. Perhaps they thought the description needed no contradiction since it was only the absurd and unwarranted fear of the "wicked servant." But they would hardly have added such a characterization to the story; thus it was found in the prechristological structure of the parable. This fact reveals that in reinterpreting them the evangelists do not always reshape parables so completely that their more original form is erased. The original form in this case clashes with their interpretation.

Other indications suggest that the image of the master was negative in the original structure of the parable. The economic system generates opportunity for those who are willing to abandon covenant values and for whom capital is for private use, even if that use contravenes the Torah. The actions that the master commends could create tensions or conflicts for Torah-abiding Jews. First, the recommendation to gain interest through moneylenders suggests a tension with, if not contradiction to, laws against lending at interest to a fellow Israelite.[93] Although Psalm 15:5 says a wicked but not a just person receives interest on loans, standards might have changed to such an extent that usury had become customary and acceptable, as Luke 19:23 may assume. It is possible that these laws, like Jubilee laws, were ideal but never actual. But it is also possible that the parable directly calls attention to the master's casual commendation of actions contradicting Torah, in which case he is indeed a "hard man."

Second, the command in Luke that the servants should trade with the money, as well as Matthew's matter-of-fact statement that the first two "traded with them," raises questions. Trade in postexilic Palestine remained largely in the hands of foreigners,[94] and thus traders would likely be at least marginally suspect. Trading would inevitably involve the sort of engagement with the Gentile world that compromises the standards of the Torah; many hearers would immediately know that the departing master's command is at best suspect.[95] Further, the expansion of trade in Hellenistic and Roman

---

93. According to the Torah (Deut. 23:19–20), "You shall not charge interest on loans to another Israelite, interest on money, interest on provisions, interest on anything that is lent. On loans to a foreigner you may charge interest . . . so that the LORD your God may bless you in all your undertakings in the land." Cf. Ex. 22:25: "If you lend money to my people, to the poor among you, you shall not deal with them as a creditor; you shall not exact interest from them." (Cf. also Lev. 25:35–38.)

94. G. A. Barrois, "Trade and Commerce," *Interpreter's Dictionary of the Bible*, 4:681.

95. David Flusser, "The Social Message from Qumran," *Jewish Society Through the Ages*, ed. H. H. Ben-Sasson and S. Ettinger (New York: Schocken Books, 1969), 108.

times (as in Solomon's time—see 1 Kings 10:15) tended to involve luxury goods, slaves, fine wines, all beyond the reach of ordinary people and thus revealing the class divisions of Roman Palestine.

Possibly for these sorts of reasons, the Essenes taught that trading with those outside the community defiles the faithful.[96] The Essenes' attitude has precedent in Hebrew scripture. Zechariah says that in the final days no trader will be found in the house of the Lord (14:21), presumably because trading would defile and thus a trader would defile the Temple. Ben Sira reflects a similar sentiment: "A merchant can hardly keep from wrongdoing, nor is a tradesman innocent of sin" (Sirach 26:29; compare James 4:13). Economic developments had possibly so eroded these standards that many might not have noticed the problem. Examples from the Essenes and James show, however, that the standards had not disappeared. The Essenes, John the Baptist, and Jesus all reveal a concern for sharing wealth. The Essenes and the early church (at least in Luke's description of it) held property in common. John the Baptist called for sharing with the poor, as did Jesus, with no evidence that either advocated full community of goods.

The astute hearer of this parable would not miss in it a criticism of the attitudes of the master. Both Jesus and his audience would be suspicious of the master's command, the attitudes it reflects, and the first two servants' responses.

Jesus did not decry such attitudes because he advocated poverty as an ideal for his followers.[97] As I have argued in chapter 4 above, Jesus did not find poverty a good thing in itself, but he advocated renunciation of private acquisitiveness in favor of social justice. The early church at least for a time

---

96. Flusser, "The Social Message from Qumran," 107–15, points to the Essenes as a source of teaching that trading, etc., with those outside the community is a defilement. Restrictions on trading with those outside the community are found in Qumran scrolls as part of the maintenance of purity from outside influence. The Community Rule V: "No member of the Community shall . . . take anything from them [the men of falsehood] except for a price." The Damascus Rule XII prohibits the sale of certain items to Gentiles—clean birds or beasts, grain, and wine; it also requires informing the Guardian of the camp of the formation of any association for trade. If Josephus is correct (*Jewish Antiquities* XVIII.19) that the Essenes were devoted entirely to agriculture, the prohibited products would seem to leave little for them to trade with. Josephus says the Essenes did not buy or sell among themselves but freely gave to one another (*Jewish War* II.127). Thus, while trade was not forbidden, it was strictly limited.
97. Flusser, "The Social Message from Qumran," 109, concludes too quickly that Jesus did not share the attitudes of the Essenes but instead advocated absolute poverty for his followers. See chapter 4 above.

continued to maintain property values derived from Jesus, influenced by Qumran and John the Baptist.

These considerations lead one to question the morality of the absent master, who expresses concern about only one thing: return on his investment. He leaves entirely to his servants the decision about how best to control those resources for maximum return. In both Luke and Matthew, he says the third servant should have invested with the bankers (or moneylenders). There is no expression of concern for the effects of the investments: (1) To whom would bankers lend? (2) At what interest rate? (3) With what consequences to the impoverished who temporarily needed help?

Granted that one parable does not contain all Jesus' teaching, surely he would not expect his audience to ignore the callousness of the master. It is more likely that the master's taken-for-granted attitudes relate to the primary point the parable seeks to make. The recognized greed and severity of the master do not support the notion that the departed master represents Jesus. He does not portray himself as such to the disciples, nor do the Gospel writers generally give him such traits. Nor could the absent master symbolize God. More likely, the human master is a negative example, mirroring the situation that diminishes people's lives in Jesus' time, a symbol of the rapacity and lack of conscience that dominate the wealthy aristocracy who cooperate with the ruling overlords. Like the theme of absentee landlords in general, what was originally a negative image has through the association of Jesus with the absent master been transformed into a positive image. The absentee landlord in the Palestinian context can hardly have been a positive figure.

Why is the returning master not condemned in the parable for his acquisitiveness? Is it because he has now been equated with an absent Jesus due to the shift from a social-economic to an eschatological context? Could Jesus have been so positive about him in comparison with the rich young man or the farmer with abundant crops? Why is this master's self not "required" this night? Looked at from the perspective of concern for social justice, this parable can hardly make a single point about responsible stewardship. When the stewardship allegedly called for conflicts both with Torah norms and Jesus' attitudes toward property, it would be as trivial as it is misleading to see responsible stewardship as the theme of the parable.

Fearful of wrath, ignorant of mercy, the distrustful servant does nothing. He knows the present time is dangerous, due to the character of those who control. But he finds that danger lies in inaction as well as in action.

Concerned for preservation of the treasure, he loses it, and is thus finally judged irresponsible. "Something other than preservation was called for."[98]

The fate of the one-talent man mirrors the harshness of the system to those who do not fully participate in it according to its rules. The hearers would have had some sympathy for him, not because he acted wisely or morally, but because he is trapped between two systems, one deriving from past covenant traditions and the other deriving from present economic realities.[99] If they so perceive him, Jesus' hearers might think the servant acts as he does because he fears to go against God's commands, though this motive is not attributed to him in the narrative. In Luke those who hear the king's command object to taking the pound from the third man and giving it to the first. Although this objection is not original, it suggests that Luke understands why the hearers agree with the depiction of the master as cruel and sympathize with the third man.

Parable of the Banquet: Luke 14:16–24; *Gospel of Thomas* 64; Parable of the Wedding Feast: Matthew 22:1–14

Matthew and Luke include such different versions of this parable that some have questioned whether they both draw from Q.[100] *Thomas* is closer to Luke, but all three have the same basic plot and considerable verbal agreement. Luke and *Thomas* are more true to life than Matthew, conforming more to standards of banquet etiquette in Jesus' time.[101] Luke puts the parable in the context of other sayings and stories about hospitality at meals; it especially illustrates Luke's verse, "When you give a banquet, invite the poor, the crippled, the lame, and the blind" (Luke 14:13). Nevertheless, Luke's version ends with the note that the banquet (=kingdom) finally is for those who are among the poor and distressed, and that the privileged and well-to-do exclude themselves. *Thomas* expands the groups who reject the invitation, including one who can't attend because he has scheduled dealings

---

98. Borg, *Conflict, Holiness, and Politics in the Teaching of Jesus,* 118.

99. Judging that Matthew's version (burying) is more original than Luke's (hiding in a napkin), Scott, *Hear Then the Parable,* 224, suggests that the original created sympathy for the third man, for burying was a responsible act. In neither version is that sympathy maintained fully because of the changes Matthew and Luke make. I suggest that the sympathy was for a different reason.

100. See Kloppenborg, *Q Parallels,* 166.

101. See the treatment especially in Bailey, *Through Peasant Eyes,* 94–95, for a description of those true-to-life details.

with merchants, and it ends with the servants being sent into the street, bringing whomever they find but also being warned that "buyers and merchants will not enter the places of my Father."

Matthew changes the person who gave the banquet into a king who gives a wedding feast for his son. He also transforms the theme of rejection into that of hostility and violence, as those rejecting the invitation murder those who deliver the invitation and are in turn destroyed by the angry king's troops. Matthew has obviously allegorized a simpler parable, retelling it so as to reflect the history of God's dealings with Israel. For Matthew, the king is God, the son's marriage feast is equivalent to a messianic banquet, those bearing the invitation are God's messengers (prophets, John the Baptist, Jesus, and the early Christian missionaries), the destruction of the city is the destruction of Jerusalem. Those unworthy of the invitation are the Jewish leaders or possibly the Jewish people as a whole or the elites among them. Those who are finally accepted are members of the church, possibly both Jews and Gentiles. Matthew places the parable in the context of other parables dealing with Christ's return, further indicating that God's judgment of Israel is his major point. Matthew's addition of the man without proper wedding attire (Matt. 22:11–14) underscores the theme of judgment.

All three versions thus reflect the interests of the Gospel writers, but as Breech has shown, a simpler, authentic parable lies behind them: A man gave a dinner, invited guests in the customary fashion, but they did not come, offering weak excuses for their nonattendance. The man then sent his servant to invite anyone he met on the street.[102]

Even though each of the three versions has allegorized the theme according to its own perspective, eating and drinking were standard symbols for the kingdom of God. This parable builds upon the tradition of a banquet of the Lord, who prepares a table even in the presence of enemies (Ps. 23:5). In Isaiah 25:6–9, "all peoples" and "all nations" will be present at the table of the Lord, and death will be overcome forever. Intertestamental writings developed the banquet theme and related it to the coming messiah, often without Isaiah's inclusion of the nations (=Gentiles).

The Messianic Rule of the Qumran community prescribed the procedures for each meal at which at least ten men were present, ordering those meals in anticipation of the messianic banquet: "All the wise . . . , the learned and the intelligent men . . . [will gather]. And then [the Mess]iah of Israel shall

---

102. Breech, *Silence of Jesus*, 114–23.

[come], and the chiefs of the [clans of Israel] shall sit before him, [each] in the order of his dignity, according to [his place] in their camps and marches."[103] Excluded from participation is anyone who is "smitten with any human uncleanness . . . or paralysed . . . or lame, or blind, or deaf, or dumb, or smitten in his flesh with a visible blemish."[104]

Gathering for meals, eating and drinking together, and table etiquette (hospitality) are frequent, interrelated themes in the Gospels, especially in Luke. Jesus' final meal with his disciples draws upon standard imagery of a messianic banquet. Just as Jesus' eating and drinking were the subject of controversy, the original version of this parable may make the simple point that surprising groups of people will participate in the coming messianic banquet. Those deemed "worthy" prove not to be so. The parable in Jesus' context could express disappointment over the poor reception of his message, as well as his expectation that the common folks encountered in the streets rather than the elites will know the joy of the kingdom.

Other elements in the parable suggest problems within the upper classes. The elite context of the banquet is evident in the double invitation,[105] the presence of servants, and the signs of economic well-being. In Matthew, one went off to his farm, presumably from his residence which was elsewhere, while another went to his business. In Luke, in two cases the invitees have made purchases beyond the means of a peasant. In *Thomas,* at least three excuses indicate wealth, while the fourth (giving a dinner for a friend getting married) probably does also. The rude and inconsiderate responses of the well-to-do toward their would-be host may purposefully insinuate the pettiness of the ruling class. Unable to maintain a genuine community among themselves, the elite compel the poor to provide what they cannot provide for themselves, not out of a sense of community but out of a sense of aloneness. The well-off host has guests only when he turns to the common people or, especially in Luke's account, precisely those excluded from the Qumran meals: the poor, the lame, and the blind.

Matthew brings the narrative to a closure. The banquet takes place, the

---

103. The Messianic Rule, II, tr. G. Vermes, *The Dead Sea Scrolls in English* (Baltimore: Penguin Books, 1965), 120, 121.

104. The Messianic Rule, II, in Vermes, *The Dead Sea Scrolls,* 120.

105. Jeremias, *Parables of Jesus,* 176: "The repetition of the invitation at the time of the banquet is a special courtesy, practised by upper circles in Jerusalem." The double invitation is implied but not stated in *Thomas.*

king inspects the guests, and he ousts the one who is improperly attired. By this means Matthew makes one of his persistent points: The good and the bad are alike invited into the kingdom (the church), but repentance and "bearing fruit" are required before salvation is assured. Luke's version leaves the story moderately open-ended,[106] implying the inclusion of the poor and Gentiles but not narrating the closure. The originating structure probably ended with the host sending servants out to the streets to bring in the poor.[107] In both Luke's version and in the originating structure, hearers do not fully know the outcome. The hearer completes the story by responding to the implied question: Will you come to the banquet or not?

In keeping with the general pattern of transference, the man in the parable has come to be associated with God, who invites people into the kingdom. The man thus provides a positive image with a slightly different cast in the three versions: In Matthew, as the one who graciously invites good and bad but who also judges harshly their response to that grace; in Luke, as the one who shows special kindness to the neglected; in *Thomas*, as the one who accepts all except merchants. In the originating structure, the man is not God, and the audience would have seen him in a less sympathetic light. They might think he got what he deserved from his wealthy neighbors. By inviting common people to dinner in his home to replace the absent elite, he has in fact not only been dishonored by the elite but also joined the common people. "The parable reverses and subverts the system of honor."[108] It provides social criticism, while it invites a recapturing of covenant community hospitality.

A Man Had Two Sons: Luke 15:11–32

Luke places this parable last in a group of three concerned with finding the lost and the consequent rejoicing. The usual title, "The Prodigal Son," suggests that the parable concerns the recovery of the younger son. Traditional interpretation does make that assumption and pays too little

---

106. Bailey, *Through Peasant Eyes*, 111.
107. Scott, *Hear Then the Parable*, 168.
108. Scott, *Hear Then the Parable*, 173–74. Is the host's invitation to the poor his one good deed, like the parable of Bar Maayan (see Scott, 172, and Jeremias, *Parables of Jesus*, 178–79). Unlike Bar Maayan, this man is anonymous, so that we don't know whether he was overreaching to invite respected people.

attention to the fact that the parable concerns a father with two alienated sons.[109]

Luke does see in the parable an evocative portrait of God's concern for the "lost." But Luke sees in it a social meaning as well: "Righteous" people ought to share God's concern for the lost. For Luke, as 15:1–2 indicates, Jesus primarily addressed the Pharisees; in Luke's view, they fail to understand God's love for the lost and thus turn away in hardness of heart from the "sinners" who do not conform to Pharisaic standards of purity. One need not deny that the relationship between humans and God is germane to the parable in order to look for other dimensions.

Paying closer attention to the social relationships contained in or presupposed by the parable leads to different questions and different answers. The family problems revealed here were commonplace in the Roman Palestine of Jesus' day. That fact alone does not establish the authenticity of the parable, but it provides a basis for regarding it as authentic. Seen in its social context, the parable concerns the father's attempts to reconcile two sons who have chosen very different ways of life.

The parable presents a complex of broken family relationships. The younger son is either sufficiently alienated from home or sufficiently attracted to a new way of life outside the family (we are not told the specific motivation) to break with tradition and ask for the right to dispose of his inheritance before the father's death. He reveals no concern for the future, totally neglecting the need for responsible stewardship of what is entrusted to him. Perhaps he correctly thinks his father has enough wealth to care for himself in his old age. But he neither keeps his inheritance to support his father in his old age nor manages it out of concern for his own future children. Instead, he cashes in his inheritance and then squanders it in a dissolute, hopeless life.[110] In effect he pronounces his father already dead and

---

109. Donahue's interpretation of the parable is typical of those who focus more on the human-divine than the human-human relationship: "The understanding of God as 'king' and 'father,' with its accompanying images of power and dominance, is challenged and transformed when one enters the world of this parable. The parable speaks of that change of heart (*metanoia*) which is necessary to respond to the presence of God. . . . It summons to a deep faith that one is loved as son or daughter and created as such, not according to conditions of acceptance which are dictated in advance, but because of the shocking, surprising, and outgoing love of God" (Donahue, *Gospel in Parable*, 158).

110. Breech, *Silence of Jesus*, 192, says he squandered it on "loose living" which is a Greek word referring to the way "gluttons, voluptuaries, or transvestites live. The original meaning is 'incurably ill.' "

the future nonexistent.[111] As a consequence of his choices, he lives like a Gentile, feeding swine, fulfilling the curse pronounced on the Jew who breeds or raises swine.[112] He thus exemplifies those Jews who have abandoned their inherited values and whose humanity has been lost in aping the Hellenistic world.[113] He seeks independence but finds oppressive dependency in an alien situation. Even without establishing independence from his father, he now develops a dependency on his new associates: He joins himself in a dependent relation to a citizen of the country to which he goes. There is no indication that finally the son "repented"—he "came to himself" and wished to return to his father only when he wanted something—when he was hungry. When he "comes to himself," he thinks of himself.[114]

Although the father is usually regarded as a perfect exemplar of fatherly love and forgiveness, his own behavior is not beyond censure. He allows his younger son to treat him as though dead, he gives away his property rights,[115] and he makes no effort to dissuade his younger son (in contrast to his later entreaty to his elder son). The father, in fact, exemplifies those qualities that are often seen in stories of parents who indulge younger sons and treat them as favorites at the expense of their older brothers. Nevertheless, he does yearn for reconciliation within the family and expresses a genuine love for both his sons. In his yearning love he offers the best hope for the renewal of the family; whether his hope is fulfilled, the story does not say.

The father must be a person of significant wealth, since he has enough

---

111. Scott, *Hear Then the Parable*, 108–13, provides documentation for this interpretation.

112. Breech, *Silence of Jesus*, 193–94, maintains one cannot assume that Jesus as narrator was deliberately placing the son in an occupation abhorred by Jews, swine herding, because there is no evidence that he told parables only to Jews. That seems an extremely weak argument. Even if there were non-Jews in the audience, both they and the Jewish hearers would know the distastefulness of the son's situation.

113. Ernest Wiesenberg, "Related Prohibitions: Swine Breeding and the Study of Greek," in *History of the Jews in the First Century of the Common Era*, vol. XI of *The Origins of Judaism* (New York: Garland Press, 1991), 580 (reprinted from *Hebrew Union College Annual* 27 [1956]: 213–33). Swine were especially abhorrent in the New Testament period, as the story of the Gadarene demoniac (Mark 5:1–20) shows. Wiesenberg cites Mishnah, *Baba Qamma* vii.7: "A Jew must not rear pigs anywhere." A further saying, "Cursed be the man who will rear pigs! and cursed be the man who will teach his son Greek!" comes from the Talmud and dates to the Hellenistic or Roman phase. But even though the saying may be post-70, the idea was not new.

114. Breech, *Silence of Jesus*, 196.

115. Breech, *Silence of Jesus*, 191. The father, however, through allowing himself to be treated as dead and giving away his property rights, does something unparalleled in the parabolic narratives that survive from antiquity. The man completely altered his relationship with his sons—they are no longer bound to him through property.

resources to make the division and still have adequate support for himself, his servants, and his elder son; to put symbols of wealth on the returning younger son; and to have at hand a fatted calf for a feast. There is no indication here that his wealth is ill-gotten, but he does belong to that group who have benefited from the changes brought by the Hellenistic environment in which the younger son wants to immerse himself. Do his laxity and sentimentalism derive from that influence? The father "ran" to him. It is considered extremely undignified for an Oriental man to run.[116] In not even hearing his son's weak repentance but immediately honoring him, does he betray too casual an attitude toward the social and religious bonds that stabilize Jewish families? The older son thinks so.

The elder son, though dutifully working and fulfilling commands, seems utterly joyless. Not willing to embrace the alien world to which his brother goes, but also not sufficiently convinced of the real worth of his own commitment to past traditions to enjoy them, he has lapsed into resentment and churlishness. His self-righteousness destroys family bonds just as surely as does the younger son's bad behavior.[117] He not only despises his brother (with good reason), but he also insults and dishonors his father: "The anger and refusal to participate on the part of the older son are profoundly deep public insults against the father."[118] Not only so, his address to his father is the first time in the narrative that no title of courtesy is used in direct discourse.[119] His father does not respond in kind, but addresses him with the tenderest term used in the parable, "Child."[120]

Unlike elder brothers who are cast off in other stories, unlike rejected Israel in Luke's theology, unlike Esau whose inheritance God laid waste (Mal. 1:2–3), the elder brother will inherit all the father has. But even that prospect does not enable him to live with joy; he sees only threat in his brother's presence.

The parable is thus about a family and its inheritance, and its struggles to deal with that heritage. Metaphorically it may be about God and God's relation to those who are God's children. But more likely it is about heritage—a heritage of values that are being eroded, lost sight of, neglected, even abandoned. And a heritage of values that are confused with self-

---

116. Breech, *Silence of Jesus*, 196.
117. Donahue, *Gospel in Parable*, 156.
118. Bailey, *Poet and Peasant: A Literary Cultural Approach to the Parables in Luke* (Grand Rapids: Wm. B. Eerdmans Publishing Co., 1976), 196.
119. Bailey, *Poet and Peasant*, 196.
120. Scott, *Hear Then the Parable*, 121; *teknon* is more affectionate than *pais*.

righteousness and lack of love. Nobody in the parable provides an adequate answer to the problem posed by the corrosive power of Hellenistic social and economic values. The father comes closest. At least he wants a reconciliation and adopts a mediating stance, but he himself has more sentiment than backbone.

Since inheritance is a standard metaphor for the land and people of Israel, the parable implies that in leaving his inheritance and departing to Gentile territory, the younger son has relinquished his claim on the kingdom. The elder son has saved his inheritance, leaving it intact for the future. But though he has not squandered it, neither has he enjoyed it. If the two sons represent different responses to the pressures of hellenization, neither provides a model for the future. Joylessly despising those who fraternize with the Gentiles presents no better hope for the future kingdom that God is at work establishing than does mindless aping of Gentile ways in abandonment of Israel's heritage. Whether the father finally provides an adequate and effective mediation between these extremes is not stated, for the plot remains incomplete. The father attempts to respond to each of the sons in the way most appropriate to their condition and attitude.[121] He acts to overcome the alienation that drove the younger son from his heritage, as well as the alienation that causes the elder son to look with contempt upon those who have been so enticed by the alien culture. The father seeks reconciliation and unity, and he inaugurates a feast of life.[122]

Usually it is assumed that the younger son has been fully restored, that his alienation has been overcome. But that is not so clearly stated. What he will be in the future when his immediate want is satisfied is not clear. Whether he reciprocated his father's lavish love remains unstated. And it is even less clear that the elder son's rigid and loveless obedience, and its concomitant resentment, will be overcome. The parable, then, concerns community reconciliation. The shadow side of the elder son's rigid obedience is resentment. The parable in its originating structure addressed such tensions within Jewish society.[123]

The parable shows the difficulty of reconciliation between two whose very

121. Perkins, *Hearing the Parables of Jesus*, 56.
122. Donahue, *Gospel in Parable*, 157.
123. Perkins, *Hearing the Parables of Jesus*, 60–62, thinks that reconciliation within the community of disciples is part of Luke's use of the parable. Luke uses the Pharisees not historically of those opposed to Jesus but metaphorically of those within the church whose resentment of others makes reconciliation impossible. While I agree with that perception of Luke's intent, a similar point was made by Jesus himself.

different actions are both destructive of family (=community). It involves the renewal of those lost to the Gentile world and the reconciliation of those "who have slaved." The parable suggests not only the problem of reclaiming those lost sons who have strayed into Hellenistic ways but also the problem that their return raises for those affected by their return. The elder son's attitude is similar to that of the resentful day laborers in the vineyard, who thought the vineyard owner discounted their day-long hard work. The father wants to lose neither of his sons but finds no solution other than pleading for acceptance and reconciliation based on the model of his own acceptance. The parable leaves the hearer wondering whether that acceptance can overcome the destructive power of the forces at work within the society of first-century Palestine. Can such a society come to know the things that make for peace?

Parables and Revolution

There are no surviving parables that are overtly anti-Roman or prorevolution. That fact has been taken as evidence that Jesus did not oppose Roman rule, that he taught of the kingdom in such a way that the authorities had no legitimate reason to be concerned about his activity or his message, and that if there was cause for concern, it was only due to Jesus' hearers misunderstanding and becoming excited. The fact could also be explained by the church's tendency to depoliticize, to attribute all the conflict that led to Jesus' death to the Jewish religious authorities.

In examining selected parables I have attempted to show that Jesus did in fact address social and economic issues in ways that challenged the status quo. But that message does not overtly call for political revolution. His social criticism did not necessarily demand an end to Roman rule, though it did demand revolutionary social change.

There are, however, a few parables that could originate in a more explicitly political context. Within the parable tradition there is plenty of material suggesting that Jesus did attack Jewish authorities who participated in and profited from Roman rule. Some of the material critical of Jewish religious authority is patently influenced by the continuing and growing hostility between church and synagogue, and must be discounted accordingly. But there are some parables that go beyond that conflict and raise intriguing questions. Especially because of the way the parables have been shaped by the communities that preserved them, the Gospel writers did not record them with political themes in mind.

One such parable[124] concerns a king preparing to go to war (Luke 14:31–32; compare *Gospel of Thomas* 98).[125] Luke places this brief parable in the context of the high cost of discipleship (Luke 14:25–35), making it part of Jesus' admonitions to the large multitudes who surrounded him and who clamored to be his disciples. The entire Lukan paragraph is made up of a Q passage (14:26–27)[126] that Luke has introduced editorially (14:25), plus a Markan saying (14:34–35), between which Luke places two brief parables warning against beginning a building or a war without adequately considering the costs necessary for a successful conclusion.

Luke's context cannot be confirmed as authentic, for he has built up the passage to match his theme; the theme is not derived from the parable. The parable is in effect a proverb that could be applied in any particular circumstance, including business or war. The motivation for calculating the prospects for success in the twin parable of the tower builder is avoiding ridicule when faced with failure. But the consequence of inadequate reckoning in the case of going to war is more serious: If one miscalculates, one may have to sue for peace on terms less favorable than one could have gotten before the conflict began.

What the application might have been in Jesus' speech is only hypothetically available. Luke's application, that one should not become a disciple unless one has first made a careful calculation, can hardly be original; that message would be discordant with Jesus' radical demands of discipleship.[127] Derrett thinks the twin parables refer not to human calculation but to God's:

> Jesus reassures the people who raise reasonable objections to his call to discipleship—a highly speculative project—viz. that whether his recruit is to

---

124. One can question whether this is a parable. Fitzmyer calls it that (*Luke*, 1062), but Scott does not treat it at all in either of his two books on Jesus' parables, nor does Crossan (*In Parables*) deal with it, nor does Perkins (*Hearing the Parables of Jesus*). Jeremias (*Parables of Jesus*) does include it. The Jesus Seminar regards it and the tower builder (Luke 14:28–30) as inauthentic; see Funk, Scott, and Butts, *Parables of Jesus: Red Letter Edition*, 75.

125. Compare with *Gospel of Thomas* 98: "Jesus said: 'The Kingdom of the father is like a certain man who wanted to kill a powerful man. In his own house he drew his sword and stuck it into the wall in order to find out whether his hand could carry through. Then he slew the powerful man.'" Jeremias, *Parables of Jesus*, 196–97, finds this application: "Just as this political assassin first makes trial of his strength before he embarks on his dangerous venture, so should you test yourselves to see whether you have strength to carry the adventure through."

126. See Kloppenborg, *Q Parallels*, 170, on whether both verses are from Q.

127. See J. Duncan M. Derrett's description of the large variety of comments to this effect in his *Studies in the New Testament* (Leiden: E. J. Brill, 1982), 3:90–91.

be understood as a builder of a new city or as a soldier in the continuing fight for righteousness he can be sure that, once he has actually enlisted, however vast the undertaking, and however substantial the risk, the architect has already calculated the costs, and the general has calculated the balance between the forces in array against each other.

In this view, God is architect and general. Faith in God, not calculation, provides the basis for the decision to discipleship, or to any other of life's major decisions.[128]

In a Jewish context, based on the notion that if God fights for Israel, Israel will win, and if God does not, Israel will not win, regardless of the human resources at the commanders' disposal, calculation of readiness for battle would certainly entail discernment of whether God is actually on one's side. Josephus reports cases in which would-be messiahs miscalculated, and God did not assist them in overcoming Rome. Does Jesus have such circumstances in mind?

There is a close verbal relation between the words here and those in Luke 19:42: "the things that make for peace."[129] In the latter case, Jesus laments that Jerusalem does not know the things that make for peace and thus will be destroyed. In this parable, the calculating king sues his opponent for peace while he is yet distant.

Jesus could have told a parable that warned against Zealot-type revolutionary activity that avoids an accurate calculation of the strength available for rebellion. It could imply not only that rebellion without sufficient troop strength makes such an undertaking foolish, but also that the expectation that God will provide the necessary power will also misunderstand God's intention. Before God can be counted on to bring freedom from outside oppression, changes within the social structure must take place. Knowing the things that make for peace is a prerequisite for making peace. Without the relationship with God that makes covenant society possible, without a social order based on standards of covenant justice, rebellion is futile, for God will not sustain it. Those who undertake it will be required to sue for peace under even more unfavorable circumstances, facing an invading army one cannot withstand.

---

128. Derrett, *Studies in the New Testament,* 3:93.
129. Fitzmyer, *Luke,* 1065.

Summary and Conclusion

Jesus used parables instrumentally, to convey his criticism of the social order and to present his vision of its renewal. The reapplication of the parables in the process of transmitting the tradition and in the writing of the Gospels obscures but does not erase the dimension of social criticism.

The parables contradict conditions existing under Roman rule. The social order—with large landowners, many of them absentees, tenants and stewards, and day laborers—is held up for observation and critique. Pursuit of wealth at the expense of the poor and dispossessed places one on the negative side of the prophetic judgment parables convey.

Jesus' parables call for a changed perception of the relationships among covenant people. The hierarchical patterns that mimic Hellenistic culture contradict covenant norms of a society of equity and justice. The ways in which land, wealth, and power were distributed and used are subjected to norms derived from scripture and tradition. Those in power rightly perceived that Jesus told parables "against them," or at least against the violations of covenant responsibility their way of life represented. Those on the underside of social justice would have seen the parables as "for them," in that the way of seeing the self and others in relation to God would transform society. In that transformation they would be the beneficiaries.

CHAPTER SIX

"They Left Everything and Followed"

The Gospel accounts say Jesus attracted crowds of followers, some of whom went about with him from place to place. He issued general appeals for followers, promising benefits and warning of difficulties for those who responded. He issued specific invitations to particular individuals, some of whom accepted while others rejected and still others wished to defer a decision. He taught the disciples, and he commissioned some with the particular tasks of itinerating, spreading the message of the kingdom, casting out demons, and healing.

The Gospels use three overlapping and not easily distinguished terms in referring to Jesus' followers. "Disciple" usually refers to the special group of twelve, though it can refer to the broad group of followers (Luke 6:17).[1] Mark is especially fond of "the Twelve" as a designation for the group closest to Jesus (Mark 3:14; 4:10; 6:7; 9:35; 10:32; 11:11; 14:10, 20, 43). Luke uses the term "apostle" several times (Luke 6:13; 9:10; 17:5; 22:14; 24:10) to describe the inner circle of twelve, whereas Matthew uses it only once (10:2), as does Mark (6:30). "Disciple" means learner or student, with the additional

---

1. See, for example, Luke 6:17; also Matt. 10:42, "little ones"; Matt. 27:57, Joseph of Arimathea; Matt. 28:19, "make disciples"; Luke 6:13, he chose from his disciples twelve; Luke 6:17, a large crowd of disciples; Luke 14:26, 27, 33; 19:37, a whole multitude of disciples.

connotation of personal loyalty or devotion to the person or the teaching. "Apostle" means one who is sent on a mission and connotes an authoritative representative of the one sending. Outside the Gospels in the New Testament, "apostle" suggests one whose authority derives from being a witness to the event of Jesus' resurrection. "Twelve," recalling the traditional number of Israelite tribes, symbolically represents Israel and suggests the whole people of God.

Scholars debate which if any of these terms goes back to Jesus. "Apostle" seems least likely, since it carries connotations associated with the world mission of the early church. During Jesus' ministry the term "disciple" was more likely applied to Jesus' followers. Greek philosophy and religion used the term with associations similar to those in the Gospels. Josephus reflects a similar usage in talking about the relationship between Elijah and Elisha and in describing Hyrcanus as a disciple of the Pharisees.[2] The Gospels confirm this general use of the term "disciple" by speaking of the disciples of John the Baptist and of the Pharisees. The rabbis had disciples, as the Talmud attests. Thus there is no good reason to doubt that Jesus' close followers were described by him and others as his disciples.

The tradition of the Twelve is more problematic. However, it is documented in early traditions such as 1 Corinthians 15:5, and in the Q passage in Luke 22:30=Matthew 19:28. Since Jesus was engaged in a movement for the renewal of all Israel, the number twelve provided an appropriate symbol.

This chapter will argue not only that Jesus had disciples but that he used the number twelve to symbolize the renewal of all Israel, that he assigned them special tasks and special responsibilities, and that his words to them show the radical nature of his own activity. His relationship with his disciples demonstrates that others recognized him as a person of authority, that he asserted authority over others, and that he had an authoritative message to impart. The disciples, especially the Twelve, were to share that authority, both in the present and the future. The disciples formed a community of those who were receiving the kingdom and who were beginning to be its instruments.

---

2. For Hyrcanus as a disciple of the Pharisees, see Josephus, *Jewish Antiquities* XIII.289; for Elisha as a disciple of Elijah, VIII.354. For other examples, see Karl Rengstorf, "Manthanō," *Theological Dictionary of the New Testament,* ed. Gerhard Kittel, tr. and ed. Geoffrey W. Bromiley (Grand Rapids: Wm. B. Eerdmans Publishing Co., 1967), 4:439–40.

"Calling" Disciples

All four canonical Gospels have stories of Jesus calling disciples. The stories emphasize the decisiveness of Jesus' call and thus the seriousness of the disciples' response.

In Mark 1:16–20 (followed by Matthew but not by Luke), Jesus calls two pairs of brothers who were fishermen: Simon and Andrew, James and John. The very simplicity of the wording enhances the complete abandonment required by the call. "Follow me" sounds more like a command than a gracious invitation. Those who follow will become "fishers of men," a term not used elsewhere as a symbol for disciples and of uncertain meaning. Described by George Buttrick as "a genial and dramatic metaphor,"[3] the term has rather ominous associations, which are "dramatic" but hardly "genial." Fishing provides a congenial diversion for a sport fisherman (though it was evidently not practiced as a sport in ancient Israel). However, it is hardly congenial for the fish, and probably not for those who must make a living at it. Other instances of related imagery suggest more negative than positive associations. In Matthew 13:47–50, the dragnet is a symbol for judgment. In Amos 4:2, Habakkuk 1:14–15, and Jeremiah 16:16, as well as in a Qumran Psalm (1QpHab 6:1f.), fishing is a symbol of judgment. There are no instances in Hebrew scripture of the metaphor being used positively.

The fishing metaphor raises the question as to why Jesus called disciples. In Matthew, Jesus enters the scene like a rabbi, teaching in a synagogue and debating theological and moral issues with opponents.[4] That picture probably is Matthew's own contribution; he does not derive it from Mark or from Q. Matthew presents a view of the disciples similar to rabbinic disciples. The rabbis had pupils who followed them, studying Torah by hearing words of their teacher and by seeing the practical application of teaching in the life of the rabbi. Similarly, Matthew has Jesus call disciples (Matt. 4:18–22); then after a general summary of his activity (teaching, preaching, healing), Matthew has Jesus begin to expound a new edition of Torah (in a sermon delivered on a mountain). But Mark, Matthew's source for the ingredients in this sequence, has Jesus call disciples (Mark 1:16–20), and, following a general summary (1:21–22), he presents Jesus' ministry of mighty works.

---

3. George Buttrick, "The Gospel According to St. Matthew, Exposition," *The Interpreter's Bible,* ed. George Buttrick et al. (Nashville: Abingdon Press, 1951), 7:276.
4. Günther Bornkamm, *Jesus of Nazareth,* tr. Irene and Fraser McLuskey with James M. Robinson (New York: Harper & Brothers, 1960), 96.

Matthew's insertion of the Sermon on the Mount between the call and the specific stories of healings heightens Jesus' image as primarily a teacher of a new rule for the messianic community within Judaism.

Luke presents a different picture and reveals further development in the stories of the call of disciples (see Luke 5:1–11). He combines the call of the fishermen with a miraculous catch of fish, which makes the whole event more awesome and miraculous, thus making the disciples' acceptance of the call more psychologically understandable. Luke's story has much in common with the postresurrection story of John 21:1–19. The disciples respond to one who does awesome things, invites their repentance, and offers forgiveness. Like Mark, Luke presents a Jesus who astounds his disciples and others by the miracles he performs and the forgiveness he brings (Luke 5:12–32).[5]

Are disciples leaving their nets to follow an itinerant rabbi with a new law (Matthew)? Or to follow a worker of miracles (Luke and Mark)? Or to follow one who proclaims the coming of God's kingdom and prepares Israel for God's impending judgment (suggested by Mark's "fishers of men")?[6] The stories of the call of disciples and the sequence of events in the Gospel narratives do not provide full answers to the question of Jesus' purpose. They intend to emphasize the authority of Jesus' call and the seriousness and decisiveness of the disciples' response more than to answer that historical question. We must look further for other clues concerning the disciples' activity and purpose.

The Twelve

Apostolic lists appear in Mark 3:16–19; Matthew 10:2–4; Luke 6:13–16; and Acts 1:13. The number is always twelve, but the names vary. Some names remain consistent in all lists, such as Simon (nicknamed Cephas or Peter) and his brother Andrew, and the brothers James and John; but others vary. The disagreement can be accounted for in a variety of ways. Some of the Twelve might have had more than one name. The notion of the Twelve is a later invention to symbolize the church's supersession of Judaism. While there

---

5. Like John 21:1–19, Luke's story involves a large catch of fish; the catch signifies to Peter the awesome majesty of Jesus. (Peter asks Jesus to "depart" in Luke, while in John Peter "put on some clothes.") In both Peter is called to new work of "fisherman" (Luke) or "shepherd" (John). Some have said Luke's version is a "resurrection" story out of place. Probably Luke has recast Mark's call story in light of resurrection experience, perhaps in light of the same resurrection story John possesses.

6. The Q saying about judging the twelve tribes of Israel can support Mark's picture of Jesus' intent in calling disciples, but see the discussion below.

really were Twelve, not all their names were remembered when the Gospels were written. This last option, I think, provides the best explanation. The Twelve neither as a group nor as individuals continued for long to provide the leadership of the emerging Christian communities; some of their names simply were not widely remembered.

This view finds confirmation in the fact that only rarely do individual disciples speak or act as individuals in the Gospel narratives, leading to the frequent statement that they are a "shadowy" group around Jesus. Gospel narratives give them more importance as symbol and/or group than as individuals. Because the number suggests the early church's expectation of the return of Christ and the renewal of Israel, as well as the church's belief that it constitutes the core of the new Israel, some have doubted that Jesus used it.

However, the tradition of the Twelve existed before Paul, for he cites a tradition that includes resurrection appearances to the Twelve (1 Corinthians 15:5). A further argument that the tradition goes back to Jesus' own practice is the fact that one of the Twelve, Judas, turned Jesus over to the authorities. The church would not have invented the embarrassing story of Jesus' betrayal from within his closest circle.[7] Since Jesus embarked on a mission to renew the covenant life of Israel, "the Twelve" provides a fitting symbol of God's covenant with the twelve tribes of Israel. There is evidence that even though the ten northern tribes had been destroyed, hope remained for the reestablishment of the twelve tribes. That hope finds expression as early as Isaiah 49:6 in the promise to "raise up the tribes of Jacob and to restore the survivors of Israel." Two passages in Sirach express the same hope in the early second century B.C.E.: Sirach 36:13–16 ("Gather all the tribes of Jacob, and give them their inheritance, as at the beginning") and 48:10 (the returning Elijah will "calm the wrath of God" and "restore the tribes of Jacob"). Further evidence for that hope comes from *Psalms of Solomon* 17:21–46, where the author speaks of God raising up as king the "Lord Messiah" who will restore the people who have been scattered and bring renewed good fortune in the "assembly of the tribes." In expectation of such a restoration, the Qumran community organized itself around a leadership representing the twelve tribes of Israel.[8]

---

7. Horsley, *Jesus and the Spiral of Violence,* 200. For a fuller discussion of authenticity, see Sanders, *Jesus and Judaism,* 98–106. Sanders thinks the tradition "probably goes back to Jesus." Horsley (199–208) is more positive, using the Twelve as a clue to the meaning of kingdom of God in Jesus' teaching.

8. See Horsley, *Jesus and the Spiral of Violence,* 199–208, for additional evidence and argument.

Little is said of the background or personal qualities of the Twelve, and the little that is said may not be reliable historically. The stories of the call identify four as fishermen, an occupation providing relatively low social status (as did other crafts).[9] Most of the Twelve were apparently from Galilee, though Judas might have been from the Kerioth, a town south of Hebron in Judea. Andrew is a Greek name, as is Philip. Luke describes the second Simon in the list as a zealot. Whether Luke uses that term to imply that Simon belonged to the revolutionary group who led the revolt against Rome in 66 is unclear. Luke probably draws his clue for the epithet from Mark's term translated in NRSV as "Cananaean" but which probably derives from the Aramaic word qanah, to "be zealous" for something. If Iscariot derives from sikarios and means "assassin," Judas could have been a resistance fighter as well. Not enough is known about either Simon or Judas Isacriot to know whether Jesus included within his group one or more who supported violent revolution. One of the Twelve might have been a tax collector; Matthew identifies the Levi of Mark 2:13–14 with the disciple that Mark 3:18 names "Matthew" (compare Mark 3:18 with Matt. 10:3, and Mark 2:13–14 with Matt. 9:9). A tax collector would likely be a despised person (and that is the main point Mark makes by following Levi's call with a quarrel over table fellowship [Mark 2:15–17]). Even if the telōnēs was a minor subordinate and not the higher tax contractor, the office offered opportunities for greed, required constant contact with foreigners, and thus tended to alienate these revenue officers from the Jewish population. This occupation would suggest to many not only ceremonial uncleanness but traitorous collaboration with the Romans or their agents.

The Gospels thus suggest a diverse group of disciples (and that may reflect the Gospel intent more than historical fact), so that the group as a whole represents those to whom the coming of God's kingdom would be good news. For the most part, they do not reflect the well-connected and the well-to-do, but common folk from rural more than urban areas. Only John's Gospel suggests strongly that a disciple (presumably one of the Twelve) has close acquaintance with the Jerusalem aristocracy (John 18:15–16). It is possible that the Gospel writers, in order to enhance the message that the gospel is for the poor, the despised, and the outcasts, have exaggerated the lowliness of the disciples. Horsley thinks interpreters have exaggerated the view that Jesus' followers were the dregs of society.[10]

---

9. W. H. Wuellner, "Fishermen," *Interpreter's Dictionary of the Bible,* Supplement, ed. Keith Crim et al. (Nashville: Abingdon Press, 1976), 338.
10. Horsley, *Jesus and the Spiral of Violence,* 212–28.

In the Gospels Jesus' enemies accuse him of fraternizing with tax collectors, "sinners," and prostitutes, but that accusation may be false. "Sinners" may designate not the notoriously wicked but the careless who did not closely observe the ceremonial requirements advocated by some groups. It seems clear, as Horsley maintains, that Jesus did associate with the poor, a term that "may refer to the oppressed and suffering Jewish peasantry generally."[11] Jesus conducted his ministry among the common people, and it is likely that most of his closest disciples came from that group. His message was addressed to their needs, and they were the ones most responsive to it.

It is very unlikely that Jesus intended the Twelve to be the foundation of an institution of any sort. There is no convincing evidence that Jesus organized a community or that he intended one separate from the rest of Judaism, either on the model of the Qumran sect or on the model of Matthew's or Luke's community. Matthew suggests that he did, especially in chapter 18, where he has Jesus articulate rules for his community. Luke is more likely correct in showing the origins of community organization to lie in the period after Jesus' removal from their presence, as he does in the beginning chapters of Acts. The roots of that community, however, may lie in the table fellowship Jesus and his followers practiced. The hospitality within the group loyal to Jesus both expressed the ideals of covenant community Jesus advocated and formed the basis for the continuation of the disciples as a recognizable community after Jesus' departure.

The Role of the Disciples

Table fellowship provides an important clue for discerning the role the disciples were to play in the renewal of Israel. That activity forms part of the task given the disciples in the accounts of Jesus' commissioning and sending the disciples throughout the region.

Both Mark and Q contain an account of the sending out of disciples. Mark has two accounts, located at 3:14–15 and 6:6–13 (see parallels in Matt. 10:1, 9–14, and Luke 9:1–6). Luke 10:2–12 and Matthew 9:37–10:15 contain the Q version. Luke uses the Markan account to describe the mission of the Twelve (Luke 9:1–6) and the Q account to describe that of the Seventy (Luke 10:2–12). Matthew conflates Mark and Q into a single account. The accounts suggest that Jesus sends out disciples to do the same things he does: preach,

---

11. Horsley, *Jesus and the Spiral of Violence*, 225.

teach, heal, exorcise, and announce the good news of the kingdom of God. Jesus sends disciples out two by two on a mission so urgent that they travel lightly and move on rapidly, not wasting time on those who refuse to hear. Their mission is a metaphor, an acted parable, underscoring the urgency with which Jesus conducted his ministry. As now written, the descriptions also reflect the urgency felt by the first Christian evangelists who were expecting the return of Jesus in the very near future.

Matthew's version (10:1–42) of the sending of the disciples uses the Markan narratives (plus some verses from Mark 13) to build a "missionary sermon" that provides Matthew's community with a model for their own itinerating missionaries. By this means, Matthew shows that discipleship entails sharing in Jesus' ministry. Disciples must adopt his style of life, which is not a principled asceticism but a practical simplicity that will allow the disciples to carry out the urgent mission of evangelizing.

Contained within the instructions to the missionaries in both Mark and Q is the admonition to go to houses and to accept the hospitality offered. The instructions are directed to the Twelve in Mark and to "seventy" in Luke's version of Q. One cannot assume the accuracy of either, since the Gospel writers and not their sources provide the context for the instructions.[12] Itineration for missionary activity was characteristic of the early church, as the Q document shows, as do the book of Acts, the New Testament letters, and Jesus' own example. Thus, it is likely that limiting such tasks to a one-time mission by the Twelve would be historically inaccurate, as Luke recognized when he included also the mission of the Seventy. As Crossan says, "The 'mission' may well have been a more or less standard phenomenon for those who wished to participate more actively in the Jesus movement."[13]

Whether applied to the larger group or only to the Twelve, the tasks of the missionaries included participating in hospitality, healing, and preaching. These tasks characterize Jesus' own ministry, and they are to characterize those who follow him. Referring to participating in hospitality as a "task" may seem odd, but in Jesus' context it is not. Receiving hospitality, eating and staying in someone's house implies acceptance as a member of a fellowship; rejecting hospitality means the rejection of the person who offers it (as in the case of the parable of the banquet). Jesus went in to eat with those who were "sinners," that is, those who were not considered part of the faithful

---

12. Crossan, *Historical Jesus,* 334.
13. Crossan, *Historical Jesus,* 334.

community by those with the power to define that membership. Jesus defied that definition; he crossed the boundaries of established social custom and religious authority, accepting the hospitality and table fellowship of all who would share in the festival of renewal.

Table Fellowship

The large amount of attention given to food, eating, and sharing hospitality in the Gospels reflects a very important aspect of Jesus' historical ministry and that of his followers. Not only in the Jewish context but generally, sharing food at table symbolizes and establishes close relationships. To admit one into the home or to the table is to admit that one into the family; to join someone at home or at table implies accepting an invitation into the family. Sharing food provides the context for some of the most important affirmations about Jesus in the Gospels: The temptation story includes the temptation to provide food for himself in desert isolation, removed from the problems of fellow Israelites; Jesus does not succumb to the temptation to live by his own bread alone. The stories of the feeding of the multitudes express Jesus' concern for the crowds, not merely for their food, which God's gift provides, but also because they need "teaching" and leadership (Mark 6:34); John correctly sees the implications of this community feast in the wilderness when he says the crowd wanted to make Jesus king (John 6:15). Eating provides the context for sayings that break the boundaries between clean and unclean (see Mark 7:1–23). Sharing food symbolizes the inclusion of the outsiders (Mark 7:24–30). A final supper marks the separation of Jesus from his disciples (Mark 14:17–25), shows the horror of betrayal (Mark 14:20), and provides the symbol for the renewal of that fellowship through a community celebration (Luke 22:19) as well as in resurrection (Luke 24:28–35, 41–42; John 21:9–14).

One need not argue for the historicity of these stories to affirm that they represent the historical reality that table fellowship and the sharing of food were characteristic ways in which Jesus included common people in the renewal of community. Cultural (and crosscultural) understanding of the importance of sharing food argues the case in a general way that Jesus must have used these occasions. More specifically, the great importance placed on the meal in the celebrations of Christian fellowship after Jesus indicates that the communities remembered him in a context that he had made memorable. The book of Acts may well idealize the common sharing of house and food by the early community in Jerusalem, but that ideal draws on the church's historical memory of Jesus himself.

In describing the mission of Jesus' disciples, then, the emphasis upon going to houses, sharing in the meal of whatever house they entered, was not merely a means of missionary support (though it was also that); it was a manner in which the mission expressed itself. Hospitality provides an opportunity for estrangement to be overcome. Depriving others of food expresses the strongest sort of alienation; neither words nor actions, from either God or neighbor, can overcome that alienation so long as food is denied. Accepting food and hospitality, entering into close relationships within homes, was thus, as Crossan expresses it,

> a strategy for building or rebuilding peasant community on radically different principles from those of honor and shame, patronage and clientage. It was based on an egalitarian sharing of spiritual and material power at the most grass-roots level.[14]

Kingdom of Equals

Sayings regarding the egalitarian relationship among the disciples supports this interpretation of the mission instructions. Mark 10:35–45 contains the incident of James and John requesting positions of honor and power in Jesus' "glory," Jesus' negative response, the other disciples' criticism of James and John, and Jesus' statement contrasting the hierarchical arrangement of the "Gentiles" with that appropriate to the disciples. While much of this passage is of dubious authenticity since it reflects the church's understanding of Jesus' death as well as the leadership struggles within the early church,[15] the egalitarian principles go back to the historical Jesus. The insistence on service and the rejection of hierarchical arrangements coheres with the social vision of Jesus, and it goes against hierarchical tendencies that soon developed within the early church itself.

"You know that among the Gentiles those whom they recognize as their rulers lord it over them, and their great ones are tyrants over them. But it is not so among you" (Mark 10:42). The disciples here are represented as being

---

14. Crossan, *Historical Jesus,* 344. See his important discussion of this point on pp. 332–44.

15. Funk and Smith, *Gospel of Mark,* 167–69.

tempted by a Gentile style of political rule that permeated Israelite society
from the Hasmonaeans on, and which came to even fuller expression as the
Romans ruled through Jewish elites. Jesus rejects the appropriateness of that
style of government for a covenant community of equals. The Son of Man,
possibly symbolizing the "people of the holy ones of the Most High" (Dan.
7:27), provides a counter example as a community of servants. "Among you"
the Gentile mode is inappropriate.

A questionable saying in Luke 17:7–10 (from L) apparently runs counter
to this egalitarian ideal: The servant, even after plowing all day, will not be
invited to sit at table with the master but will rather be expected to prepare
supper for the master, and even then remain "unworthy." If the servant sits at
table with the master, it is only by an act of grace. Such a hierarchical
arrangement is typical of the social structure of Roman Palestine, and Luke
thinks it provides an appropriate symbol for the relationship of the Christian
to Christ: The Christian should never presume on the grace of the master,
whose condescension is the necessary foundation for any relationship at all.
The master-slave relationship, just as the patron-client and the absentee
landlord–tenant relationship, has been transformed into a positive symbol.
But authentic tradition shows it was not so for Jesus. Imagery of sharing
common meals, giving and accepting hospitality, building a community of
equals goes contrary to both the practice of the Palestinian power structure
and of theological developments in the church, and thus has strong claim to
authenticity. The saying in Luke could be authentic only if it is understood
ironically: Such attitudes toward master-slave relationships exist, but they are
contrary to the kingdom of equals Jesus seeks to establish.

How far this kingdom of equals extended toward the inclusion of Gentiles
and women is much controverted. The story of the sending out of the Twelve
(and also that of the Seventy) suggests that the missionary effort included
only men. Cultural context would argue for that understanding as well. But
Jesus' countercultural tendencies in many regards leave open the possibility
that he disregarded the barriers of gender and ethnicity as well. While I have
argued that Jesus rejected Gentile ways of organizing social and economic life
and called for a return to covenant norms instead, that does not mean he
rejected Gentiles as such. The early church apparently opened Gentile
missions very soon, a fact arguing that Jesus himself had set the tone and
direction of the future covenant community. Likewise, women had important roles to play in the Jesus' movement and in the early church.

While the issue of Gentiles and the issue of women are not the same, they
are interrelated in that Jesus' activities and teachings express concern for

those on the margins of society and called for a social renewal that eradicated barriers and ended domination by the powerful. Even if Jesus did not directly address issues of particular structures of oppression, he "implicitly subverts them by envisioning a different future and different human relationships on the grounds that *all* persons . . . are created and elected by the gracious goodness" of God.[16] I think it highly unlikely that Jesus inaugurated or conceived a "mission to the Gentiles," since his own mission focused on the renewal of Israel. Such a renewal could in theory have been strongly anti-Gentile (if Gentile dominance were thought to be the essential problem in Palestine), or it could have included Gentiles (if social renewal and justice were the key issues). Not all Palestinian Gentiles were among the wealthy and powerful, just as not all Jews were poor and oppressed.[17]

An effort to renew society through the process of hospitality could pose a threat to the dominant forces in society. Especially if that renewed society began to see itself as the heir of God's promised kingdom, a society in which God's will came to expression for all Israel. A second aspect of the disciples' mission likewise posed a threat: healing. Mark reports that Jesus commissioned the disciples with "authority over the unclean spirits" (Mark 6:7). He then reports that they "cast out many demons, and anointed with oil many who were sick and cured them" (Mark 6:13). Q apparently included "healing" as one of the tasks Jesus gave the disciples (Luke 10:9; Matt. 10:8). Beyond the general reports of healing and exorcism, the Gospels do not narrate any specific incidents of the disciples' healing; one specific incident of failure is reported (Mark 9:18). The Acts account of the early church includes acts of healing (for example, Acts 3:1–10) and exorcism (Acts 16:16–18) by missionaries. Paul includes healing and miracle working among the gifts the Spirit provides the church (1 Cor. 12:9–10, 29–30).

Spiritual Healing

There is little room to doubt that the tradition of spiritual healing goes back to the historical Jesus and that the disciples carried on that work both simultaneously with Jesus and subsequently. Questions about "miracles"

16. Elisabeth Schüssler Fiorenza, *In Memory of Her: A Feminist Theological Reconstruction of Christian Origins* (New York: Crossroad, 1983), 142. See her provocative discussion, pp. 105–54.

17. See Sanders, *Jesus and Judaism*, 212–21, for a brief but judicious discussion of this issue.

have dominated discussion of the healings to such an extent that the social-political implications have often been overlooked. Questions about who can heal, who should receive healing, and under what conditions are political questions in any society. In Jesus' day, illness was often associated with sin, so that to heal implied bringing forgiveness, as the story in Mark 2:1–12 shows. Access to the power of forgiveness was guarded by the same authorities who governed access to political and economic power. Thus, to challenge them by unauthorized healing, based on the claim of direct access to God's healing power, constituted a threat no less than would a direct political challenge.

When Jesus commissioned disciples to tasks that included healing, therefore, he set the stage for even greater opposition to his ministry than he had already generated by his own activity. Crossan expresses well the implications of Jesus' activity, and implies that of his followers as well:

> There is . . . a terrible irony in [the] conjunction of sickness and sin, especially in first-century Palestine. Excessive taxation could leave poor people physically malnourished or hysterically disabled. But since the religiopolitical ascendancy could not blame excessive taxation, it blamed sick people themselves by claiming that their sins had led to their illnesses. And the cure for sinful sickness was, ultimately, in the Temple. And that meant more fees, in a perfect circle of victimization. When, therefore, John the Baptist with a magical rite or Jesus with a magical touch cured people of their sicknesses, they implicitly declared their sins forgiven or nonexistent. They challenged not the medical monopoly of the doctors but the religious monopoly of the priests. All of this was religiopolitically subversive.[18]

Itinerating missionaries, operating under Jesus' direction, would only spread the subversion as they went about healing.

Hospitality and healing are combined in the summary of the itinerating missioners with their proclamation of repentance. Again, the Gospels contain no specific stories of the disciples' preaching, and it may be questionable whether or how much they engaged in such activity during the ministry of Jesus. The instructions nevertheless express the nature of the historical ministry of Jesus. The renewal movement inaugurated by Jesus necessitated a change of outlook and action, a new understanding of the covenant com-

---

18. Crossan, *Historical Jesus*, 324.

munity, its relationship to past traditions, and the relationship of persons within that community. Such a change is appropriately called "repentance," a turnaround, a fundamental change.

A Q saying provides evidence for the role of the disciples that confirms their participation in a renewal movement that had political and social ramifications: "I confer on you, just as my Father has conferred on me, a kingdom, so that you may eat and drink at my table in my kingdom, and you will sit on thrones judging the twelve tribes of Israel" (Luke 22:29–30; compare Matt. 19:28). The first part of this saying, including the emphasis on hospitality, is likely Luke's editorial expression, as a comparison with Matthew shows. The sitting on thrones (Matthew says twelve thrones), however, likely belongs to Q.[19] The question as to whether it goes back to Jesus may be tied to the meaning of "judging." Usually "judging" has been understood in the context of the judgment associated with the coming of the Son of Man at the end time. That idea more likely belongs to the early church than to Jesus, and thus the association of the disciples with that activity would also belong to a later time. However, as Horsley has persuasively argued, the translation "judging" misleads the reader into thinking of judicial activity.[20] If "judging" is not end time judicial activity, and if it is analogous to the work of "judges" in ancient Israel, a different conclusion is warranted. The term often means "establishing justice" or right social relations when justice has been denied by some inside or outside power. Thus, God's judging includes deliverance or salvation from oppressive power and the renewal that comes to society when such power has been removed. Jesus' disciples, in that understanding of the term, were participating in the same renewal of society that Jesus pursued. Like the Messiah, Son of David described in *Psalms of Solomon* 17:26–32, the disciples participate in "gathering" the people, leading them in righteousness, and effecting their liberation.[21]

Discipleship and Jesus' Radical Demands

Many of Jesus' sayings that present discipleship as radical demand derive from Q. Luke 9:57–62 (Matt. 8:19–22)[22] reports an exchange between Jesus

---

19. See Kloppenborg, *Q Parallels*, 202.
20. Horsley, *Jesus and the Spiral of Violence*, 201–6.
21. Horsley, *Jesus and the Spiral of Violence*, 205.
22. Whether the whole Lukan block is derived from Q, see Kloppenborg, *Q Parallels*, 64.

and three persons who express a willingness to follow him at present or in the future. In each case Jesus' statement demands such a radical change as to discourage the would-be follower. The story of the rich man who "went away grieving, for he had many possessions" (Mark 10:17–22) also exemplifies that point.

To one who professed willingness to "follow you wherever you go," Jesus said, "Foxes have holes, and birds of the air have nests; but the Son of Man has nowhere to lay his head" (Luke 9:58).[23] This saying could be a general proverb, comparing the difficulty of a human life (son of man = human being) with that of an animal. Or it could apply to the conditions (homelessness) in which people were placed due to the economic stress of Jesus' time. Or it could mean the particular circumstances of uprootedness in which Jesus' ministry placed him (Son of Man = I). In the latter case, following Jesus involves renouncing any security one may have in order to follow one whose life is completely insecure by worldly standards. The only security for the disciple comes from placing oneself at the disposal of God and God's kingdom and its agent, Jesus.

A second, to whom Jesus issued the invitation to follow, requests, "Lord, first let me go and bury my father." This request for delay probably could mean the father has died and the funeral must be attended. In this case, Jesus' harsh reply, "Let the dead bury their own dead" (Luke 9:59–60), makes loyalty to his cause a higher claim than a demand of the Torah. Burying dead parents was understood to be a part of the commandment to honor father and mother, a commandment that could be transcended only in extreme cases, such as a priest in a state of ritual purity (see Lev. 21:11) or one who has taken a Nazarite vow (see Num. 6:6–7). For Hasidic Pharisees "the last offices for the dead had gained primacy among all good works."[24] Jesus' attitude has prophetic precedence in Ezekiel 24:15–24. Even when his own wife died, Ezekiel heeded Yahweh's word forbidding mourning or weeping for the dead as a sign of the inexpressible grief facing the people.

"To bury one's father" in traditional idiom, however, probably meant performing a son's duty to stay home and care for parents as long as they are

---

23. NRSV translates literally "Son of Man," but I regard this as equivalent to "one" meaning "this one" or "I." In Q it would have meant "Son of Man," for as Edwards says, " 'Son of Man' has a specific, future, judgmental meaning for the Q community" (Richard A. Edwards, *A Theology of Q: Eschatology, Prophecy, and Wisdom* [Philadelphia: Fortress Press, 1976], 101).

24. Martin Hengel, *The Charismatic Leader and His Followers,* tr. James Greig (New York: Crossroad, 1981), 8.

alive.[25] But since the command to honor father and mother was understood to include such care, following Jesus still transcends demands of Torah. In either case, Jesus' saying puts obligations of family loyalty, even commanded by religious duty, lower than demands of discipleship. Hengel states the matter too christologically in speaking of Jesus' "sovereign freedom in respect of the Law of Moses,"[26] but he points to the truth that the urgencies of the situation cause Jesus to reject conventional requirements in order to pursue unconditionally the will of God for the present crisis.

A third exchange repeats Jesus' emphasis on the precedence of kingdom claims over the most basic claims that humans experience. "Another said, 'I will follow you, Lord; but let me first say farewell to those at my home.' Jesus said to him, 'No one who puts a hand to the plow and looks back is fit for the kingdom of God' " (Luke 7:61–62).

Another Q saying expresses even more forcefully the renunciation of family ties and obligations that Jesus' discipleship demands: "Whoever comes to me and does not hate father and mother, wife and children, brothers and sisters . . . cannot be my disciple" (Luke 14:26; compare Matt. 10:37 and *Gospel of Thomas* 55).

If home, family, and religious obligations do not cushion one from the demands of the kingdom, then nothing will. That precisely is the nature of the radical demands that Jesus makes on his disciples. His way of life was a call to repentance, to conversion, a turning about. The turning about involved a rejection of the values most highly praised in the conventional wisdom of Jesus' society: family, wealth, honor, and religion.[27] None of these values provided an acceptable substitute for the radical renewal demanded by God's kingdom. All of them in Jesus' prophetic view were used as a shield against seeking first God's kingdom and God's righteousness.

Therefore, without repentance one cannot participate in God's kingdom as Jesus' disciple. Repentance means turning to God and away from the pursuit of any other end than God's kingdom. It also means turning to the neighbor, a recapturing of the notion that the kingdom of God and the blessing of God are inseparable from the well-being of the community of God's people. The proclamation of the kingdom is directed toward all; the invitation and the demand and their promises of healing (salvation) are for all. The disciples are

---

25. Bailey, *Through Peasant Eyes*, 26.
26. Hengel, *Charismatic Leader*, 11.
27. Borg, *Jesus: A New Vision*, 104–6.

to join in that proclamation; thus they are to exemplify through their radical commitment the urgent demands of the kingdom.

> Thus, the following of Jesus does not simply mean imitation of him, but entering into the very conditions of his life, ministry, and lot. It calls a person to a sacrifice of security (Case I), filial duty (Case II), and family affection (Case III).[28]

The story of the rich man (Mark 10:17–26) dramatizes the difficulty posed by the radical demands of Jesus. It presents a stark contrast to the repentance required of those who would be disciples. Regardless of the historicity of the particular narrative, the saying at the story's climax has a good claim to authenticity: "Children, how hard it is to enter the kingdom of God! It is easier for a camel to go through the eye of a needle than for someone who is rich to enter the kingdom of God" (v. 25). The man exemplifies the values of conventional wisdom; there is no suggestion that he is a particularly "evil" person. Quite the contrary; he is an admirable person. Nonetheless, what he represents is a denial of the kingdom of God. He belongs to the class that benefited from the present social, economic, political, and religious structures under Roman rule. It was the group to which he belonged that more than any other needed to change, to repent, to gain a new vision of self and society in order to accept God's just rule in Israel. Jesus put the demands in the strongest, most uncompromising terms: "Go, sell what you own, and give the money to the poor . . . ; then come, follow me" (Mark 10:21). The man preferred his own accumulations of both goodness and goods, and the security they offered, to the uncertain future Jesus offered. So, finally, did most others in Israel like him. If only they had known the things that made for peace, but those things were hidden from their eyes. The camel did not go through the eye of the needle.

Jesus' Relationship with His Disciples

How well those who did follow Jesus understood him and his purposes is debatable. Mark presents a dismal picture of the failure of the disciples to comprehend and/or accept the way of Jesus; Luke and Matthew follow him partially. Mark has some purpose in mind for portraying the disciples so negatively; probably he wants to correct false adulation or exaggerated claims

---

28. Fitzmyer, *Luke*, 834–35.

for them that give positions and status to those who were their heirs in the church. Mark's theology also requires that Jesus alone must bear desolation and separation from God in order that he might be a ransom for many (10:45). Thus he may exaggerate their failure, an exaggeration in some ways overcompensated by Matthew's investing them with the ability to have the church built upon them (Matt. 16:18–19; 18:18; 28:16–20). We simply have too little information to trace their experience with Jesus, including the impact upon them of his death.

Regardless of what happened with the Twelve, a significant movement of disciples following Jesus helps account for his execution. If the crowds had not followed, the authorities could have ignored Jesus. His following was strong enough to disturb them. Hengel says the only reason for such a large following was that people misunderstood Jesus and followed him for the wrong reasons.[29] While that may explain some of his following, it is more plausible that many understood him all too well and responded enthusiastically to his call for renewing covenant traditions in ways that would radically change the status quo.

The fact of Jesus' calling disciples thus confirms that Jesus was a charismatic leader and that he had a prophetic message that made him a potential agent of renewal. That combination made him attractive to many and threatening to many others. Unfortunately for his cause, those who saw in him a threat were the ones who had the power to control his fate.

---

29. Hengel, *Victory Over Violence*, 47–51.

CHAPTER SEVEN

"Pray Then in This Way"

The Gospels portray Jesus as a person of the Spirit, upon whom the Spirit of God came at baptism, whose mission to the poor, the blind, the captive, and the oppressed resulted from the presence of the Spirit (Luke 4:18–19). He prays after a full day of healing and at the beginning of another (Mark 1:35), as well as after feeding the multitudes and before walking on water (Mark 6:46). Praying in the midst of miracle working implies the need for replenishing the spiritual power that miracle working requires. Luke especially has Jesus pray in connection with important events: his baptism (Luke 3:21); the disciples' recognition of his messiahship (Luke 9:18–20); the transfiguration (Luke 9:28–29); the arrest and trial (Luke 22:40–46, follow Mark 14:32–42). Jesus also encourages his disciples to pray with the confidence that God will hear (Luke 18:1; Mark 11:24=Matt. 21:22).

The stories of Jesus at prayer may not derive from historical remembrance of particular events. In fact, the most compellingly human of them all—Jesus' struggle in Gethsemane—purportedly happens while all potential eyewitnesses were asleep. Even if Mark introduces the disciples' sleep to portray Jesus' solitary agony, an agony that no one can share, still one questions whether the disciples were present to witness Jesus' prayer.

Yet Jesus must have been the kind of person who expressed a close relationship with God. Just as his teachings about God's kingdom do not derive from institutionalized authority but from his own immediate understanding of God's will, so his understanding of God and his relationship with God do not derive from priestly authority either. They come from his own personal experience and his immediate interpretation of that experience.

Jesus was a charismatic personality. Jesus manifested a power that his contemporaries regarded as spiritual, deriving either from God or from some demonic force. His followers, of course, believed that he, like prophets of past and present, was inspired by God's Spirit. While the endowment by God's Spirit is not reducible to personal spiritual experience, it bears a close relationship to it.

Jesus' personal religious experience is a difficult subject to deal with, and one enters the discussion with much trepidation. The difficulty of that daunting task no doubt accounts for the frequency with which interpreters of Jesus avoid the topic. Notice, for example, the recent treatment by E. P. Sanders, who in many ways enlightens and enlivens the discussion of Jesus within the context of Judaism. Indices to his book do not reveal any discussion of the subject of prayer; no mention is made of the Lord's Prayer; the word "*abba*" or "father" does not occur in the index, nor are the relevant texts listed in the index of passages cited.

There are good reasons to avoid discussion of such issues. The Gospels themselves are reticent to speak about Jesus' inner thoughts or his spiritual life (John being less so than the Synoptics). This reticence may be related to the fact that Jesus himself spoke little of his inner, spiritual life. The Gospels concentrate instead on the message of the kingdom that dominated his thinking and acting. Thus there exists very little data on which to base any discussion of the spiritual life of Jesus.

Attempting to address the question of Jesus' spiritual life suggests the discredited quest of the historical Jesus; most recent interpreters have correctly steered clear of any assumption that one could write a biography of Jesus, complete with a portrayal of his inmost thoughts about himself, God, and the world. Few would want to resurrect such a quest; it has been appropriately abandoned.

Nevertheless, to discount completely any speaking of Jesus' spiritual life may be to reject useful historical knowledge unnecessarily. If one judges on the basis of wide attestation, Jesus knew himself to have a close relationship with God. All the strata of the Gospel tradition portray Jesus as addressing God as "Father."[1]

---

1. Joachim Jeremias, *The Prayers of Jesus,* tr. John Bowden et al., Studies in Biblical Theology, 2d series, no. 6 (London: SCM Press, 1967), 54–57.

Since the early church especially emphasized Jesus' unique relationship to God, that wide attestation loses some to its persuasive power. Instead of the term going back to Jesus, the Christian way of addressing God might have permeated even the earliest sources.

Jesus and the Lord's Prayer

The "Lord's Prayer" begins with this mode of addressing God (Luke 11:2–4; Matt. 6:9–13). Since the early church used this prayer extensively,[2] the authenticity of the prayer as a whole may be suspect.[3] However, apart from the address to God, the prayer does not reveal the Christian church's reflection upon Jesus' experience with God, or his intimate prayer life.

In its most rigorous application, the criterion of dissimilarity tends to discount the prayer's authenticity. There is nothing in it that could not derive from Judaism,[4] with the possible exception of *abba*, Father. The first two petitions are very similar to the Jewish Kaddish, which was probably familiar in Jesus' time:

> Exalted and hallowed be his great name
>   in the world which he created according to his will.
> May he let his kingdom rule
>   in your lifetime and in your days and in the lifetime
>   of the whole house of Israel, speedily and soon.
> And to this, say: amen.[5]

In fact, Jesus' prayer is so thoroughly Jewish and so untypically Christian, Elliott thinks any Jewish rabbi or prophet could have taught it. Elliott speculates that it comes from John the Baptist, since for the more ascetic John prayer was more

---

2. Its appearance in the *Didache* in Matthew's version attests to this wide usage, as do the different versions in Luke and Matthew. See *The Didache or the Teaching of the Twelve Apostles* 8:2.

3. See, for example, Crossan, *Historical Jesus,* 441, who lists it with texts whose core does not derive from Jesus.

4. Fitzmyer, *Luke,* 900, says the prayer is "thoroughly Jewish" and that its petitions can be found in Jewish prayers, though he follows Jeremias's questionable interpretation that Jesus' use of *Abba* was distinctive. Fitzmyer thinks the earliest form was "Father! May your name be sanctified! May your kingdom come! Give us this day our bread for subsistence. Forgive us our debts as we have forgiven our debtors. And bring us not into temptation."

5. Jeremias, *Prayers of Jesus,* 98.

important than for Jesus.[6] But when the criterion of dissimilarity requires that Jesus must be separated from Judaism, that criterion can no longer be valid. Jesus' prayer life must have been thoroughly Jewish. What else could it have been?

The evidence of the prayer's continued use in the early church might also make it suspect. But the prayer contains no distinctively Christian theology, no explicit Christology, no expectation of the return of Christ, no assertion of the role of Christ in the kingdom or of his triumph over his enemies. The fact that the church continued to use a Jewish prayer that did not distinguish the church from rival Judaism argues strongly for its early origin and authority as a genuine prayer of Jesus.

The prayer's authenticity finds support in that it coheres with the teaching of Jesus precisely at the point where church practice was departing from the practice of Jesus: social-political renewal. More important, it does cohere with the picture of Jesus and his activity derived from other authentic tradition. The prayer authenticates both his spiritual life and his social engagement, for it connects an intimate relationship with God ("Father") and Jesus' message of the kingdom. Thus, if the Lord's Prayer is a construction by the church and does not derive directly from Jesus, those who constructed the prayer discerned the way Jesus connected spiritual life and social renewal. God's kingdom encompasses both. Jesus' spirituality engaged the world; it did not negate the world or leave it to hostile powers. His spirituality did not lead to ascetic withdrawal, either as a goal or as a tactic. The prayer combines intimacy with God and concern for community.

The Lord's Prayer thus provides a good way to focus our concluding discussion of Jesus' work, and a way of connecting that work with the practice of prayer and spirituality.

Luke's version (Luke 11:2–4) is most likely very close to Q in the petitions it includes, while Matthew (6:9–13) may preserve some more original wording that Luke translates for a Gentile audience.[7] Matthew's version is more liturgically full, but it adds nothing materially to Luke's version.

---

6. James Keith Elliott, "Did the Lord's Prayer Originate with John the Baptist?" *Theologische Zeitschrift* 29 (1973): 215.

7. Some think Matthew and Luke had different versions and that the prayer was generally and widely known. See Kloppenborg, *Q Parallels*, 84; Jeremias, *Prayers of Jesus*, 93.

Father

The prayer addresses God with the intimate term "Father." Matthew's "Our Father in heaven" is more liturgical and more formal than Luke's simple "Father." The intimacy implied in the Lukan form coheres with Jesus' attitude of trust in God contained in other sayings: "Your Father knows that you need" all these things (Luke 12:30; Matt. 6:32). Since God knows, and since God exercises a parent's care, one need not be anxious but may trust in God.

Jeremias argues that (1) *abba* is Jesus' authentic address to God, (2) it conveys Jesus' understanding of God, and (3) it reveals Jesus' view of his uniquely intimate relation to God. His treatment of this topic has been widely influential and deserves attention. His first point can be accepted, for *abba* was already applied to patriarchal heads of households as well as to regional authorities, and to refer to scholar-teachers, such as some Pharisees.[8] The early church used both the Aramaic *abba* and the Greek *patēr* ("father") to refer to God, suggesting that the intimate way of referring to God goes back to the earliest Palestinian tradition. There is no adequate reason to deny that Jesus adopted an emerging Jewish practice and gave it his own distinctive meaning. The trust in God Jesus advocated supports the view of God that the use of "father" implies. The use of a familial term to refer to God also coheres with Jesus' use of egalitarian social ethic and the sense of a close-knit community.[9]

Jeremias's second point is also valid: The mode of address does reveal Jesus' understanding of God. Jeremias's third point contains two implications concerning Jesus: his intimacy with God and his uniqueness. Jeremias argues on the basis of his investigation of the use of *abba* in Hebrew scripture and other literature that Jesus' utterances were "without contemporary parallels. As a form of address to God the word *abba* is without parallel in the whole of late Jewish devotional literature."[10] For Jeremias, Jesus' unique use of this term indicates an unparalleled intimacy between Jesus and God. Even though he allows the disciples to "share in his relationship with God," Jesus himself has unique authority; he provides "complete divine revelation."[11]

Jeremias overdoes Jesus' intimacy with God. Since *abba* was the standard

---

8. Horsley, *Jesus and the Spiral of Violence,* 241.

9. Horsley, *Jesus and the Spiral of Violence,* 241, 244.

10. Joachim Jeremias, *The Problem of the Historical Jesus,* tr. Norman Perrin (Philadelphia: Fortress Press, 1964), 18. For his fuller treatment, see *Prayers of Jesus* and *The Central Message of the New Testament* (New York: Charles Scribner's Sons, 1965).

11. Jeremias, *Prayers of Jesus,* 63, and *Problem of the Historical Jesus,* 21.

Aramaic word for "father," and father can denote authority and status as well as familiarity, the term itself does not require Jeremias's understanding.[12]

Even if the term should denote unusual intimacy, Jeremias exaggerates in maintaining that Jesus' use of *abba* shows his sense of unique filial relationship with God.[13] Jesus teaches his disciples to address God in the same way, and even if one argues that their intimate relationship with God is through Jesus, that still does not distinguish the quality of their relationship from that of Jesus. They are related to God through him in the sense that following his teachings and his way puts them in a new situation, but their spiritual life is to be analogous to his, not derivative. He does not teach them to consider him an intermediary, but rather to imitate him in approaching God without intermediary. There is no solid evidence that Jesus taught them that they derived their relationship with God from him.

Particularly if one understands the "unique" relationship of Jesus with God in ontological rather than experiential terms, theirs is not derivative from his. It is not, in other words, because of who Jesus is *in essence* that they can be related to God in a new, more intimate way.[14]

To think of God as Father implies a familial rather than an institutional framework for relationships within the disciple community.[15] The prayer thus confirms the egalitarian community advocated in other sayings. Matthew's saying that the disciples should call no one father because they have one Father (Matt. 23:9) suggests that understanding. Matthew's fuller liturgical version suggests that familial understanding: "Our Father" (6:9)

---

12. Krister Stendahl, "Your Kingdom Come," *Cross Currents* 32 (1982): 260: "Such speculation is unwarranted, since Abba is the standard Aramaic term for 'father.'" See James D. G. Dunn, *Jesus and the Spirit* (Philadelphia: Westminster Press, 1975), ch. 2, note 55, for more scholars who doubt Jeremias's views. Dunn (23) agrees with Conzelmann that Jeremias "has pressed his argument too far," but he nonetheless maintains that "Jesus said 'Abba' to God for precisely the same reason that (most of) his contemporaries refrained from its use in prayer—viz., because it expressed his attitude to God as Father, his experience of God as one of unusual intimacy."

13. Dunn agrees with this judgment; *Jesus and the Spirit*, 24ff.

14. The Q saying, "No one knows the Son except the Father, and no one knows the Father except the Son" (Matt. 11:27; compare Luke 10:22; I regard the Matthean wording as more likely authentic, since Luke's has been shaped more completely by the notion of the hidden identity of Jesus) is sometimes interpreted as Jesus' assertion of his own uniqueness and that the Father reveals himself only to the Son and those associated with him. See, for example, J. C. O'Neill, "The Charge of Blasphemy at Jesus' Trial Before the Sanhedrin," 74, who supports the validity of the accusation by pointing among other things to this saying.

15. Horsley, *Jesus and the Spiral of Violence*, 242–44.

rather than simply "Father"; "in heaven" in contrast to earthly fathers, of which there are to be none in Matthew's view.

Some suggest that Jesus' thinking of God as Father provided an alternative to a political solution to the problems of Judaism in Jesus' day. Jesus did not offer social programs to deal with the deep-rooted social ills; rather he offered "unconditional trust in the goodness of the Father."[16] In Hengel's view Jesus' most provocative act was linking unconditional love and forgiveness with his own messianic claim to be Son of Man. That combination made Jesus' message socially and politically explosive, even though it was not political.

Two related criticisms of this interpretation of Jesus are warranted. Trusting the goodness of the Father as a solution to political issues only provides an opiate unless one has confidence that God will act—or is acting—to rid society of those social ills. The trust that Hengel suggests may produce endurance in an evil world but not active hope for social or political change. Second, if such a message is socially and politically explosive, then it must have been related, or perceived to be related, to those very issues and not merely to the character of an absent God. By praying to the Father, therefore, the disciples are praying to one who transforms society into the kingdom of God. Father and family go together; the father who cares for the family will not merely love the family while allowing it to languish in poverty. If he can do something to change the family's situation, he will do so. The rest of the prayer confirms the view that the prayer anticipates that God will act and that those who join God's family will join in the action.

Name

"May your name be sanctified." Similar to the Jewish Kaddish, "May his great name be extolled and hallowed in the world which he has created according to his will," this petition expresses concern for the vindication of God's honor or glory. Both Jesus' petition and that of the Kaddish use a passive voice which in Jewish custom often means the active voice when used of God: "Sanctify your name." Sanctifying or hallowing God's name requires recognizing the reality and effective power of God. Prophetic voices connected that recognition with the character and fate of God's people. If they honor God with their lips while their hearts remain far removed, they deny God's honor; God's vindication requires that they reap the consequences of

---

16. Hengel, *Victory Over Violence*, 51; see also 54–56. Riches, *Jesus and the Transformation of Judaism*, pursues a similar thesis.

their lack of genuine honor (Isa. 29:13). If God's people languish or if they remain a prey to the nations, God's honor suffers. God's name can be profaned either by the people violating the covenant or by the nations oppressing Israel, or by the scorn heaped upon Israel because of God's allowing them to suffer for their misdeeds. These sentiments are expressed especially in Ezekiel during the Babylonian exile (see Ezek. 36:20–22 for a good example).[17] According to Ezekiel, God's name will be vindicated by God's action. Ezekiel speaks of God making a "covenant of peace," with Israel (34:25). God will remove the oppressive power, renew the fertility of the land, increase its productivity, establish a special relationship between people and God, and cause surrounding nations to recognize that Israel's God has blessed them (Ezek. 34:25–31).

Seen against the background of prophetic thought, Jesus' prayer for vindicating God's name stands in close correlation with his concern for social justice, freedom from internal or external oppression, economic well-being, and spiritual vitality. The petition for the honoring of God's name precedes petitions for the coming of God's kingdom, for bread, for debt relief, and for success in the struggle against temptation. But it is more than merely prior to them. Those other petitions best express what it means for God's name to be held in reverence.

One should note also that the petition is expressed in the aorist imperative. This Greek verb form indicates, first, the coming about of a situation different from the prior situation.[18] Thus, the petition implies that the present circumstances do not vindicate God's name; the vindication will occur at a point in the future. Secondly, the aorist imperative "usually has a note of urgency in it,"[19] suggesting that Jesus prays for a vindicating activity that could be recognized as such in the near future. The prayer thus requests God's action to renew and restore Israel so that Israel's life will bring honor and not shame to God's name.

Kingdom

"Your kingdom come" connects the changed circumstance Jesus anticipates with the dominant symbol of his whole ministry. I have already argued

---

17. Fitzmyer, *Luke*, 898.
18. F. Blass and A. Debrunner, *A Greek Grammar of the New Testament and Other Early Christian Literature,* tr. Robert W. Funk (Chicago: University of Chicago Press, 1961), 173.
19. W. D. Chamberlain, *An Exegetical Grammar of the Greek New Testament* (New York: Macmillan, 1954), 86.

that the kingdom for whose coming Jesus prays includes the renewal of the whole life of God's people. Matthew more explicitly expresses this meaning when he places in parallel an explanatory petition: "Your will be done, on earth as it is in heaven" (Matt. 6:10).

Bread

"Give us this day our daily bread" demonstrates the connection Jesus makes between concern for God's will and the social-economic circumstances in which God's people live out their lives. The use of bread as a metaphor for all that is needed to sustain life is appropriate from one whose ministry and teaching made substantial use of receiving and giving table hospitality.

The translation of "daily bread" (*artos epiousios*) is problematic. It could mean "bread for today," reminiscent of the Israelites' gathering "manna" each morning for the day, or "tomorrow's bread," suggesting the Israelites' gathering of two days' supply of manna on Sabbath eve. The deeply ingrained story of God feeding the people of Israel in the wilderness supports a material understanding.[20] Or it could mean "bread for subsistence" or "necessary for existence." In any event, it means bread to fill hungry stomachs, not merely a "spiritual" bread unrelated to the problems of the poor.

> The kingdom-banquet was not just a symbol of spiritual bliss but also of the kingdom where there would be no starvation. . . . The petition for the bread thus holds together material and spiritual needs without making one more important than the other. The daily bread was a token of the messianic banquet—and the messianic banquet a reminder of the sanctity of the daily bread.[21]

The story of Jesus' feeding the multitudes in the wilderness reflects this same theme of concern for the daily existence of those who live with poverty, hunger, and injustice.

Forgiveness

"Forgive us our sins, for we ourselves forgive everyone indebted to us" (Luke 11:4). Matthew's version is more likely original: "Forgive us our debts, as we also have forgiven our debtors" (Matt. 6:12). Palestinian Jews could

---

20. Fitzmyer, *Luke,* 900.
21. Stendahl, "Your Kingdom Come," 262–63.

understand "debt" to refer to "sins," but there is no evidence for similar use in Hellenistic Greek; thus Luke likely changed it for his Gentile readers.[22] Either reading connects God's forgiveness with human forgiveness. In the context of Jesus' debt-ridden society, the debt might well have been meant literally and not merely as a metaphor for personal sins. The petition makes connections with the Jubilee theme of remitting debts as part of the observance of the Jubilee year.[23]

It may not be coincidental that the petition for forgiveness stands next to the prayer for bread, for the two were linked in the lives of ordinary people. Indebtedness disrupted the possibility of earning daily bread in Jesus' day.[24] Again, Jesus' prayer addresses the direct experience of the people. It brings the kingdom of God into contact with the need for liberation from privation and oppression. God's sovereignty over the social life of Israel will end the dehumanizing patterns that indebtedness and consequent subsistence living have established.[25]

Forgiveness is generally associated with repentance, so this petition should be placed in the context of Jesus' call for repentance in light of the coming of the kingdom. Renewing the community of God's people requires the change in attitude and action expected in the call to repentance. Forgiveness of debt, love for the neighbor, renunciation of greed are ingredients in that repentance without which God's restoring forgiveness is impossible. Human forgiveness of debts provides a model for God's expected forgiveness of sins,[26] and its condition as well.

Trial

"Do not bring us to the time of trial" (Luke 11:4). Matthew characteristically adds a parallel petition that expresses Matthew's understanding of Jesus' prayer: "But rescue us from the evil one" (Matt. 6:13). This petition requests that God will not lead the petitioner into trial, testing, or temptation. Two basic meanings are possible here, neither without difficulty. The term can mean "test" or "trial," in which case the reference could be any time of testing or the particularly difficult time of testing associated with the coming of the end time. With this meaning, the petitioning community, out of anxiety that

22. Fitzmyer, Luke, 906.
23. Ringe, Jesus, Liberation, and the Biblical Jubilee, 83.
24. Oakman, Jesus and the Economic Questions of His Day, 155.
25. Ringe, Jesus, Liberation, and the Biblical Jubilee, 79.
26. Horsley, Jesus and the Spiral of Violence, 252ff.

it will fail to remain firm in faith to the end time, asks that God not lead them to such a time. A second possible meaning is "temptation," or enticement to sin. With that meaning, the petitioning community requests that God not entice them to do evil. With either meaning, the petition seems stranger to modern ears than to people in Jesus' day who thought of God as in some sense responsible for both good and evil, of enticing to sin or apostasy those whom God might consequently destroy.

This petition more than any other retains the eschatological note that is an ineradicable element of Jesus' teachings. Apocalyptic thought is laden with the notion that the end time brings unusual danger even to the faithful. Since God will bring the end time, so God also brings with it the accompanying tests of faithfulness. Jesus' petition here echoes that thought. What he believed would happen in the future is not discernible; that he expected a consummation of God's activity in renewing Israel and establishing the kingdom of God seems indisputable. As in other apocalyptic thought, the future that Jesus envisioned contained both threat against losing connection with renewed Israel and promise of a secure future to those who are steadfast. The apocalyptic language in the final petition reminds that God's historical renewal of God's people leads to the ultimate renewal of all history. No social order can claim to be fully the manifestation of God's kingdom, for that kingdom always lies beyond the historical manifestation as its challenge and its criterion.

Conclusion

The piety of Jesus expressed in the petitions of the Lord's Prayer corresponds to the character of Jesus shown in his teachings and actions. His piety does not mask the self and hide from God and neighbor; rather, it fully opens the self to the claim of God that comes through the neighbor. His piety does not diminish the neighbor by claiming goodness or right for himself; rather, it acclaims God as the source of good both in the self and in the neighbor. His piety does not deceive the self into thinking it belongs to God when in reality it claims God for itself; rather, it claims that the self derives from God and finds its own good only in obedience to God. His piety does not divorce him from the community that shapes and is shaped by his vision of self; rather, his piety connects him to the traditions of the community, even when his prophetic vision contradicts the present structures and implicit values of his community. His piety does not divorce him from the pain, suffering, and privation produced by injustice; rather, it places him within that pain even when he could avoid it, because his piety demands that his immediate happiness give way to the well-being of the community to which he is bound. Jesus' piety is a piety of obedience, in which "not my will but yours be done" are not mere words but lived reality. Jesus' piety, as seen in the Lord's Prayer and elsewhere, is not merely personal and devotional; even more it combines those dimensions with the ethical and political. Luke successfully captures in Mary's Magnificat (Luke 1:46–55) those traditional expressions of piety that Jesus had learned from scripture and that he lived.

CHAPTER EIGHT

"Who Do You Say That I Am?"

No interpreter from H. S. Reimarus to S. G. F. Brandon has been able to convince the scholarly world that Jesus was a political messianic figure. The dominant religious and theological view has been that Jesus regarded himself as Messiah but reinterpreted Messiah in purely spiritual and nonpolitical terms. Historically, scholarly interpretation of Jesus originated largely within Christian circles. It is not surprising, therefore, that much scholarly interpretation has shared the view that Jesus was a nonpolitical Messiah, or else has advocated a view that Jesus deflected messianic hopes.

The view that Jesus was a spiritual and not a political Messiah has its roots in the Gospel tradition. In Mark's story of the "confession" of Peter (Mark 8:27–33; compare Matt. 16:13–28; Luke 9:18–22), Jesus tacitly accepts the title "Messiah" but reinterprets it in terms of suffering and death rather than triumph over Israel's enemies. The contrast between Jesus and his disciples provides a powerful set of images: The disciples want a crown, Jesus chooses a cross; they want triumph, he chooses humiliation; they want prestige, he chooses denigration/degradation; they want power, he chooses weakness.

This picture of Jesus presents serious historical problems. While Jesus' own piety led him to place concern for community above self, the contrasting images reveal church reflection more than direct historical knowledge. The church faced the fact that it was impossible for Jesus to fulfill the messianic hopes that his followers had lodged in him; yet they continued to place their hope for the future in the experience they had had with him. The two facts together necessarily refocused any messianic expectations he had aroused. They could not have retained an emphasis on the political nature of Jesus, for that would imply that he pursued a course doomed to fail.

Therefore, political elements have been reduced in the overarching grander purpose that the church attributed to him after his death. The historical dimension of the Gospels is seen in their retaining evidence for the more political Jesus; the church's theological creativity is revealed in the transformation of Jesus' political particularities into an image of a universal savior. But Jesus himself did not address the issue of "human" salvation so much as he addressed the social and political issues of his own society on the basis of the covenant traditions of Israel. That effort brought him into the conflict that resulted in his execution. The Romans, assisted by the Jewish authorities, saw in him the social and political threat associated with Jewish messianism, and thus they executed him.

The question of whether Jesus thought of himself as Messiah has been left aside throughout this study. One reason for leaving it aside is the impossibility of answering it satisfactorily. Another reason is that claiming the title or having others bestow it is not the decisive factor. The question of titles that Jesus or others applied to him is much less important than the attention it often receives would suggest. The people around Jesus probably did not spend much time wondering what title to give him. That is a preoccupation of one looking back.

Noting the difference between John and the Synoptics in regard to titles illustrates this point. John looks back and speaks of Jesus as the Lamb of God (John 1:36) who takes away the sins of the world; the Logos (Word) of God (John 1:1–14); God's only-begotten (John 1:18); Son of Man who descended from heaven (John 3:13); Messiah (4:25–26). Mark also reveals Jesus' identity to the reader through using titles: Son of God (Mark 1:1; 15:39), Son of Man (Mark 8:31), and Messiah (Mark 8:29). The major difference between John and the Synoptics lies not merely in the wide array of titles John applies to Jesus, but in the exalted claims Jesus makes for himself. John has Jesus boldly proclaiming that he is Messiah (John 4:25–26), the "bread of life" (6:48), the one whose flesh and blood give eternal life (6:54), "the light of the world" (8:12; 9:5), "I am he" (8:28),[1] "the gate" (10:9), the "good shepherd" (10:11), "the resurrection and

---

1. Either "I am [the Son of Man]" or "I AM" (equivalent to the divine name, YHWH). Cf. John 8:58, where Jesus says, "Before Abraham was, I am." Cf. also John 9:35–37, where Jesus tells the man born blind that he is the Son of Man.

the life" (11:25), "the way, and the truth, and the life" (14:6), "the true vine" (15:1). Even beyond these titles and metaphors, Jesus boldly asserts himself, his authority, his unity with God, his origin in God. The self-assertive Jesus of John has none of the reticence of the Synoptic Jesus. Of the two pictures, the Synoptic one bears more resemblance to the historical Jesus. Jesus gave his attention to God's kingdom as the renewal of the people, not to a self-identity that might be expressed through titles.

Titles provide only one way of speaking about Jesus' identity. Another way is to speak of his *being:* Was Jesus God? Was he human? Was he both? The church followed this way as it struggled with doctrinal controversies, especially in the fourth and fifth centuries, culminating in the Nicene Creed and the Definition of Chalcedon. That concern belonged neither to Jesus nor to the authors of the New Testament, not even to John.

Another way to speak of Jesus' identity is to speak of his *action:* What did he do, and how do his deeds reveal his understanding of himself? I have chosen the third way, both because I think it corresponds more to Jesus' own Hebraic way of thinking, and because historical inquiry can deal more effectively with it. Nevertheless, the question of whether Jesus thought of himself as Messiah or wanted his followers to think of him as such inevitably forces itself on the interpreter of Jesus' actions.

If Jesus preached the coming of the kingdom as the renewal of Israel, what role did he assign himself? How did he understand his mission? What role did he expect to play in the coming kingdom? Was he the announcer of its coming or a chief actor in bringing in the kingdom? Did Jesus think of himself as the Messiah? What would it mean to do so?

In a Jewish context, even though prophets and others might be anointed (*massiah*), to claim to be the Messiah would amount to a claim to be king, the person God has chosen and anointed to be ruler of God's people. In a Roman Palestinian context, that claim would mean rebellion against the rule of Rome. For neither Romans nor Jews would it mean what Christians came to understand as incarnation, the presence of God in human form. That later theological understanding depends on Christian interpretation of Jesus rather than on Jesus' Hebraic background or Jesus' self-perception. Nor could it mean that Jesus was a "spiritual Messiah" who rules not over Israel but over the human self.[2] To

---

2. John probably intends this meaning when he has Jesus say to Pilate, "My kingdom is not of this world" (John 18:36, RSV). This saying can mean that Jesus does not derive his power from the political authorities (as the NRSV translation "*from* this world" suggests [italics added]). John, however, more likely means that the spiritual realm in which Jesus rules is different from the political realm in which Pilate governs.

test whether this view can go back to the historical ministry of Jesus, one can ask four questions.

1. Did the *authorities* think of Jesus as a spiritual Messiah whose rule would not impinge on their political authority? The execution of Jesus by crucifixion argues tellingly against that view. As I have argued above, while the suggestions in the narratives of Jesus' trial and crucifixion could lead to the conclusion that the religious authorities had Jesus executed for religious reasons, historical probability strongly opposes it.

2. Did the *crowds* Jesus addressed think of him as a spiritual Messiah whose rule would not bring about change in the holders of power or its use? The answer is almost certainly not. Hengel inadvertently shows the implausibility of such a view when he says the crowds followed Jesus because they misunderstood him: They thought he was political, but they were mistaken; they would not have followed him if they had known his kingdom was not of this world. The point here is that the crowds thought of Jesus as political, whether or not they explicitly associated his activity with the title Messiah.

3. Did the *disciples* think of Jesus as a spiritual Messiah? Again, the answer is almost certainly not. The Gospels (especially Mark) portray the disciples as also misunderstanding Jesus. Jesus tries to teach them the true understanding of messiahship, but they cannot learn. They continue to cling to messianic hopes and to reject the notion of messianic suffering for spiritual salvation. Luke provides insight into the disciples' political-messianic expectations by having them (a) still harboring political expectations at the Last Supper (Luke 22:24–30); (b) asking permission for armed resistance at Jesus' arrest (22:49); (c) even after Jesus' death expressing their disappointed hope that Jesus was the "one to set Israel free" (Luke 24:21, NRSV margin); (d) ask, even after the resurrection, "Lord, is this the time when you will restore the kingdom to Israel?" (Acts 1:6).

The evidence points strongly in the direction that the disciples saw in Jesus a political figure. Why all this political expectation in the narratives? It was not generated by the church, for the church tradition very quickly moved away from the political. Perhaps it came from the disciples in spite of Jesus' attempts to restrain political hopes. Perhaps it was generated innocently by Jesus' talk of the kingdom, which was wrongly understood. More likely Jesus generated it himself, not inadvertently but intentionally. Because his notion of the kingdom of God involved the renewal of Israel's life as God's people, his message directly and inevitably raised such expectation. God's will for God's people was as thoroughly political as it was religious.

4. Did *Jesus* understand himself as a spiritual and nonpolitical Messiah? While it is not impossible that he did, I find it implausible. Spiritual messianism

depends on the perspective of Jesus' death and resurrection, and Jesus did not have the advantage of that perspective. Jesus did not choose death and resurrection as the means to accomplish his mission. They were not actions he performed but events that happened to him. His willingness to take his cause of renewal to Jerusalem and to place himself at risk for the kingdom does not mean that he saw his death as the way to establish God's kingdom.

If my answers to these four questions are historically valid, then Jesus and his contemporaries, including both friends and foes, saw him as politically important, as either a threat or a promise. I believe that perception of Jesus has been confirmed by the foregoing study of his actions and words. He proclaimed God's kingdom as hope for the poor, as liberation for the oppressed, as good news for Israel's future. He unleashed a charismatic movement of helping, healing, and renewing community. He spoke with the directness of Spirit-filled authority to challenge Israel toward peaceful, nonviolent, nonegoistic dealings with each other. He called for new trust and confidence in God's goodness and power as antidote to the anxiety that drove some to aggression and others to despair. He challenged the holders of institutional religious power with bold manifestations of God's immediate presence. His vision of a just society of equals threatened those whose economic advantage was backed by the coercive power of Roman troops. He celebrated fellowship meals anticipating the time when the renewed covenant community would find fulfillment in the kingdom of God.

If Jesus was political, what happened to his work? He did not succeed in restoring the kingdom to Israel or in setting Israel free or in transforming Palestinian Judaism into a covenant community of justice. His lack of success in these regards has provided the major reasons used by those who argue against seeing Jesus' aims as in any real sense political. Most of his interpreters, ancient or modern, have not wanted to allow him the possibility of failing to accomplish his goals. But honest historical judgments cannot be predicated on preferred outcomes.

Jesus does not seem to have prepared for what was to come, or at least for what came. What did he expect to be the result of his direct challenge to authority in Jerusalem? He did not attempt a military overthrow, nor did he try to wrest control of political power from those who held it. His march into Jerusalem and his demonstration at the Temple were symbolic, not attempts at gaining power from the authorities.

What Jesus expected is not what happened. "Jesus expected the kingdom, and what came was the church," expresses one dimension of the difference. That dimension concerns the political realm, according to the interpretation of the kingdom given in the preceding chapters. Whether Jesus expected to become a messianic king or not, his aims included the reconstitution of the covenant community of Israel. That community was not merely "Judaism" understood as a religion but Israel as a political-religious entity. Not merely the religious views and practices of the people and the religious leaders would have changed if Jesus' aims had been fulfilled; the social and political structures would have changed as well.

The surviving tradition about Jesus does not allow us to know what Jesus had in mind for political structures. His sayings suggest charismatic more than institutional/hierarchical structures, perhaps recalling the premonarchical understanding that God rules through "judges," or charismatic leaders (see chapter 6 on disciples). What is not likely, since it contradicts his vision of society, is a hierarchical government, certainly not one in control of the current incumbents.

As far as changes within society are concerned, Jesus anticipates a situation in which the poor receive a just portion of the wealth available to the community. He does not, in the traditions that have survived, provide any clear plan by which equity would be achieved. He calls for voluntary action by the wealthy that would correspond to covenant community norms, and he implies God's judgment and removal of those who refuse to comply. He might have called for an observance of the year of Jubilee. He did not call for an armed revolt to expel the Romans as a way of restoring the kingdom. The saying regarding tribute to Caesar can imply such a revolt, but that understanding finds no confirmation in the surviving tradition.

Could Rome have continued to rule in the presence of the kingdom? Very unlikely, it seems to me. If Jesus did not think it according to God's will for Rome to rule in Palestine, and if he did not advocate armed revolt, two options remained: (1) Nonviolent noncooperation and/or demonstration as a tactic of political pressure to make Roman government either impossible or too costly for the Romans. These sorts of actions were not new in Roman Palestine as the cases cited in chapter 1 show. (2) He could have expected God to act to overthrow or remove the Romans. In support of the former is the march to Jerusalem and the Temple demonstration. In support of the latter are the sayings leading to the view that the kingdom will be God's gift, not something violent persons can force.

Israel's history contained sufficient examples of God's acting on behalf of God's people for Jesus, like Second Isaiah, to believe that "the Creator of the ends of the earth . . . does not faint or grow weary" and that "all the nations are as nothing before him; they are accounted by him as less than nothing and emptiness" (Isa. 40:28, 17). In Jesus' view, as in the view of many prophets, Israel's strength lay not in the power of arms but in practicing righteousness within the community of God's covenant people. Isaiah's affirmation that "Zion shall be redeemed by justice" within society (Isa. 1:27) differs little from Jesus' belief that Jerusalem (Zion) must practice "the things that make for peace" (Luke 19:42) in order to avoid catastrophe and to gain liberty. If the notion that political liberation can result from social justice seems too farfetched for modern readers to think Jesus could have believed it, that only shows how far removed the modern reader is from the faith that Jesus shared with Israel's prophets.

Just what Jesus thought God would do to restore Israel's liberty cannot be said. Either Jesus himself did not answer that question clearly or else the church has not preserved his words. What does not seem likely to me is that Jesus advocated a violent revolt during which God would empower a successful armed overthrow of the Romans. Though some doubt the authenticity of the sayings on nonviolence and nonretaliation, I think their arguments fall short. I find no basis for Horsley's view, appealing as it might be, that such words concerned only internal enemies, not external ones like the Romans.[3] The action in the Temple had the potential of becoming violent, and it was provocative, but it was not likely an armed attack. It would surely have been promptly quashed had it been violent. The presence of swords in Jesus' group at the time of arrest argues that Jesus' disciples might not have been pacifists; but swords for personal protection represent very different attitudes and tactics than does armed revolt.[4] Thus, while it is not inconsistent with Jesus' belief that God would restore the kingdom to Israel, I do not think Jesus thought armed revolt would be the way to trigger God's intervention. Rather, establishing that degree of social justice and renewal possible to the Jews even under Roman rule would prompt God to act in a manner God would determine to deliver a faithful people from their oppressors.

3. Horsley, *Jesus and the Spiral of Violence*, 255–71, provides an excellent analysis of sayings related to hate, violence, and resistance. While I agree with the major thrust of his analysis and argument, I think he unnecessarily restricts the application of the "focal instances."

4. Available evidence does not contradict, even if it does not confirm, a resistance movement that was not an armed revolt. Brandon's suggestion that Jesus hoped for an armed insurrection within Jerusalem as a result of his Temple demonstration is highly speculative and not supported by any substantial evidence. It contradicts Jesus' admonitions against hate and for love of enemies (Brandon, *Jesus and the Zealots*, 350–56).

Conclusion

The historical Jesus resists attempts to modernize him. He was not a modern capitalist intoning the values of individualism and free enterprise, nor was he a modern socialist calling for a bureaucratic state. He was not a militarist who believed the sword can make the world safe for his values, nor was he a pacifist who thought conflict must be avoided at all costs. He was not a freedom fighter who believed that justice can come only through violence, nor did he turn aside from the struggle for human dignity because politics is a dirty business. He was not a champion of modern women's rights, nor did he promote male power and prerogative as the bastion of civilized values. He was not a racist, hating Gentiles as foreigners, nor was he a world citizen who knew all people to be the same underneath a veneer of cultural difference. He was not a secularist who tried to establish separation of religion and politics, nor was he a fundamentalist who wished to impose a narrow, doctrinaire tradition upon all members of society. He did not intend to be the savior of the world; he intended to be a good Jew, faithfully following the path of conscience inspired by tradition and by the fresh presence of God.

Above all else, he was a prophet, in word and deed. He did not curry favor with the wealthy and powerful in order to garner their support for his reform movement. Neither did he pander condescendingly to the poor in order to use them in his enterprise. Like true prophets of the past, he fearlessly proclaimed God's will as he saw it, letting offense or approval be the result of his message, not the shaper of it. He engaged the real issues of a society torn by religious faction, divided by selfish interests, dominated by powerful elites who used society's resources for their personal benefit, heading toward war and catastrophe. If his message did not deter the race toward social self-destruction, the fault lay not in the message or messenger but in individual and collective resistance to pursuing justice.

A study of the historical Jesus provides an image of a powerful individual whose concern for the well-being of the community dominates his personality, his words, and his actions; who does not let traditional values prevent the direct power of God's presence, and who yet understands tradition, and is nourished by it; whose intimate relation to God provides a motivating power for social action rather than a withdrawal into an egocentric religious mysticism; whose vision of society renews the prophetic vision of God's kingdom and makes that vision vital and active.

A CONCLUDING
THEOLOGICAL POSTSCRIPT

"This Jesus God Raised Up"

Christian faith has preserved memories of Jesus and has used those memories to provide a challenging model for human living. Nevertheless, Christian faith has not centered on the historical Jesus. The Apostles' Creed demonstrates the truth of this statement, for it moves from "born of the Virgin Mary" to "crucified under Pontius Pilate." The Creed's omission suggests that the intervening years and activities of Jesus were of no real consequence to faith. That tendency began as early as the apostle Paul, for whom the death and resurrection (and perhaps incarnation) were the pivotal events that brought salvation. One purpose of this book has been to challenge the adequacy of that theological perspective on Jesus, not to question its validity.

Since this book is about the historical Jesus, the resurrection faith of the early church and the narratives by which they expressed that faith might be declared out of bounds. And I will not treat them fully. But I do want to suggest some of the implications of affirming the resurrection of a political Jesus. Theologically and ethically, it is not enough to say that a death and resurrection have occurred. Who Jesus was whom the Romans executed and God raised from the dead matters not only for the historian but for the theologian and the believer. The historical character of Jesus, and not merely a spiritual Christ, provides Christian faith with its reason for being and its power to bring about change in personal and social life.

It matters which Jesus was raised from the dead and who engages his modern followers in dialogue about his history and theirs, about his world and theirs, about what commitment to God's kingdom means for him and for them.

If Jesus was a violent man, a freedom fighter, who failed in his attempt to overthrow the Romans, the affirmation that he has been raised from the dead as Lord and Christ could mean that his followers too should take up the sword against the enemies of God's people.

If Jesus' main purpose was to tell people how to get to heaven and to provide the means to do so, then the risen, heavenly Christ bids his followers to leave the world behind. Following that Christ would lead to otherworldliness, resulting in a lack of concern for the historical lives that people live now.

If Jesus was primarily a mystic who taught his followers how to experience oneness with God, the risen Christ could lead his followers on a quest for mystical ecstasy. He might not lead them to agonize over the state of the ordinary world or to work for its transformation.

If Jesus was a spiritual teacher, concerned only that our hearts be right with God and unconcerned about political, social, and economic ills of his time, the risen Christ would have little to do with political life. He would rather encourage his followers to develop a spiritual life that focuses upon the soul's health, and the individual's practice of piety, and not be bothered by the plight of the poor, the oppressed, and the marginalized.

If Jesus was a prophet calling for the renewal of Israel, for a return to the covenant traditions that would produce a society of peace and justice, the risen Christ could call his followers to do the same in their time. Following him would require a commitment to examine human abuses of social, economic, political, and military power; to envision their world as a place of justice, peace, and reconciliation; to strive for a new social, political, economic, and religious order in which God's will can come to fruition.

If none of these images does full justice to the historical Jesus, they do show that not all images of Jesus have the same consequences for those who intend to be followers of the risen Christ. Nor do all images of Jesus have the same claims to historical truth. Some visions of Jesus do not withstand close historical, theological, or ethical scrutiny.

The disciples' belief in Jesus' resurrection was an act of defiance and of affirmation. Those who claimed that God pronounced a different verdict on Jesus and his actions defied the authorities who put him to death. Depending on the place and manner in which they made that act of defiance, Jesus' followers risked the same fate that had awaited Jesus.

Belief in Jesus' resurrection was also an affirmation of the continuing validity of Jesus' vision of society, an affirmation of hope that the future lies with that vision more than with present injustice, an affirmation that God's kingdom will come, that God's will will be done on earth as in heaven.

The affirmation of the resurrection of Jesus means that those who take him seriously in the present must continue their dialogue with his history, with his historic activity, with his social and political message, as well as with their own personal and social history. Only by such a dialogical process can Jesus' prophetic vision have significant effect on our time.

Jesus' vision was too large for his time, or for any time. It remains as challenge more than achievement. No age and no people have "practiced" it, for it may finally be impractical. Even the most just do not fully achieve the justice of the kingdom; not even the most peaceful secure the peace promised in its vision. Yet its power to evoke sympathetic response in many persons in various ages shows that it is not irrelevant. It remains relevant as vision, offering criticism of the present and promise of a future. It lies beyond, and yet it demands to be present.

Index of Scripture
and Other Ancient Writings

Index of Names and Subjects